Survival

GLOBAL POLITICS AND STRATEGY

Volume 60 Number 3 | June–July 2018

'Just as at the turn of the twentieth century American policymakers set out to "make the world safe for democracy", so, at the start of the twenty-first century, their Chinese counterparts are attempting to make it safe for authoritarianism.'

Aaron L. Friedberg, Competing with China, p. 25.

'Ultimately, the Rites Controversy had less to do with Chinese civilisation than with religious rivalries in Europe, with China getting caught in the middle of a civil war between Protestantism and Catholicism … It would eventually drag in three popes, two Chinese (Manchu) emperors, hundreds of Christian missionaries and the entire theological faculty at the Sorbonne, the intellectual citadel of the Counter-Reformation.'

Lanxin Xiang, China and the Vatican, p. 91.

'The post-bipolar euphoria of the West created an impression that the old rules of behaviour that helped us survive the East–West confrontation had lost their importance once that confrontation ended.'

Nadezhda Arbatova, Reaching an Understanding on Baltic Security, p. 118.

Survival

GLOBAL POLITICS AND STRATEGV

Volume 60 Number 3 | June–July 2018

Contents

On the cover
President Richard Nixon, his wife, 'Pat' Ryan Nixon, US secretary of state William Rogers, Chinese deputy premier Li Hsien-nien and his wife, Lin Chia-mei, visit the Great Wall of China on 24 February 1972.

On the web
Visit www.iiss.org/publications/survival for brief notices on new books on Africa, Latin America, Europe, and Environment and Resources.

***Survival* editors' blog**
For ideas and commentary from *Survival* editors and contributors, visit www.iiss.org/politicsandstrategy.

Survival
GLOBAL POLITICS AND STRATEGY

The International Institute for Strategic Studies

2121 K Street, NW | Suite 801 | Washington DC 20037 | USA
Tel +1 202 659 1490   Fax +1 202 659 1499   E-mail survival@iiss.org   Web www.iiss.org

Arundel House | 6 Temple Place | London | WC2R 2PG | UK
Tel +44 (0)20 7379 7676   Fax +44 (0)20 7836 3108   E-mail iiss@iiss.org

14th Floor, GBCorp Tower | Bahrain Financial Harbour | Manama | Kingdom of Bahrain
Tel +973 1718 1155   Fax +973 1710 0155   E-mail iiss-middleeast@iiss.org

9 Raffles Place | #51-01 Republic Plaza | Singapore 048619
Tel +65 6499 0055   Fax +65 6499 0059   E-mail iiss-asia@iiss.org

Survival Online www.tandfonline.com/survival and www.iiss.org/publications/survival

Aims and Scope *Survival* is one of the world's leading forums for analysis and debate of international and strategic affairs. Shaped by its editors to be both timely and forward thinking, the journal encourages writers to challenge conventional wisdom and bring fresh, often controversial, perspectives to bear on the strategic issues of the moment. With a diverse range of authors, *Survival* aims to be scholarly in depth while vivid, well written and policy-relevant in approach. Through commentary, analytical articles, case studies, forums, review essays, reviews and letters to the editor, the journal promotes lively, critical debate on issues of international politics and strategy.

Editor **Dana Allin**
Managing Editor **Matthew Harries**
Associate Editor **Carolyn West**
Editorial **Jessica Watson**
Production and Cartography **John Buck, Kelly Verity**

Contributing Editors

Gilles Andréani	Bill Emmott	Jeffrey Lewis	Teresita C. Schaffer	David C. Unger
Ian Bremmer	John A. Gans, Jr	Hanns W. Maull	Steven Simon	Ruth Wedgwood
David P. Calleo	John L. Harper	Jeffrey Mazo	Angela Stent	Lanxin Xiang
Russell Crandall	Pierre Hassner	'Funmi Olonisakin	Jonathan Stevenson	
Toby Dodge	Erik Jones	Thomas Rid	Ray Takeyh	

Published for the IISS by
Routledge Journals, an imprint of Taylor & Francis, an Informa business.

Copyright © 2018 The International Institute for Strategic Studies. All rights reserved. No part of this publication may be reproduced, stored, transmitted or disseminated, in any form, or by any means, without prior written permission from Taylor & Francis, to whom all requests to reproduce copyright material should be directed, in writing.

About the IISS The IISS, a registered charity with offices in Washington, London, Manama and Singapore, is the world's leading authority on political–military conflict. It is the primary independent source of accurate, objective information on international strategic issues. Publications include *The Military Balance*, an annual reference work on each nation's defence capabilities; *Strategic Survey*, an annual review of world affairs; *Survival*, a bimonthly journal on international affairs; *Strategic Comments*, an online analysis of topical issues in international affairs; and the *Adelphi* series of books on issues of international security.

**Director-General
and Chief Executive**
John Chipman

President Emeritus
Michael Howard

Vice-President
Yoshio Okawara

Chair of the Council
François Heisbourg

Chair of the Trustees
Fleur de Villiers

Trustees
Bill Emmott
Chris Jones
Sophie-Caroline
  de Margerie
Nigel Newton
Risto Penttilä
Lord Powell
Catherine Roe
Thomas Seaman
Matt Symonds

**Members of the
Council**
Carl Bildt
Joanne de Asis
Karl Eikenberry
Bill Emmott
Michael Fullilove
Lord Guthrie
Marillyn A. Hewson
Peter Ho
Badr Jafar
Bilahari Kausikan
Ellen Laipson
Chung Min Lee

Eric X. Li
Jean-Claude Mallet
Moeletsi Mbeki
Lord Powell
Michael Rich
Lord Robertson
Andrés Rozental
Ghassan Salamé
Grace Reksten Skaugen
Anne-Marie Slaughter
Hew Strachan
Amos Yadlin
Igor Yurgens

SUBMISSIONS

To submit an article, authors are advised to follow these guidelines:

- *Survival* articles are around 4,000–10,000 words long including endnotes. A word count should be included with a draft. Length is a consideration in the review process and shorter articles have an advantage.
- All text, including endnotes, should be double-spaced with wide margins.
- Any tables or artwork should be supplied in separate files, ideally not embedded in the document or linked to text around it.
- All *Survival* articles are expected to include endnote references. These should be complete and include first and last names of authors, titles of articles (even from newspapers), place of publication, publisher, exact publication dates, volume and issue number (if from a journal) and page numbers. Web sources should include complete URLs and DOIs if available.
- A summary of up to 150 words should be included with the article. The summary should state the main argument clearly and concisely, not simply say what the article is about.

- A short author's biography of one or two lines should also be included. This information will appear at the foot of the first page of the article.
- *Survival* has a strict policy of listing multiple authors in alphabetical order.

Submissions should be made by email, in Microsoft Word format, to survival@iiss.org. Alternatively, hard copies may be sent to *Survival*, IISS–US, 2121 K Street NW, Suite 801, Washington, DC 20037, USA.

The editorial review process can take up to three months. *Survival*'s acceptance rate for unsolicited manuscripts is less than 20%. *Survival* does not normally provide referees' comments in the event of rejection. Authors are permitted to submit simultaneously elsewhere so long as this is consistent with the policy of the other publication and the Editors of *Survival* are informed of the dual submission.

Readers are encouraged to comment on articles from the previous issue. Letters should be concise, no longer than 750 words and relate directly to the argument or points made in the original article.

ADVERTISING AND PERMISSIONS

For advertising rates and schedules

USA/Canada: The Advertising Manager, Taylor & Francis Inc., 530 Walnut Street, Suite 850, Philadelphia, PA 19106, USA Tel +1 (800) 354 1420 Fax +1 (215) 207 0050.

UK/Europe/Rest of World: The Advertising Manager, Routledge Journals, Taylor & Francis, 4 Park Square, Milton Park, Abingdon, Oxfordshire OX14 4RN, UK Tel +44 (0) 207 017 6000 Fax +44 (0) 207 017 6336.

SUBSCRIPTIONS

Survival is published bi-monthly in February, April, June, August, October and December by Routledge Journals, an imprint of Taylor & Francis, an Informa Business.

Annual Subscription 2018

Institution	£505	$885	€742
Individual	£144	$243	€196
Online only	£442	$774	€649

Taylor & Francis has a flexible approach to subscriptions, enabling us to match individual libraries' requirements. This journal is available via a traditional institutional subscription (either print with online access, or online only at a discount) or as part of our libraries, subject collections or archives. For more information on our sales packages please visit http://www. tandfonline.com/page/librarians.

All current institutional subscriptions include online access for any number of concurrent users across a local area network to the currently available backfile and articles posted online ahead of publication.

Subscriptions purchased at the personal rate are strictly for personal, non-commercial use only. The reselling of personal subscriptions is prohibited. Personal subscriptions must be purchased with a personal cheque or credit card. Proof of personal status may be requested.

Dollar rates apply to all subscribers outside Europe. Euro rates apply to all subscribers in Europe, except the UK and the Republic of Ireland where the pound sterling rate applies. If you are unsure which rate applies to you please contact Customer Services in the UK. All subscriptions are payable in advance and all rates include postage. Journals are sent by air to the USA, Canada, Mexico, India, Japan and Australasia. Subscriptions are entered on an annual basis, i.e. January to December. Payment may be made by sterling cheque, dollar cheque, euro cheque, international money order, National Giro or credit cards (Amex, Visa and Mastercard).

Survival (USPS 013095) is published bimonthly (in Feb, Apr, Jun, Aug, Oct and Dec) by Routledge Journals, Taylor & Francis, 4 Park Square, Milton Park, Abingdon, OX14 4RN, United Kingdom.

The US annual subscription price is $842. Airfreight and mailing in the USA by agent named Air Business Ltd, c/o Worldnet Shipping Inc., 156-15, 146th Avenue, 2nd Floor, Jamaica, NY 11434, USA. Periodicals postage paid at Jamaica NY 11431.

US Postmaster: Send address changes to Survival, C/O Air Business Ltd / 156-15 146th Avenue, Jamaica, New York, NY11434.

Subscription records are maintained at Taylor & Francis Group, 4 Park Square, Milton Park, Abingdon, OX14 4RN, United Kingdom.

ORDERING INFORMATION

Please contact your local Customer Service Department to take out a subscription to the Journal: **USA, Canada:** Taylor & Francis, Inc., 530 Walnut Street, Suite 850, Philadelphia, PA 19106, USA. Tel: +1 800 354 1420; Fax: +1 215 207 0050. **UK/ Europe/Rest of World:** T&F Customer Services, Informa UK Ltd, Sheepen Place, Colchester, Essex, CO3 3LP, United Kingdom. Tel: +44 (0) 20 7017 5544; Fax: +44 (0) 20 7017 5198; Email: subscriptions@tandf.co.uk.

Back issues: Taylor & Francis retains a two-year back issue stock of journals. Older volumes are held by our official stockists: Periodicals Service Company, 351 Fairview Ave., Suite 300, Hudson, New York 12534, USA to whom all orders and enquiries should be addressed. *Tel* +1 518 537 4700 *Fax* +1 518 537 5899 *e-mail* psc@periodicals.com *web* http://www.periodicals. com/tandf.html.

The International Institute for Strategic Studies (IISS) and our publisher Taylor & Francis make every effort to ensure the accuracy of all the information (the "Content") contained in our publications. However, the IISS and our publisher Taylor & Francis, our agents, and our licensors make no representations or warranties whatsoever as to the accuracy, completeness, or suitability for any purpose of the Content. Any opinions and views expressed in this publication are the opinions and views of the authors, and are not the views of or endorsed by the IISS and our publisher Taylor & Francis. The accuracy of the Content should not be relied upon and should be independently verified with primary sources of information. The IISS and our publisher Taylor & Francis shall not be liable for any losses, actions, claims, proceedings, demands, costs, expenses, damages, and other liabilities whatsoever or howsoever caused arising directly or indirectly in connection with, in relation to or arising out of the use of the Content. Terms & Conditions of access and use can be found at http://www.tandfonline.com/page/terms-and-conditions.

The issue date is June–July 2018.

The print edition of this journal is printed on ANSI conforming acid free paper.

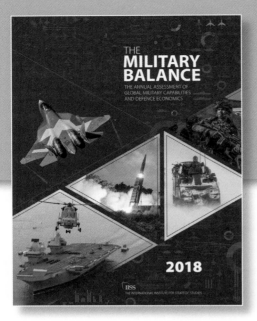

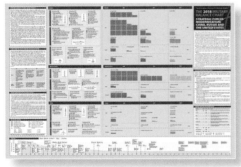

THE MILITARY BALANCE 2018

The annual assessment of global military capabilities and defence economics

The Military Balance is the annual IISS assessment of the military capabilities and defence economics of 171 countries. It is an indispensable handbook for anyone conducting serious analysis of security policy and military affairs.

NEW FEATURES

- Complementing its regional military analysis, the book carries detailed assessments of defence developments in China, Russia and the United States, as well as France and the United Kingdom. There are also features on Norway, Qatar, Sudan, Taiwan, Uganda and Venezuela, among others.

- New thematic texts analysing Chinese and Russian air-launched weapons; big data, artificial intelligence and defence; and Russia's strategic-force modernisation.

- A new *Military Balance* wall chart, focused on strategic-forces modernisation in China, Russia and the US.

- New regional arms orders and deliveries sections, outlining significant defence-procurement events in 2017.

- Updated comparative defence-statistics section, with graphics showing key data relating to defence economics and major land, sea and air capabilities, including global UAV sales and Chinese and Asia-Pacific regional naval shipbuilding since 2000.

- Updated summaries of national military capability, at the start of each country entry.

- New maps comparing selected military training exercises in Europe and Russia and Eurasia in 2016–17.

- Updated entries relating to national cyber capabilities.

LAUNCHED/PUBLISHED

14 February 2018

 THE INTERNATIONAL INSTITUTE FOR STRATEGIC STUDIES

Competing with China

Aaron L. Friedberg

There appears to be a growing consensus in Washington, and in the capitals of many other advanced industrial democracies, that prevailing policies towards China have failed and that an alternative approach is now urgently required. In a recent, widely read article in *Foreign Affairs*, two former Obama-administration officials conclude that, after years of 'hopeful thinking' about China's future, the United States finds itself confronting 'its most dynamic and formidable competitor in modern history'.[1] Republican Senator Marco Rubio describes the challenge in similar terms, noting that in the 240 years since its founding, the United States has never before 'faced an adversary of this scale, scope, and capacity'.[2] 'Decades of optimism about China's rise have been discarded', declares *The Economist*.[3] 'We got China wrong', writes an editorialist for the *Washington Post*. 'Now what?'[4]

The answer is by no means obvious. To put the matter in medical terms, while there may be increasingly widespread agreement about the existence of certain troubling symptoms, there is much less regarding a diagnosis of underlying causes, and virtually none at all on the appropriate prescription. Despite the evident severity of the challenge, debate on how to respond remains nascent and fragmentary.

For its part, in its formal statements the Trump administration has adopted an unprecedentedly combative stance towards China, describing it as a 'revisionist power … that seeks to displace the United States in the

Aaron L. Friedberg is Professor of Politics and International Affairs at Princeton University.

Survival | vol. 60 no. 3 | June–July 2018 | pp. 7–64   DOI 10.1080/00396338.2018.1470755

Indo-Pacific region',[5] and 'a strategic competitor' that is using 'predatory economics', as well as its growing military capabilities, 'to intimidate its neighbors'.[6] These harsh words are offset, to a degree, by the president's own odd expressions of personal admiration and affection for his opposite number in Beijing.[7] Notwithstanding these effusions, however, the administration's general stance, at least for the moment, seems clear enough: the United States must shed its illusions and gird for a 'long-term strategic competition' with China, one that will require 'the seamless integration of multiple elements of national power', including 'diplomacy, information, economics … and military' capabilities.[8]

But why is such a competition necessary, and what are its stakes? What are China's aims in this intensifying rivalry, and how do its leaders intend to achieve them?[9] And how should the United States redefine its goals and reshape its strategy in response? The purpose of this essay is to provide one possible set of answers to these questions.

If there is a single theme that unifies much of what follows, it is the often underestimated importance of political beliefs and ideology. America's post-Cold War strategy for dealing with China was rooted in prevailing liberal ideas about the linkages between trade, economic growth and democracy, and a faith in the presumed universality and irresistible power of the human desire for freedom. The strategy pursued by China's leaders, on the other hand, was, and still is, motivated first and foremost by their commitment to preserving the Chinese Communist Party's monopoly on domestic political power. The CCP's use of militant nationalism, its cultivation of historic claims and grievances against foreign powers, and its rejection of the idea that there are, in fact, universal human values are essential pieces of its programme for mobilising popular support and bolstering regime legitimacy. It is impossible to make sense of the ambitions, fears, strategy and tactics of China's present regime without reference to its authoritarian, illiberal character and distinctive, Leninist roots.

The intensifying competition between the United States and China is thus driven not only by the traditional dynamics of power politics – that is, by the narrowing gap between a preponderant hegemon and a fast-rising challenger – but also by a wide and deep divergence in values between their respective regimes. The resulting rivalry is more intense, the stakes are higher, and the likelihood of a lasting *entente* is lower than would otherwise be the case. The two powers are separated not only by divergent interests, some of which could conceivably be reconciled, but by incompatible visions for the future of Asia and the world. China's current rulers may not be trying actively to spread their own unique blend of repressive politics and semi-market economics, but as they have become richer and stronger they have begun to act in ways that inspire and strengthen other authoritarian regimes, while potentially weakening the institutions of young and developing democracies. Beijing is also using its new-found clout to reach out into the world, including into the societies, economies and political systems of the advanced industrial democracies, to try to influence the perceptions and policies of their people and governments, and to suppress information and discourage the expression of opinions seen as threatening to the CCP.

The stakes are higher

If they wish to respond effectively to these new realities, American and allied policymakers cannot afford to downplay the ideological dimension in their own strategy. Beijing's obsessive desire to squelch dissent, block the inward flow of unfavourable news and discredit 'so-called universal values' bespeaks an insecurity that is, in itself, a form of strategic vulnerability. China's rulers clearly believe the ideological realm to be a crucially important domain of competition, one that they would be only too happy to see the United States and the other Western nations ignore or abandon.

Assuming that China's power continues to grow, the United States will need to cooperate even more closely with its friends and allies, mobilising a coalition of like-minded countries to check Beijing's predatory economic practices, oppose its attempts to close off portions of the global commons, deter Chinese aggression and keep the peace. With only a handful of exceptions, the members of this coalition, which must include European as well as Asian nations, will be liberal democracies. Whatever their differences over trade, climate change or other issues, and notwithstanding the temporary frustrations caused by elected leaders who appear indifferent to these facts, the nations of the liberal-democratic West continue to have far more in common with one another than they do with the authoritarian powers.

Like it or not, if they do not wish to hang separately, they are going to have to hang together.

Last but not least, the experience of the past century suggests that, if America's leaders are serious about mobilising and sustaining the bureaucratic focus, domestic political support and economic resources necessary to wage a protracted strategic competition against a powerful and determined rival, they are going to have to cast the challenge, at least in part, in ideological terms. Geopolitical abstractions and economic statistics may be important, but historically what has moved and motivated the American people is a recognition that the principles on which their system is founded are under threat. There is an undeniable risk here of fear-mongering and overreaction, but at this point excessive caution and a continuing refusal to face facts may be an even greater danger. What is needed instead is a sober assessment of the challenge in all its dimensions, a clear articulation of the measures necessary to meet it, and leaders in Congress, the executive branch and the private sector who are capable of conveying both to the public.

America's failed China strategy

For almost a quarter-century after the end of the Cold War, the United States had a broadly stable, two-part strategy for dealing with China. On the one hand, in a continuation of a process that began with the Nixon/Kissinger 'opening' in the late 1960s, the United States sought to engage China across a wide variety of fronts: diplomatic, cultural, scientific, educational and, above all, economic. These efforts grew broader and deeper over time, and from the early 1990s onwards, after a brief period of uncertainty and debate in the wake of the 1989 Tiananmen Square massacre, the economic element of engagement, in particular, expanded at a rapid pace.

Contrary to what some recent commentary might suggest, however, the United States did not simply throw caution to the wind and embrace China without restraint. At the same time as it pressed ahead with engagement, from the mid-1990s onwards Washington also began to work harder to preserve a favourable balance of power in the Asia-Pacific region. The balancing part of US strategy had several subsidiary components. In addition to maintaining its own forward-based forces, the United States sought to strengthen its traditional alliance partnerships with Japan, Australia, South Korea and, albeit with more limited success, Thailand, the Philippines and New Zealand. Successive presidents restated the long-standing US commitment to Taiwan, and Washington also began to build new, quasi-alliance partnerships with other countries in the region to which it did not extend security guarantees, but which shared with the US a concern over the implications of China's growing power, including Singapore, India and, more tentatively, Vietnam.

The goal of balancing was to preserve stability and deter attempts at coercion or overt aggression while waiting for engagement to work its magic. Engagement, in turn, had three interlocking objectives. By welcoming Beijing into the existing, largely US-built and -led international order, Washington hoped that it could persuade China's leaders that their interests lay in preserving that order rather than seeking its overthrow or substantial modification. In the words of George W. Bush administration official Robert Zoellick, the United States wanted China to become a 'responsible stakeholder' in the existing international system.[10] It was expected that the process of inclusion, most notably China's 2001 admission into the World Trade Organization (WTO), would accelerate its transition away from state-directed economic planning and towards a more open, market-driven model of development. Finally, although they were blunter in saying this in the 1990s and early 2000s than in the years that followed, US policymakers continued to hope that engagement would promote tendencies – including the growth of a middle class, the spread of liberal ideas, and the development of the rule of law and the institutions of civil society – that would lead eventually to democratising political reforms.[11]

As it was in Europe, so too in Asia at the end of the Cold War was the ultimate aim of US policy to build a region 'whole and free', filled with democracies tied together by trade, investment and regional institutions, and integrated into a global system built along similar lines – a free and open region in a free and open world. The incorporation and eventual transformation of China were central to this ambitious vision.

Since the turn of the century, and especially in the past ten years, it has become increasingly evident that US strategy has thus far failed to achieve its objectives. Thanks in large measure to its rapid integration into the global economy, China has grown richer and stronger far faster than would otherwise have been possible. Rather than loosen its grip, however, the CCP regime has become even more repressive and more militantly nationalistic. In the economic domain, instead of shifting towards greater reliance on market forces, as had been expected after 2001, the party-state has maintained and, in certain respects, expanded its use of mercantilist policy tools. As regards its external behaviour, instead of evolving into a mellow, satisfied, 'responsible' status quo power, Beijing has grown more assertive and, at times, aggressive. The sustained build-up of China's armed forces is making it increasingly difficult for the United States and its allies to maintain a favourable balance of power in the Western Pacific. Meanwhile, China's leaders have become more open about their intention to use their growing military strength, new-found economic clout and expanding repertoire of 'soft' and 'sharp' power tools to try to reshape the existing Asian regional system and some aspects of the wider international order.[12]

Why did US strategy fail? And why were American and other Western policymakers so slow to acknowledge reality and to adjust their policies accordingly?

At the deepest level, the failure of America's China strategy is a grim tribute to the resilience, resourcefulness and ruthlessness of the Chinese Communist Party and the determination of its leaders to retain their monopoly on domestic political power. Even as it opened China to the West, the CCP found ways to maintain control over the direction of the national economy, while preserving its hold on the population through an evolving mixture of surveillance, coercion, co-option and ideological indoctrination. During the early stages of the process of 'reform and opening up', initiated by Deng Xiaoping in 1978, there may have been some in the top ranks of the Party who favoured political liberalisation, but these figures and their followers were purged after Tiananmen, never to re-emerge.[13]

Like the Sovietologists who debated whether Lenin led inevitably to Stalin, future generations of China specialists will no doubt argue over whether Xi Jinping was the natural heir to Deng, or perhaps to Mao Zedong himself.[14] Whatever the verdict of history, there is certainly a strong case to be made that, from the early 1990s onwards, China was launched on a trajectory that would lead toward increasing authoritarianism, as the regime redoubled its efforts to contain and neutralise the potentially disruptive effects of rapid economic growth and societal development. This was not immediately obvious at the time. Nonetheless, despite the mea culpas of some former officials, it is simply not the case that everyone 'got China wrong'. As early as the turn of the century, a number of observers had begun to write of what they described as China's 'authoritarian resilience',[15] noting that instead of making steady progress towards democracy and markets, China appeared 'trapped' in a form of 'developmental autocracy',[16] and arguing that visions of imminent liberalisation were, in fact, a 'fantasy'.[17] But these voices remained discordant exceptions in a general chorus of optimism.

Both sides believed that time was on their side

American and other Western leaders gambled that engagement would tame and transform China, even as it enabled the country to get richer and more powerful, thereby obviating the need for endless and increasingly costly balancing. China's leaders, on the other hand, calculated that they could continue to enjoy the fruits of engagement, growing stronger and less vulnerable to what they saw as Western pressure and attempts at ideological subversion without having to fundamentally alter the character of their system or abandon their broader ambitions. Both sides believed that time was on their side. It would appear, at least for now, that Beijing got the better of that bet.

Despite accumulating evidence that its initial wager was not paying off, Washington continued to double down on engagement without pausing periodically to reassess the costs and potential risks. While they did make some adjustments, successive US administrations also neglected to hedge adequately against the possibility of failure by investing sufficient resources in balancing. This pattern reflects the relative strengths of the bureaucratic and domestic political coalitions favouring the two halves of America's mixed strategy.

Throughout the 1990s and into the 2000s, even as they began to focus more attention on the problem, US intelligence agencies tended to underestimate the pace and scope of China's military build-up and to understate the true nature and extent of its revisionist aims.[18] Defence planners generally acknowledged the importance of the balancing mission, but they held varying views about the extent to which the locus of national strategy should shift towards the Asia-Pacific. Even within the US Navy and Air Force, the services that would naturally have the greatest role to play in that theatre, there was an inclination to regard the emerging challenge as relatively distant and most likely manageable with weapons systems and concepts of operation that were already on the books. To a surprising degree, many professional military officers also seem to have internalised the hopeful conventional wisdom of the day regarding the transformative effects of engagement and the danger that, by appearing to treat China as an enemy, they might cause it to become one.[19]

Things began to change after the turn of the century, as the Bush administration took a series of steps intended to start what one top official described as a 'long-term shift in focus' towards the Asia-Pacific.[20] By bolstering the US military posture in the region and strengthening defence ties with and among local friends and allies, the administration hoped to preserve a balance of power so overwhelmingly favourable that it would dissuade China from trying to mount a serious challenge for many years to come.

Many of these initiatives continued throughout the 2000s, laying the ground for the Obama administration's subsequent 'pivot' to Asia. But the 9/11 attacks, and the protracted, wasteful conflicts in Afghanistan and Iraq that followed, deflected money, intelligence resources and organisational energy away from the task of waging a long-term military competition with China and towards the more immediate problems of counter-terrorism and counter-insurgency. The Obama administration's efforts to pick up where its predecessor had left off and redirect America's strategic attention back to Asia were stymied by a variety of factors, including the persistence of fiscal constraints (made worse in some respects by the aftermath of the 2008 financial crisis) and the re-emergence of challenges in other regions, including the Middle East and Eastern Europe.

Support for investing more in the balancing portion of the American strategic portfolio was thus intermittent, divided and, in some periods, strikingly weak. By contrast, at least until quite recently, the coalition favouring ever more engagement was broad but largely unified, and consistently influential.

Starting in the 1980s, engagement accumulated a widening circle of supporters that quickly grew to include business executives, economists, China experts at universities and think tanks, politicians, former government officials, and most members of the foreign- and defence-policy establishments of both political parties. These people were motivated by varying mixtures of material self-interest (including the prospect of trade, investment, employment and professional advancement), combined in many cases with a sincere belief that deeper engagement with China would be good for all involved and that it would promote peace as well as prosperity. Keenly aware of the potential economic and strategic benefits of deepening engagement, Chinese interlocutors, including organs of the party-state, worked hard to encourage and reinforce such tendencies in the United States and other Western countries.

> *The pro-engagement coalition lobbied actively*

In addition to making the case for expanding economic and societal openness, the pro-engagement coalition also lobbied actively against policies that its members saw as threatening to disrupt the overall political relationship between China and the West. It was in part for this reason that the US, and other Western governments, became more circumspect about voicing criticism of China's human-rights policies, and chose not to apply more pressure on trade issues. Efforts at enhanced balancing, including proposals for new military capabilities, more aggressive operational concepts, or closer strategic cooperation with friends and allies, also typically had to overcome objections that such measures were unnecessary and wasteful at best, if not provocative, dangerous and destabilising.[21] Even certain words and phrases were barred from the official lexicon on grounds that they might appear offensive or unnecessarily combative to Beijing.[22] Although they were supposed to go hand in hand, the West's enthusiasm for engagement tended over time to undercut its commitment to balancing.

Rather than being the result of a single decisive event, the current crisis of strategic confidence in the United States and across the West is the product of disturbing developments on a wide range of fronts. For the first time since the start of the post-Cold War era, these have begun to raise widespread doubts about the continuing efficacy of engagement, as well as adding to concerns over the eroding balance of power. As a result, the pro-engagement coalition has begun to fragment, even as the balancing coalition gains in strength. In addition to the testing of new weapons and the construction of artificial islands in the South China Sea, the past decade has seen a brutal crackdown on lawyers, dissidents, foreign media and non-governmental organisations, the roll-out of a massive, Orwellian national-surveillance system, a steadily worsening climate for foreign firms seeking to do business in China, and a growing chorus of complaints about intellectual-property theft, cyber espionage and political-influence operations.

The list is long and it continues to grow. Some experienced observers speculate that, by highlighting the anti-democratic character of the Chinese regime, the March 2018 constitutional revision that enables Xi Jinping to serve as president for life could have 'a stunning effect on the American public comparable to the Soviet Union's successful launching of Sputnik'.[23] Whether or not this turns out to be the case, recent events have helped spark the most serious debate over China policy in more than a generation.

The sources of Chinese conduct

While novel in certain respects, the policies now being pursued by Xi Jinping are a response to the same forces, and to a similar blend of ambition and anxiety, as those that shaped the policies of his predecessors. Indeed, rather than being a radical departure from the past, Xi's approach is actually a lineal descendant of the one put in place under Deng in the early 1990s. Before turning to a brief description of current Chinese strategy and the process through which it evolved, it is important to identify the underlying factors that have been central in shaping it. Three, in particular, stand out.

Geopolitics

Like virtually every other fast-rising power in history (including the United States), China seeks to reshape the international environment, starting with its immediate neighbourhood, in ways that better reflect its strength and serve its interests. The nation's rulers want to secure China's 'place in the sun': they aim to alter geographical boundaries, institutional structures, rules, norms and hierarchies of prestige that were put in place when their country was relatively weak, and which they therefore regard as illegitimate and, in certain respects, threatening.

History

China is not just any rising power; it is a nation with a long and proud history as the leading centre of East Asian civilisation and a more recent, inglorious experience of domination and humiliation at the hands of foreign intruders. China's leaders see their country as not merely *rising,* but rather *returning* to a position of regional pre-eminence that it once held and which they (and many of their people) regard as natural and appropriate.

Regime

China is ruled by a one-party authoritarian regime that is determined at all costs to retain its exclusive grip on political power, and which feels itself to be constantly under threat from enemies, foreign and domestic. These facts have a profound impact on every aspect of policy, internal and external. A democratic China would no doubt have its differences with other countries, including the United States. But the illiberal character of the current regime shapes how it perceives threats, and how it defines its interests and goes about pursuing them.

CCP leaders believe that the United States and its liberal-democratic allies are implacably opposed to them on ideological grounds and that the US, in particular, seeks not only to encircle and contain China but to undermine its current regime by promoting 'splitism' (that is, separatist movements in Tibet, Xinjiang and Taiwan) and 'peaceful evolution' (that is, the spread of liberal-democratic beliefs among the Chinese population).[24] Warding off these threats requires that Beijing exert greater control over events around

China's periphery and in the international system as a whole, while continuously refining its capabilities for domestic surveillance and repression.

In addition to coercion, the regime has sought to guard against ideological subversion and to bolster domestic political support; it has done this by managing the national economy in ways intended to sustain growth and employment, and by promulgating a distinctive, state-manufactured form of popular nationalism. China's pervasive (and still expanding) system of domestic propaganda and 'patriotic education' emphasises the wrongs done to China by foreign powers during the 'century of humiliation' and the essential (and as yet unfinished) role of the CCP in righting those wrongs. Together with the promise of continuing improvements in living standards, nationalism is the primary prop on which the regime relies for its legitimacy.

In recent years Beijing has also made increasing use of crises and confrontations over issues of history, territorial control and national pride to mobilise popular sentiment and deflect the frustrations of the Chinese people outwards, toward alleged foreign enemies, including Japan and the United States. Especially if economic growth falters, militant nationalism and 'standing up' to foreign enemies are likely to become increasingly important parts of the CCP's strategy for retaining its hold on power. Insecure about their own legitimacy, China's rulers believe that the stronger their country appears abroad, the stronger the regime will be at home.

The evolution of Chinese strategy

Shaped by these forces, China's post-Cold War strategy has evolved through three phases: a foundational period extending from 1991 to 2008, a period of transition between 2008 and 2012, and a new and distinctly more aggressive stage that began in 2013.

Founding

Just as the United States pursued a consistent set of policies towards China, so also, for the better part of two decades after 1989, did China have a broadly stable strategy for dealing with the United States. The essential theme of China's approach during this period was expressed in Deng's '24 Character Strategy' formulated in the aftermath of Tiananmen and shortly before the final collapse and disintegration of the Soviet Union. Here Deng advised that, in light of its relative weakness, diplomatic isolation and potential susceptibility to economic pressure, China should 'hide its capabilities and bide its time'.[25]

Adhering to this dictum, throughout the 1990s and into the early 2000s Deng, and his successors Jiang Zemin and Hu Jintao, worked to avoid conflict and improve relations with the United States and the other major advanced industrial nations, while at the same time strengthening ties to virtually all of China's neighbours. At home, despite the objections of some Party elders, the CCP regime resumed its pursuit of reform and opening up, but it also took care to preserve control over key sectors of the economy, as well as the overall process of development.[26] Economic growth raised incomes and helped to revive popular support for the regime, while providing the resources necessary to build every element of China's 'comprehensive national power'.[27] Beginning in the mid-1990s, Beijing launched a major military build-up aimed at improving its ability to coerce, deter and, if necessary, defeat any potential opponent. It also expanded its capacities for maintaining social control, including by bolstering the People's Armed Police (a second army dedicated to preserving domestic security), strengthening all elements of the public-security apparatus and launching the nationwide programme of patriotic education.[28]

China's leaders during this period saw themselves as being on the defensive in relation to the United States, which was nearing the apogee of its 'unipolar moment'. Having dispatched the Soviet Union, it seemed only a matter of time before the Americans turned the full weight of their attention to destroying the last bastion of socialism.[29] Chinese strategists comforted themselves with the thought that long-term historical trends would eventually promote the 'democratisation' of the international system, as other nations (most notably China) grew more rapidly and began to close the gap with the United States. But that did not mean that they could afford to remain passive. Instead, they sought to advance incrementally towards their long-term goals, holding Washington close by highlighting the mutual benefits of engagement and encouraging the belief that political liberalisation might, in fact, be imminent, while at the same time working quietly to weaken and constrict the American position in Asia.

Transition

By the turn of the century, China was markedly stronger in virtually every respect than it had been only a decade before. Growth, fuelled by trade, had reached unprecedented levels and, thanks to Beijing's entry into the WTO, the prospects for further rapid and uninterrupted progress seemed assured. China had broken out of its post-Tiananmen diplomatic isolation and enjoyed good relations with most of its neighbours and all the major powers. After a period during which it seemed that the Americans might be gearing up for an intensified strategic rivalry, the 9/11 attacks fortuitously diverted Washington's attention to other problems and other parts of the world. As Hu Jintao prepared to take office in 2002, the situation appeared so favourable that the regime officially endorsed the view that China could expect to enjoy a 20-year 'period of strategic opportunity' during which it was unlikely to face major conflict and would be free to concentrate on further enhancing its comprehensive national power.[30]

The global financial crisis of 2008 marked the beginning of a decisive shift in the tone and substance of Chinese strategy, a trend that would be consolidated and accelerated after Xi replaced Hu at the end of 2012. Coming on the heels of America's deepening difficulties in Iraq, and the seeming erosion of its stature as a global leader, the crisis and its aftermath convinced many Chinese analysts and policymakers that the relative power of the United States was declining more rapidly than had been expected. It stood to reason that China should seize the opportunity to expand its influence and advance more rapidly towards its long-term goals.[31]

Along with its beneficial effects, however, the crisis also raised the prospect of slower domestic growth, rising unemployment and an increasing risk of social unrest. This was both an immediate worry (due to an expected collapse in global demand for Chinese exports) and a longer-term concern, reflecting a deepening awareness that China's existing growth model was, in the words of premier Wen Jiabao, 'unsteady, unbalanced, uncoordinated and unsustainable'.[32] In the wake of the financial crisis, the spectre of stagnation and the potential consequences of economic failure were never far from the minds of China's rulers.[33]

Beijing's increasing assertiveness, first visible in its more aggressive prosecution of long-standing maritime disputes in the East and South China seas starting in 2009–10, was fuelled by this potent blend of ambition and fear. On the one hand, China's leaders hoped to exploit what they perceived to be a period of American weakness and preoccupation in order to create facts on the ground and improve China's relative position. At the same time, Beijing also sought to use increased tensions with other countries, including Japan, the Philippines, Vietnam and, indirectly, the United States, to stir nationalist sentiments, mobilise public support and bolster popular backing for the regime.[34]

The start of a 'new era'

The tendencies that emerged during the latter years of Hu's second term have been amplified and institutionalised under Xi Jinping. Like those who came before them, Xi and his colleagues are driven by a mixture of anxiety and optimism. They appear to be even more confident than were their predecessors a decade ago that America is in decline, that their own national power is on the rise and that the moment has come for China to reclaim its rightful place on the world stage. What they see as the recent mismanagement by the United States of the global economy, its difficulties in following through on the pivot, the intensifying division and dysfunction of its political system and its apparent inclination to turn inward under the presidency of Donald Trump have only served to reinforce these convictions.

And yet, this long-term confidence is still tinged with uncertainty and a sense of urgency. Xi and those in his inner circle know that they face serious difficulties of their own in sustaining growth, dealing with debt and corruption, addressing the needs of an ageing population and ameliorating the harmful effects of a severely polluted natural environment, among other pressing problems. Despite their increasingly open expressions of contempt for democracy, they likely also retain a healthy respect for the resilience of the United States and for its ability to mobilise resources and generate power once its leaders and people recognise that they are being challenged. As predicted by the Party's theorists, the window of strategic opportunity will not remain open forever, and may already be starting to close.

In order to seize the moment, and in keeping with this assessment of the overall configuration of forces, Xi has launched an integrated set of policies and programmes designed to strengthen his own authority and that of the CCP at home, sustaining and if possible accelerating the growth of China's comprehensive national power and applying it more boldly and more effectively to achieve the nation's objectives in Asia and beyond.

Xi's signature domestic initiatives – the anti-corruption and stepped-up patriotic-education campaigns,[35] the crackdown on dissidents and the internet,[36] the issuance of new ideological guidelines calling for increased vigilance against corrupting Western ideas[37] – are all intended to enhance his own power over the CCP, and the Party's control over the state, the military, the economy and all segments of society.

As regards China's external objectives, Hu Jintao may have harboured the hope that his country would one day be able to re-emerge as the leading power in Asia and perhaps the wider world. But he remained extremely careful not even to hint at such a possibility, and refused to dispense with Deng's 'hide and bide' as the guiding principle of Chinese strategy.

By contrast, soon after Xi's accession to power, Deng's directive was finally eased into retirement and high-ranking officials began to use the phrase 'striving for achievement' to characterise their new and distinctive approach to strategy.[38] Beyond this general statement of intent, from his earliest days in office, Xi has said that his goal is to achieve the 'China Dream' of the 'great rejuvenation of the Chinese nation', and to do so no later than the 100th anniversary of the founding of the People's Republic in 2049. While these words too are subject to interpretation, many Chinese as well as Western observers agree that, at a minimum, they imply the restoration of China to its 'rightful' place at the centre of Asia.[39] As one senior academic and government adviser explains:

> President Xi Jinping is very ambitious to increase China's growing power and even for China to take on a dominant role in the Asia and Western Pacific area. Over the long term, this power and influence will undoubtedly weaken and ultimately abolish U.S. dominance in the region.[40]

From the start of his first term in office, Xi's forward-leaning inclinations have been visible across Eurasia. Picking up where Hu left off, in his first speech on foreign policy Xi signalled a tougher stance in China's ongoing maritime disputes, warning other claimants that Beijing would 'never bargain over our core national interests'.[41] Within a matter of months, in late 2013, he authorised a series of steps that Hu had reportedly rejected as overly aggressive, including declaring an air defence identification zone (ADIZ) over the East China Sea and beginning construction of artificial islands in the South China Sea.[42]

Xi's strategic activism has not been directed exclusively to the east. Coincident with these more assertive measures in the maritime domain, he also announced what would eventually come to be known as the Belt and Road Initiative, a hugely ambitious set of proposals for investment and infrastructure development designed to stretch, over land, across Central Asia to Europe and the Middle East and, by sea, down through the South China Sea and the Indian Ocean all the way to the Persian Gulf and the Mediterranean.[43]

Accompanying all of this was a stepped-up campaign of 'peripheral diplomacy' intended in part to offset and neutralise the American pivot while enhancing Beijing's own standing and influence. Instead of being portrayed merely as relics of the Cold War that had outlived their usefulness, Chinese spokesmen began to denounce America's alliances as a source of instability and an obstacle to regional peace.[44] In place of the existing, divisive 'Cold War … zero-sum' concepts and structures, in 2014 Xi called for a new pan-Asian system to provide 'common, comprehensive, cooperative and sustainable security' for the entire region. Although he did not say so in as many words, the United States would evidently have little or no role to play in such a system. After all, as Xi told his listeners, 'in the final analysis, it is for the people of Asia to run the affairs of Asia, solve the problems of Asia and uphold the security of Asia'.[45]

Under Xi, China has intensified its use of all the instruments of national power, including military coercion, diplomatic suasion, economic leverage and 'political warfare' or influence operations to advance towards its long-standing goal of regaining a preponderant position in eastern

Eurasia. While it remains shrouded in soothing rhetoric and is still, in some respects, a work in progress even in the minds of its architects, the contours of that objective have also become increasingly evident in the past five years. What Beijing has in mind when it speaks of a 'community of common destiny' appears in fact to be a new regional sub-system, insulated to a degree from the larger and still Western-dominated global system, joined together by economic exchange, physical infrastructure, agreed rules and institutions for consultation and the coordination of policy, all with China at the centre and with the United States pushed to the periphery, if not out of the region altogether.[46]

Nor is this the limit of Xi's ambitions. Whereas previous generations of Chinese leaders went out of their way to foreswear any intention of attempting to match, still less overtake, the United States in terms of overall power and influence, Xi has made clear that he already regards what he describes as a 'new type great power relationship' as a coming together of equals.[47] As the vice-president of an intelligence-community-linked think tank explains, the 'shrinking discrepancy' between the US and China means that the relationship between them has 'graduated from superpower/major power to world's Number 1/Number 2'.[48] Left unspoken for the moment is the obvious possibility that, at some point, these rankings will be reversed.

In time, as Xi told the 19th Party Congress, China will 'move closer to centre stage', taking on a greater role as a world leader. Senior officials now openly express dissatisfaction with the 'existing world order' which they describe as 'built and led by the US', rooted in 'American or western values', and operating to Washington's 'great benefit' but to the detriment of other nations.[49] In part because change has come more quickly than expected, by their own admission, Chinese theorists have not yet advanced anything resembling a fully developed vision for what they would like a new and more 'democratic' world order to look like.[50] For the time being, Beijing will continue to take an à la carte approach to the existing system, supporting those international institutions that serve its interests (including the WTO and the UN Security Council), ignoring those that do not (such as the International Tribunal for the Law of the Sea), turning others (like INTERPOL) to its own purposes, and weakening or subverting those (like the UN Commission on Human Rights) that might otherwise pose a challenge to its legitimacy. In some areas, China has also begun to develop new institutions (like the New Development Bank) and to promote new norms (like the idea of 'internet sovereignty') that aim to circumvent those favoured by the West. Finally, instead of shying away, as it has done in the past, Beijing has embraced the idea of ideological competition, offering China's mixture of market-driven economics and authoritarian politics as 'a new option for other countries … who want to speed up their development while preserving their independence'.[51]

At home, in Asia and in the world at large, Xi is pursuing policies that, despite their evident diversity and complexity, have a strong unifying theme. Xi's strategy may not succeed, and could fail catastrophically, but the momentum and sense of purpose that drives it, and the resources being mobilised to support it, are undeniably impressive. Just as at the turn of the twentieth century American policymakers set out to 'make the world safe for democracy', so, at the start of the twenty-first century, their Chinese counterparts are attempting to make it safe for authoritarianism.

A countervailing strategy

At the end of the Cold War, the United States shifted from containment to what Bill Clinton's national-security advisor Anthony Lake labelled a policy of 'enlargement'.[52] The ultimate aim of this strategy was to hasten the transformation of China, Russia and other former communist regimes into liberal democracies by incorporating them as fully as possible into the open, liberal system that the Western powers had built for themselves in the years following the end of the Second World War. Instead of transforming them, however, incorporation made it easier for the two authoritarian great powers to gain in strength while granting them essentially unrestricted access to the economies and societies of the democracies.

The failure of their ambitious, optimistic post-Cold War strategy requires the United States and its allies to revert to a more defensive posture, protecting themselves more effectively both from external coercion or aggression and from internal exploitation or subversion. To a certain extent, the objectives of a new US China strategy can be defined in traditional terms:

- As it has done since the early part of the nineteenth century, the United States must oppose attempts by foreign powers to deny free use of the global commons. If permitted to succeed, such efforts could damage the prosperity of the United States and the other advanced industrial democracies.

- As it has done since the early part of the twentieth century, the United States must seek to prevent the direct, physical or indirect, economic and geopolitical domination of either end of the Eurasian landmass by a hostile power or coalition. A hostile regional hegemon might be able to aggregate the resources of its neighbours and could use its preponderant position as a base from which to project power in ways threatening to the United States and its interests and allies in other regions.

- As it has done since the end of the Second World War, the United States must continue to assist its treaty allies and, to the extent possible, non-allied, friendly nations in defending themselves against attack or coercion. Upholding alliance commitments is both a means to the larger end of preventing regional domination by a hostile power and, because virtually all US allies are fellow democracies, an end desirable in itself.

- As it has done since the 1960s, the United States must also continue to work to prevent the further spread of weapons of mass destruction including, for the time being, discouraging its regional friends and allies from acquiring nuclear weapons despite the fact that, in Asia, they feel increasingly threatened by the growing capabilities of China and its ally North Korea.

In addition to these more familiar, outward-looking goals, a new strategy must also look inward. Without entirely excluding the authoritarian powers, the United States and its allies will have to find ways to respond to the threats to their economies, societies and political systems that have arisen as a result of a prolonged period of excessive and imprudent openness. As regards China this will require:

- Working to neutralise Beijing's attempts to use economic lever-age, political warfare and other techniques to alter the perceptions and policies of democratic countries, including the United States.
- Defending against practices, including massive state subsidies, formal and informal barriers to foreign imports and investment, and the theft or forced extraction of technology and intellectual property that could damage the long-term prospects of US and other Western economies relative to China's.

Although this aspect of the challenge is still in its early stages, Beijing's increasing activism and ambition necessitate the addition of a final, global dimension to any new strategy:

- Together with like-minded friends and allies, the United States must work to counter Chinese efforts to exploit or weaken global rules and institutions rooted in liberal principles of political and economic openness, and its attempts to encourage the consolida-tion and spread of illiberal norms and authoritarian regimes.

As they pursue these defensive aims, the United States and its allies should continue to seek the best possible relationship with Beijing, cooper-ating where possible on issues of convergent interest and doing whatever they can to avoid a conflict that would be catastrophic for all concerned. But they must do so with a clear-eyed appreciation of the likely limits on such cooperation, without backing away from their other objectives or compro-mising their values, and without giving up on efforts, however indirect, to encourage tendencies within China that may someday result in its transi-tion to a more liberal and democratic form of government.

Engagement in its current form has obviously failed to promote this shift, but that does not mean it should be abandoned as an objective. Without a fundamental change in the character of its domestic regime, a lasting, trust-ing and mutually beneficial relationship between China, the United States and the other democracies will prove impossible to attain. Such a relation-ship may someday be within reach, but, to paraphrase George Kennan, it will have to await 'either the break-up or the gradual mellowing' of the power of the Chinese Communist Party.[53]

Alternatives

To achieve these ends, the United States need not abandon altogether the mixed strategy it has been pursuing since the end of the Cold War. But, together with its allies, it must modify substantially the mixture of elements which that strategy contains. In sum, the United States and its strategic partners should increase and better integrate their investments in balancing, while at the same time regulating more carefully – and in certain respects constricting – their present posture of open and still largely unconstrained engagement with China.

Before turning to a detailed description of the various elements of this strategy, it may be helpful to bracket it between two conceivable alternatives.[54] At one end of the spectrum of possibilities is an approach that would effectively abandon engagement in favour of a return to Cold War-style containment. The United States did, of course, pursue such policies toward China from the late 1940s to the late 1960s, cutting off virtually all trade and investment, providing armed support to separatists in Tibet, attempting to destabilise, and refusing even to recognise, the government in Beijing. Nothing of the sort is suggested here. Such a course would carry extraordinary costs and risks, and, even if it were desirable from a strategic standpoint, it could not at present win the support necessary to sustain it, either from the American public or from the people and governments of its allies.

Inverting the emphasis of containment, under a strategy of accommodation Washington would back away from balancing in favour of seeking a 'grand bargain' with Beijing, perhaps involving the delineation of spheres of influence between the two Pacific powers. But of what would such a deal consist? The notion advanced by some scholars that China might be willing to settle for a preponderant position in continental Eurasia, leaving the United States and its allies to dominate the maritime domain, is belied by Beijing's recent activism in the East and South China seas, to say nothing of the ongoing expansion in its naval capabilities.[55] Putting aside the obvious moral objections, even permitting the mainland to absorb Taiwan, as a few analysts have suggested, would probably prove insufficient to head off an accelerating strategic rivalry.[56] To the contrary, because it would enhance China's ability to project military power into the Western Pacific while shaking the confidence of America's allies, such a gesture would likely feed Beijing's appetite for further gains.

For as long as they believe that long-term trends are running in their favour, China's leaders are unlikely to be satisfied even with substantial concessions from the United States or its allies. The things that they most want, however – including not only an end to the US commitment to Taiwan, but control over the East and South China seas, the withdrawal of America's forward-based forces, the dissolution of its alliances and perhaps the eventual creation of a new Sino-centric order in eastern Eurasia – are (or should be) unacceptable to their counterparts in Washington. While it is possible that some kind of new regional modus vivendi could emerge, it is more likely to take the form of a stalemate, following a period of vigorous competition, than a coolly negotiated *entente*.

Objections

The strategy outlined here is susceptible to numerous potential objections, of which two warrant particular attention. As has happened so often in the past, some will no doubt argue that taking steps to increase balancing or constrain engagement risks triggering an arms race, a trade war, a new Cold War and perhaps even a real, hot war. While there is every reason to proceed with caution and to avoid unnecessary provocation, the fact remains that in virtually every realm an intense rivalry is already well under way. The difficulty is that, until quite recently, these competitions have been excessively one-sided. To take the most obvious examples: for more than two decades, China's defence-research and -procurement programmes have been aimed at matching or neutralising US and Western military advantages, while its state-directed economic programmes used every available method to help Chinese firms gain an edge over their foreign competitors. What has been lacking thus far is a serious, focused and coordinated Western response. Failure to react effectively now will result in a further erosion of the position of the United States and its allies, weakening their ability to protect their interests and potentially increasing the danger of future miscalculation and possible conflict. The most important thing the democracies can do to keep the peace is to look to their own defences.

A second objection to the course of action described below is that, especially in the military domain, it could prove difficult to sustain. Given the size and dynamism of the Chinese economy, and the slower growth rates and already substantial claims on the fiscal resources of the democracies, in the long run it may simply be impossible for the United States and its allies to compete effectively with Beijing. Perhaps Chinese hegemony truly is inevitable, at least in Asia, and the most prudent course for other powers is to strike the best deal they can.

Despite Beijing's efforts to promote them, such projections are premature, at best. As its leaders are well aware, China's rate of growth has already slowed substantially from a peak of over 14% on the eve of the financial crisis to under 7% today, and it could fall further in the years ahead.[57] The fact that this will be happening as the population ages means that Beijing too will face competing budgetary demands.[58] Even if present trends continue, the United States and its strategic partners (including India, as well as Japan, South Korea and Australia, among others) will still command sufficient aggregate wealth to enable them to defend their interests and preserve a favourable balance of power, should they choose to do so.[59]

The final clause is key. While it is not yet clear what level of effort will be required over the long run, and while many of the necessary measures will not be costly in monetary terms, engaging in an intense, sustained strategic competition with China will undoubtedly require the democracies to devote more money to defence. That, in turn, will demand difficult and contentious decisions about spending, taxation and debt.[60] Such choices could result from a process of informed debate guided by wise and far-sighted leaders able to mould a national consensus on the need to compete more effectively against China; or they may emerge from a severe crisis or sudden setback. The former path would certainly be preferable, but if American history is any guide, the second may be more likely.

To meet the challenge China now poses, the United States and its allies will have to craft a countervailing strategy, an approach that seeks to blunt the momentum of Beijing's recent initiatives, mobilising resources and pushing back, over a period of years and possibly decades, by matching the enduring strengths and advantages of a diverse coalition made up mostly of maritime democracies against the weaknesses and vulnerabilities of their continental, authoritarian rival. The next two sections will discuss how this might best be done.

Enhanced balancing

The two primary elements of a mixed strategy are balancing and engagement, each of which comprises two components: diplomacy and military policy, in the first instance, and economic policy and information operations (or political warfare) in the second. These can be thought of as four instruments of national power, but it is more useful to think of them as four distinct but interlocking domains of competition.

Diplomacy

The diplomatic dimension of the US–China rivalry involves a competition in alliance-making and alliance-breaking. As has been true since the early 1990s, the United States seeks to strengthen and extend its network of alliance and quasi-alliance ties in order to maintain a favourable balance of power in Asia. For its part, China is attempting to weaken those ties, fragmenting a nascent US-led coalition so that it can establish itself as the preponderant regional power.

Thanks to China's growing power and increasing assertiveness, there are now strong balancing tendencies at work across Asia. It would be a serious mistake, however, to assume that a stable balance of power will form automatically, or that it can be sustained over the long run without active US involvement and leadership. Beijing seeks to delay and diminish the responses of individual countries, as well as attempting to exploit and widen possible differences among them. Divide-and-conquer tactics can work, especially where the members of an erstwhile countervailing coalition are geographically dispersed, have little prior experience of cooperation, and are not joined together by formal collective-security commitments or institutions. In part for these reasons, some analysts have suggested that

Asia, unlike Europe, may be a region in which other states are more likely to 'bandwagon' with a rising power than to balance against it.[61]

While this could turn out eventually to be the case, the last several years have instead seen a marked uptick in strategic consultation and cooperation, not only between Washington and each of its traditional allies and new-found friends, but among the regional states. Japan has been especially active in this regard, strengthening its own bilateral ties with India, Australia, Vietnam and Europe, while India, for its part, has moved to do the same with Japan, Vietnam and Australia.[62] The United States should do what it can to encourage and enable these linkages, as well as working to give real substance to new and still relatively loose multilateral groupings in which it is actively engaged, like the US–India–Japan–Australia 'Quad'. It is possible to exaggerate the utility of such arrangements; occasional summits, exercises and even arms sales do not come close to approximating the level of coordination found in a functioning alliance.[63] But the aim of this element of US strategy should be to promote the growth of an increasingly dense, overlapping network of ties. These can ease policy consultation and coordination, build familiarity and habits of cooperation and could, if necessary, harden quickly into a true, multilateral defensive coalition.[64]

China is a permanent presence

The scope of the diplomatic competition between the US and China is no longer limited to Asia. Beijing is now trying to use its growing economic clout (and increasing uncertainty over the direction of US policy) to promote divisions within Europe, and between Europe and the United States. For its part, the United States should be doing more to mobilise the support of its European allies in pursuit of common objectives in Asia. The fact that many European governments now share US concerns over the direction of Chinese policy on a variety of fronts should make this easier than might have been the case only a few years ago. If its members can work together, a unified global coalition of democracies could exert considerable pressure on China on freedom of navigation, human rights, trade, cyber security, political-influence operations and the protection of intellectual property, among other issues.[65]

In the diplomatic realm, the most important task confronting the United States is to find ways to reassure its Asian allies and strategic partners about the depth and permanence of its commitments. This is a challenge in part because of geography: China's proximity makes it a threat, but it is also undeniably a permanent presence. The United States, by contrast, is far away, and could choose at some point to pull back from the region. In recent years Chinese diplomats have also advanced the view that America's commitments are unreliable because it is a declining power, with an increasingly narrow view of its own interests.[66]

In addition to adjustments in military and economic policy that will be discussed more fully below, Washington can help to counter this narrative by highlighting the common values that link it with most of its major regional allies and strategic partners, including Taiwan and India, as well as Japan, Australia and South Korea. Aside from commercial interests or purely geopolitical concerns, these shared beliefs provide an enduring foundation for cooperation. They also make it extremely unlikely that Washington would ever willingly cede regional preponderance to an authoritarian China. As the last 75 years make clear, the United States has a history of helping its fellow liberal democracies to preserve their open social, political and economic systems, even at some cost to itself, and even at the risk of war.

To date the Trump administration's track record in this domain of competition has been mixed, at best. Saying that the United States seeks a 'free and open Indo-Pacific' is a step in the right direction, but it should be clear that what is at stake here is not only freedom of navigation and open markets, but the continuing security and prosperity of free and open (that is, liberal-democratic) *societies* along China's maritime periphery.[67] Unfortunately, the impact of this slogan is further weakened by the president's reluctance to use the language of principle to describe America's commitments to its allies (or the failings of its authoritarian rivals) and his insistence on discussing alliance relationships primarily in transactional, monetary terms.

As it bolsters its own alliances and partnerships, the United States should also be looking for ways to exploit the problems and complications that will arise as China diversifies its own commitments. As Beijing seeks to advance and defend its far-flung interests across Central Asia and into the Middle East, Africa and Latin America, it will become more enmeshed in the internal affairs of an assortment of developing countries. China's dubious financial dealings with some of the nations along the Belt and Road are raising questions about its intentions, and ironically risk casting it in the role of a twenty-first-century neo-imperialist power.[68] It is already supporting an array of regimes with poor human-rights records, and in future it is likely to be drawn more deeply into local conflicts, possibly resulting in significant material and reputational costs.

Beijing's westward thrust is also causing it to intrude further into areas still considered by Moscow to lie within its sphere of influence, including Central Asia and parts of Eastern Europe. The Sino-Russian axis remains strong, thanks in part to the Western response to Russia's intervention in Ukraine, as well as Moscow and Beijing's shared fear of liberal democracy. In the long run, however, a continuing alignment between the two nations is not inevitable as China's growing wealth, power, influence and presence cause resentment and anxiety in Russia. Even as they oppose Vladimir Putin's attempts to bully and destabilise them, the nations of the West should not foreclose the possibility that they may one day be able to draw Russia back towards them, providing it with options other than deepening subservience to China.

Military

The Sino-American military rivalry pits a global power attempting to defend its dominant position in the Asia-Pacific against a fast-rising challenger that seeks regional preponderance and is in the early stages of projecting its own power on a wider scale. The United States seeks to preserve its ability to project power into the Western Pacific in order to support its allies and ensure freedom of navigation. For its part, China is working to neutralise US advantages in order to deter and, if necessary, to defeat any attempt at intervention. Beijing's intention is not to wage war but rather to 'win without fighting', undermining the US position by raising doubts about the viability of its security guarantees, while driving the military competition in directions that make it increasingly difficult to sustain by imposing disproportionate costs on America and its allies. This complex competition can be broken down into three parts:

US power projection versus China's anti-access/area denial (A2/AD). At the end of the Cold War, the United States had a virtually unchallenged ability to project and sustain overwhelming conventional air and naval power in the Western Pacific using local ports and airfields, surface and under-sea naval platforms, and assets based in space and deployed from facilities outside the region. In the last two decades, China has developed and is in the process of expanding its capabilities to strike at all elements of the US power-projection system. Among other weapons, Beijing has deployed conventional ballistic missiles targeted against fixed facilities and ships at sea, and large numbers of anti-ship and land-attack cruise missiles launched from air, sea, undersea and land.[69]

The Obama administration highlighted these troubling trends in the regional military balance and proposed to meet them, first in 2011 by announcing development of the so-called Air–Sea Battle operational concept (later renamed the 'Joint Concept for Operational Access and Maneuver in the Global Commons') and then in 2014 by pursuing a set of technological counters under what came to be known as the Third Offset Strategy.[70] Neither of these initiatives was brought fully to fruition, and it is not yet clear whether and, if so, in what form they will continue.[71] But the problems they were meant to address remain and have only grown more intense.

Having called attention to the challenge posed by China's A2/AD capabilities, American strategists and their allied counterparts now need to develop a credible response to them, one that can be discussed publicly in at least general terms. Whatever label is attached to it, the purpose of this response must be to bolster deterrence by eroding the confidence of Chinese planners that they could ever hope to carry out a disarming conventional first strike at the outset of any future war. In the first instance, this will require taking steps to reduce the vulnerability of US and allied forces and bases through some combination of active and passive defences, cover and deception, in-theatre dispersal, and improved capabilities for defending, reconstituting or replacing damaged satellites, cyber networks and other C4ISR assets.

Because modern wars are not won (or deterred) by adopting a purely defensive posture, the United States will also need to enhance its capabilities for conducting long-range conventional precision strikes against a large number of widely dispersed targets, including some inside China. This will require deploying more sea- and air-launched cruise missiles; developing and deploying new aircraft, both manned and unmanned, capable of penetrating Chinese air defences; and developing conventionally armed ballistic missiles, possibly including hypersonic delivery vehicles as well as more traditional intermediate-range missiles.[72] These offensive capabilities can contribute to deterrence by making clear to Chinese leaders that conventional strikes on US and allied forces and bases would be met with a prompt, proportionate response.[73]

Finally, the US and its allies should further develop their already existing capacity to respond to a large-scale use of force by China in the Western Pacific with some form of naval blockade.[74] Preparing for such a contingency might require deploying more attack submarines and more air- and submarine-launched anti-ship cruise missiles, procuring more mines and developing sophisticated unmanned underwater vehicles capable of autonomous operations. Even if it is left largely implicit, the threat of a blockade should enhance deterrence by making clear that aggression would likely result in a disruption in China's ability to use the seas to export its products or import the energy, natural resources and food it needs to keep its economy running. Beijing's anxiety over maritime interdiction is already helping drive investment in costly and potentially problematic projects designed to improve energy security, including overland pipelines. From the perspective of the long-term military competition, it would be preferable if China increased spending on these activities, rather than investing even more in its offensive aerospace and naval capabilities.

Extended nuclear deterrence versus counter-deterrence. In Asia, as in other parts of the world, America's security guarantees are backed by the promise that, if necessary, it will use nuclear weapons to defend its allies. Throughout the Cold War and into the early post-Cold War period, this promise was highly credible vis-à-vis China because, in addition to its conventional advantages, the United States enjoyed a massive margin of nuclear superiority. Although it did develop significant capabilities for striking US allies, for most of this period Beijing had little or no capacity to deliver nuclear weapons against targets on American soil. When it began to deploy intercontinental ballistic missiles (ICBMs) in the 1980s and 1990s, they were few in number and, because of their technical characteristics (fixed, liquid-fuelled), potentially vulnerable to US pre-emption.

In the past decade this situation has started to shift, as China has begun to modernise and modestly expand the size of its long-range missile forces, adding land-mobile and submarine-launched ballistic missiles and developing multiple warheads.[75] These developments may be motivated in part by a desire to maintain China's ability to threaten the United States with nuclear attack in the face of ongoing improvements in US conventional precision-strike and missile-defence capabilities. However, China's modernisation programmes (together with the ongoing development of North Korea's nuclear capabilities) are also raising questions about the continued viability of US extended-deterrent nuclear guarantees. America's allies may fear (and Chinese planners might hope) that, if they cannot do anything to prevent dozens of nuclear weapons from being detonated on their own territory, US decision-makers would hesitate to escalate to nuclear use if necessary to stop an overwhelming conventional assault, or perhaps even to retaliate against Chinese nuclear strikes on US allies.

In order to reassure its allies and deter potential opponents, the United States should maintain significant, survivable nuclear forces that can be deployed forward into the Indo-Pacific. American policymakers should also make clear that they have the ability, if necessary, to conduct limited nuclear operations and the intention to maintain intercontinental-range forces that remain larger by several orders of magnitude than their Chinese counterparts.[76] The Department of Defense should also continue to fund research and development programmes that might permit deployment of an expanded national missile-defence system in the event of an accelerating strategic nuclear competition with China.

Chinese power projection versus US (and allied) A2/AD. In addition to attempting to counter US power projection, China is beginning to develop the capacity to project military power at increasing distances from its shores. Within the First Island Chain, Beijing is working to establish a zone of effective control, using a combination of land- (and eventually carrier-)

based aircraft, surface naval vessels, submarines, maritime-patrol craft, commercial vessels and forward bases on man-made islands. If it succeeds, China will be able to dominate exploitation of the mineral, energy and food resources that these waters contain, and to regulate transit through them by the ships of other nations. Looking further afield, China is in the early stages of acquiring truly blue-water naval vessels, long-range air- and maritime-support capabilities and a network of overseas facilities that will eventually enable it to project power in and around the Indian Ocean, the Persian Gulf and off the coasts of Africa, including into the waters of the Atlantic.

Countering Beijing's efforts to enclose and control the use of its 'near seas' requires a combination of enhanced US and allied presence in peacetime, and intensified preparations for engaging and defeating Chinese power-projection forces in the event of war.[77] In peacetime, the United States and its local friends and allies, as well as countries from outside the region, need to defy any attempt by Beijing to establish air or maritime exclusion zones by operating continuously wherever international law permits.[78] This will require greater coordination of effort and would be made easier by enhanced US access to facilities close to disputed areas.

To counter China's evolving power-projection forces, the US should help its regional partners enhance their own A2/AD capabilities. This would allow them to better defend their own waters and airspace, but it would also create a significant new problem for China's military planners, one that could be very costly for them to solve.[79]

As with its expansion across continental Eurasia, China's efforts to become a truly global military power will present strategic opportunities as well as challenges for other countries. Much time and money will be required to develop long-range air and naval forces and the skills and facilities necessary to operate them effectively. In the event of war, China's overseas bases would be extremely vulnerable and, without indigenous air and anti-submarine-warfare defences, its surface ships in distant waters would be hard-pressed to survive. If it chooses to compete in global power-projection capabilities, China will be entering an arena in which the United States has some very substantial advantages.

Constrained engagement

Stepped-up balancing entails costs and carries risks, but it does not present any deep conceptual challenges. The United States and its allies know how to increase their defence capabilities and intensify their diplomatic cooperation; for the most part what is required is simply to do more of what they are already doing, and have been doing for some time.

Constraining engagement is another matter altogether. Doing so will require the democracies to re-examine their assumptions about the unalloyed virtues of openness, and to find ways to protect their economies and societies without damaging their foundational principles or lessening the vitality that comes from the freest possible exchange of goods and ideas. In practical terms this will mean recalibrating relations with China, making them less open than has been the case for most of the past quarter-century while avoiding, if at all possible, the degree of closure that characterised the early stages of the Cold War. Whether a new equilibrium can be found will depend not only on what the democracies do to defend themselves, but on how hard and in what ways Beijing tries to preserve the advantages it derives from the status quo.

Economics

Economic engagement with the West has enabled China to grow richer and stronger without compelling its rulers to liberalise politically or, beyond a certain point, economically. As a result, China today remains an authoritarian country in which the party-state exercises a high degree of control over the direction of national economic development and now has vast resources with which to pursue its external objectives.

The twin challenges that China poses in the economic domain follow directly from these features of its domestic system. For Beijing, growth and prosperity are not ends in themselves, nor are they expected to emerge from the workings of freely functioning markets. Like the mercantilists of earlier eras, China's leaders believe that wealth begets power and power begets wealth. Rather than abandoning their own liberal principles, the United States and its allies must respond with policies that offset the effects of China's economic statecraft while minimising the harms done by its industrial policies.

Economic statecraft. China's explosive growth has transformed it into the leading trading partner, and biggest export destination, for most of its Asian neighbours, as well as other countries further afield. Beijing evidently hopes that, in the long run, the desire to maintain access to its market will shape the policy preferences, diplomatic postures and perhaps even the strategic alignments of its trading partners. Regional free-trade agreements that exclude the United States could help to accelerate these tendencies, in effect amplifying the already substantial gravitational pull of the Chinese economy.

While generally cautious about drawing too direct a connection, Chinese spokesmen have become blunter in suggesting that other nations, including US allies, will have to put more distance between themselves and Washington if they want to continue to enjoy the benefits of close economic relations with China.[80] In the last several years, Beijing has also sought on a number of occasions to wield access to its market more directly in order to punish other governments for actions deemed hostile to China's interests. Without ever acknowledging the political reasons for what it was doing, the Chinese government suspended imports of salmon from Norway in 2010 to punish it for granting the Nobel Peace Prize to dissident Liu Xiaobo, stopped buying bananas from the Philippines in 2012 during its continuing maritime dispute with Manila and, among other measures, in 2017 closed down a network of South Korean department stores to discipline Seoul for permitting the deployment of American missile-defence radars on its soil.[81] None of these actions caused the target country to reverse course, but that was not really their purpose. By demonstrating its ability to impose costs, Beijing aims to shape future behaviour, discouraging repeat offences and gradually altering the strategic calculations of its trading partners, many of whom happen also to be US allies.[82]

Beijing aims to shape future behaviour

In order to prevent its Asian friends and allies from being drawn ever more tightly into a China-centred Eurasian 'co-prosperity sphere', Washington should take steps to encourage the widest possible flows of trade and investment among them, with the other advanced industrial democracies and with the United States itself.[83] For this purpose, the recently signed Comprehensive and Progressive Agreement for Trans-Pacific Partnership (CPTPP or TPP-11) and the Japan–EU Economic Partnership Agreement represent important steps in the right direction. The inclusion of the United States in a revitalised Trans-Pacific Partnership would provide further advantages, as would an eventual transatlantic trade deal between the US and the EU. Such agreements would help to limit members' dependence on the Chinese market, increasing their growth rates and creating a liberal trading bloc made up almost entirely of democratic countries whose combined GDPs could account for as much as 60% of total world output.[84] Unfortunately, despite the potential economic and strategic benefits of new multilateral trade pacts, the Trump administration remains opposed.

Along with its growing importance as a market for imports, in the past decade China has become a major exporter of capital, investing in acquiring technology from the advanced industrial countries while building infrastructure and extracting raw materials across the developing world. As has become evident especially along both axes of its Belt and Road Initiative, Beijing's role as an investor has given it another tool with which to pursue its strategic ambitions as well as its economic interests. At the same time as it buys up resources and builds roads, rail lines, ports and pipelines to bring them back to China, Beijing is using money to penetrate the societies and political systems of its partners, increasing its influence and, in some cases, gaining leverage over them.[85]

Instead of giving grants, or funding its projects directly, Beijing often lends money to foreign governments who then use it to pay Chinese companies to do the necessary work. Because the loans come without the sorts of conditions often attached to Western aid, they may be appealing to local authorities wishing to avoid outside oversight, even if the terms and conditions are relatively onerous. If the host government is unable to repay its debts, Beijing stands ready to take control of valuable assets, including ports and natural resources.[86]

Aside from the fact that in many cases they serve to strengthen corrupt and illiberal regimes, while doing relatively little to aid the development of local economies, China's investments are meant to extend its influence across a large swath of continental Eurasia, binding other countries more tightly to it while enhancing its ability to project power into the maritime domain.[87] Western governments cannot prevent all of this from happening, nor should they try; but they should resist Beijing's entreaties that they lend legitimacy by endorsing the Belt and Road Initiative or, better yet, take part in funding projects from which China will derive the great bulk of the benefits. Along with some striking successes, Beijing's massive, hasty infrastructure push is likely to result in failed projects, wasted resources and, in some places, a significant measure of political backlash.[88] This is unfortunate in many respects, but in terms of the larger strategic competition it will be a detriment to China rather than the United States and its allies.

Where it makes economic sense to do so, and where the local authorities may be receptive, democratic governments and international aid agencies should be prepared to offer a healthy alternative to Chinese loans, reinvigorating their own efforts to promote infrastructure development and providing an option to those who wish to avoid being drawn too tightly into Beijing's orbit.[89] Rather than remaining silent, or giving in to requests for their approval, the United States and its allies should also be highlighting the risks and costs that often accompany China's money (including a potential loss of control over sovereign territory) and encouraging NGOs, journalists and political leaders in target countries to do the same.[90]

Industrial policy. Even after its entry into the WTO, China continued to use a mixture of subsidies, tariffs, non-tariff barriers and other measures to protect domestically based companies and to promote their fortunes in global markets. These practices caused some grumbling, but, with China continuing to lag technologically, and supposedly transitioning towards a more market-driven model of economic growth, they were not widely seen as threatening. Now even many previously optimistic observers have concluded that this is no longer the case.[91] Beijing evidently has no intention of willingly abandoning practices that it credits for its success. And its latest trade and industrial programmes are intended to catapult it from perennial follower to a position of leadership across an array of cutting-edge technologies. The fact that many of these, including semiconductors, artificial intelligence, robots and new materials, have both military and commercial applications is fuelling concerns about the implications for the security, as well as the future prosperity, of the advanced industrial countries.[92]

China's ability to achieve its objectives will depend on whether it can continue to exploit a marked disparity in the openness of its own economy relative to that of its Western trading partners. Because they continue to lag behind in most of the sectors they hope eventually to dominate, Chinese firms, at the direction and with the assistance of the party-state, have for some time been seeking to acquire the necessary technology from foreign sources. The methods for doing this include buying up companies overseas, investing in innovative start-ups in the US and other countries, compelling foreign firms to transfer core technologies in return for access to the Chinese market, and simply stealing intellectual property in massive quantities from companies, research labs and universities using cyber intrusions and other, more traditional methods.[93] With a few scattered exceptions, the United States and its major trade and security partners have thus far done very little to close off any of these avenues of access.

Having acquired the technology it needs, China intends to build up 'national champions' in key sectors, using low-cost loans and subsidies to fund capacity expansion, and limiting competition in the domestic market with procurement regulations, tariffs and non-tariff barriers. As it has already done in older industries like steel and aluminium, Beijing aims both to achieve a high degree of self-sufficiency and to capture a significant share of the global market for a wide array of advanced products and components.[94] Chinese planners have also initiated a series of 'mega-projects' to focus research, ensure funding and stimulate the more rapid development of technologies that are expected to have military as well as commercial applications, including quantum computing, high-end chips and next-generation wireless broadband communication.[95]

Even if they are less than completely successful, the impact of China's ambitious technology-transfer and industrial policies are likely to be far-reaching. If it can gain an edge in what has been described as a fourth industrial revolution in manufacturing, while reducing its dependence on high-tech imports, China may be able to boost its own prospects for long-term growth while diminishing those of its competitors.

China's increasing level of performance in science and technology, and its growing capacity for indigenous innovation, will also yield more direct military benefits. At a minimum, the qualitative edge that the United States and its allies continue to enjoy in many areas of capability is likely to erode, and in some, China could gain a strategically significant advantage.[96] Because future products and military systems will build on them, breakthroughs in technologies such as artificial intelligence could also yield enduring advantages. As a recent report for the US Department of Defense explains, 'what is at risk is not only losing an edge in the foundational technology, but also in successive generations of uses, applications and products'.[97]

The Trump administration, and especially the office of the US Trade Representative, deserves considerable credit for raising the salience of these issues, and its decision to impose punitive tariffs on companies in sectors believed to have profited from forced technology transfer has certainly gotten Beijing's attention. What remains to be determined is whether, and if so how, the resulting stand-off can be resolved so as to produce lasting benefits for the United States and the other advanced industrial democracies.

Broadly speaking, there are three possible scenarios for the future economic relationship between China and the West. In the first, the United States and its partners remain largely open and China becomes more closed. In the second, China reciprocates Western openness by reducing its barriers to trade and investment and by forgoing the predatory practices that have provoked the current crisis. In the third, Beijing continues on its present course and the United States and other Western nations respond by imposing protective measures of their own.

The first scenario could result from a decision by the White House to accept superficial concessions that improve access for American companies in certain sectors and perhaps commit China to purchase more goods and services from the United States. This could lower the bilateral trade deficit, at least for a time (thereby addressing a major presidential preoccupation), but it would do little to resolve the underlying problems caused by China's industrial policies.[98]

The second scenario could result from a period of negotiation in which the United States, perhaps joined by its industrial allies, brought pressure to bear on Beijing, eventually compelling it to accede to a number of demands. These might include eliminating technology-transfer requirements, cutting back on subsidies and liberalising government-procurement regulations to allow greater access for foreign firms.[99] This is the course of action, and the outcome, that most economists and business analysts would probably prefer. But a number of obstacles stand in the way. Fearful of Chinese retaliation and frustrated by the Trump administration's insistence on putting 'America First', including in its dealings with them over tariffs on metals and other trade issues, US allies might choose to remain aloof. In light of its deep commitment to existing plans and policies, Beijing could well prove unwilling, or effectively unable, to change course.[100] Indeed, some observers have suggested that China may already be 'signaling that it does not want to change',[101] and that its leaders could see the current confrontation with the US as 'an opportunity to remove any and all shackles from its industrial policy machine'.[102] Finally, even a deal that levelled the commercial playing field would not alleviate concerns over the possible strategic implications of continuing to allow a military competitor and geopolitical rival ready access to advanced technologies being developed in the West.

Beijing could prove unwilling to change course

For these reasons, the third scenario is probably the most likely; indeed, there are reasons to believe that it has already started to unfold. The United States and a number of its allies have begun to tighten restrictions on Chinese investment in sensitive sectors of their economies, and China is moving to further strengthen its own restrictions.[103] Congress is considering legislation that would strengthen and expand the role of the Committee on Foreign Investment in the United States, making it easier to block proposed transactions involving Chinese entities.[104] Other bills would bar federal agencies from buying telecommunication equipment from Chinese companies,[105] and make it more difficult for private companies providing internet service in rural areas to use federal funds for the same purpose.[106] Although it has yet to take action, in its recent National Security Strategy statement the Trump administration indicated that it might restrict visas for foreign science and engineering students from unnamed countries in order 'to ensure that intellectual property is not transferred to our competitors'.[107]

One way or another, China and the United States (together with at least some of the other advanced economies) appear to be headed, if not for a complete divorce, then at least for a degree of disentanglement and separation. This outcome could take the form of a negotiated 'peaceful disengagement', in which the two sides maintain ties in many areas, but pull back in others where they perceive security risks.[108] But separation seems more likely to result from a sequence of move, counter-move and angry mutual recrimination in which China refuses to alter course and the US and its partners respond by taking steps to 'defend their companies, technology, and institutions'.[109]

If it wants to maintain a meaningful measure of advantage, the United States cannot be content simply to try to slow the diffusion of strategically relevant technologies to China. It will need to do more to boost its own capacity for innovation, running faster to stay ahead. Among other things, this will require policies that reward productive investment, promote education, fund basic scientific research and attract skilled immigrants.[110]

Political warfare

The Sino-American rivalry is ultimately a war of ideas, or, put differently, a contest between two contending visions of the future. Because neither side has sufficient power to impose its will through coercion, both are constrained to use less direct means. Much of the current rivalry between the US and China therefore involves efforts by each to influence the perceptions and beliefs, and thus the policies, of the other side's leaders, elites and wider population, as well as those of other countries.

At least until quite recently, China's rulers have tended to see themselves as being on the defensive in this aspect of their wider struggle with the United States and its Western allies, bombarded by messages calling into question the legitimacy and likely longevity of their political and economic systems, and surrounded by a structure of international institutions, norms and rules that, at least in theory, reflect liberal principles inimical to their own. It is precisely in order to counteract and neutralise what it sees as an existential threat that the CCP regime has adopted a highly aggressive posture in conducting political warfare against the United States, its allies and other nations.

For their part, by contrast, American and other Western leaders have at times seemed oblivious to the mortal challenge that their insistence on the existence of universal values, the importance of human rights and the virtues of democracy poses to their opposite numbers in Beijing.[111] Believing in the self-evident superiority of the ideas they espouse, Western leaders have tended to assume that these would spread largely of their own accord. Confident that greater openness would inevitably work to their benefit, they have also done shockingly little to defend themselves against penetration, manipulation and subversion. Both the defensive and the offensive aspects of this relaxed, laissez-faire approach to political warfare are in urgent need of change.

Since its days as a conspiratorial revolutionary party, the CCP has had a highly developed doctrine and extensive organisational machinery for conducting united-front campaigns to divide and defeat both domestic and foreign opponents.[112] At times of perceived vulnerability, China's leaders have been especially attentive to the possible compensatory uses of what chairman Mao once described as the 'magic weapon' of political warfare. More recently, however, expanded influence operations have accompanied the growth and more aggressive use of all the other instruments of Chinese power.[113] Political warfare is now being used not only to push back against a Western ideological threat, but to ease the way for the rapid outward expansion of China's power and influence.

Beijing's stepped-up political-warfare campaign presently targets a wide array of countries, including but not limited to the United States, its friends and allies. Especially as regards the US and its fellow advanced industrial democracies, these operations are intended to help gain or maintain access to foreign markets, technology, ideas, information and capital deemed essential to China's continued economic success, while at the same time discouraging foreign governments, acting separately or in concert, from adopting policies that might impede its rise or interfere with the achievement of its strategic objectives. Beijing seeks to dull the competitive reflexes of its rivals, delaying or rendering ineffective their efforts to balance against its growing power.

Towards these ends the CCP works to shape the narrative about China, encouraging views that it sees as favourable to its interests and, to the extent possible, suppressing those that are not. The regime's methods for doing this vary according to local conditions, but China's new-found wealth has given it an increasingly wide array of options for influencing the thoughts, words and deeds of foreign actors. While some of these involve activities that violate the laws of the target countries, most do not, and in many cases there is also no direct or readily visible link between the organs of the party-state and the wealthy individuals, corporations or foundations (whether Chinese or foreign) who dispense funds and favours.

Democracies have been slow to respond

Included among the CCP's current united-front tactics are offers of lucrative employment to former government officials who have demonstrated that they are reliable 'friends of China'; funding of chairs, institutes and research programmes on China-related issues at major universities and think tanks that generally do not support work on topics deemed controversial (and the threatened cancellation of funding for institutions that invite dissidents to speak or otherwise offend Beijing); expelling journalists accused of presenting an unfavourable view of China to overseas audiences; and putting pressure on movie studios, news organisations and media companies to ensure continued access to the vast Chinese market by avoiding politically sensitive content that might be subject to censorship.[114]

CCP influence operations (like those conducted by Russia) pose a particular challenge to liberal democracies because they exploit the values of openness, freedom of expression and the free exchange of ideas on which those societies are based in order to shape and distort their deliberative and decision-making processes. The democracies have been slow to respond to this threat, in part because they have been unable to come to a consensus on whether it even exists, still less how to address it without violating their own principles.

In the US, as in the other democratic countries, an adequate defence against Chinese political warfare will require action from government and, perhaps even more importantly, from the private sector. Among other measures, the federal government should boost spending on domestic counter-intelligence and tighten enforcement of regulations requiring registration by citizens acting as agents of a foreign government.[115] The United States should work together with other friendly governments seeking to harden themselves against Chinese influence operations by exchanging information about the activities of united-front-linked organisations and individuals, sharing experiences regarding laws and best practices for monitoring and controlling undue foreign influence, and forming an organisation or grouping (perhaps at the G20) to highlight the common challenges the democracies face in countering political warfare sponsored by authoritarian regimes.

If they wish to avoid an unhealthy expansion of state surveillance and regulation, private actors will have to take much of the responsibility for countering influence attempts that are inappropriately manipulative and intrusive, even if they are not at present flatly illegal. The best defence against many of these techniques is transparency. For this purpose, an independent body should track and publish information clarifying the connections between nominally private Chinese entities such as foundations and organs of the Chinese party-state. Scholars, universities and think tanks should agree to acknowledge when they accept funding from such entities, and boards of trustees should keep a watchful eye on relationships that could compromise the integrity of the institutions they supervise. Media companies, news organisations and publishing houses should strengthen their capacities for self-policing and mutual protection, publicising instances in which some appear to have been subjected to intimidation or to have engaged in self-censorship. Journalists and scholars have played a vital part in shedding light on China's influence operations in various countries including Australia, New Zealand, the United States and the Czech Republic. Private foundations concerned with the health of democracy should be eager to fund them.[116]

In addition to bolstering their own defences against political warfare, the advanced democracies must also face up to the challenge posed by China's growing presence and influence in other parts of the world. Although Xi Jinping's recent suggestion that China provides a model for others may signal a shift, the country's leaders have thus far been careful to discourage any suggestion that they see themselves engaged in an ideological struggle with the West. Rather than advance a positive programme of its own, Beijing has been content to offer a critique of Western-style capitalism, liberal democracy and 'so-called universal values', while presenting itself as a pragmatic, non-judgemental partner interested only in 'win–win cooperation'.

Despite its self-proclaimed posture of neutrality, however, China's increasing penetration into the economies and societies of other countries is also having an impact on their political systems. Beijing's willingness to lend and invest without demands for political reform helps repressive regimes sidestep the pressures they might otherwise feel from Western governments and Western-dominated institutions like the World Bank. The free flow of Chinese money is especially likely to have a corrupting effect on nations with weak political institutions, strengthening the hand of strongmen and damaging prospects for liberalisation.[117] In fragile democracies where it seeks economic access, China's increasing presence and its example lend credence to those who argue that political freedoms may not be necessary and could actually stand in the way of greater prosperity. Here, as in the advanced democracies, Beijing's influence operations also aim to shape elite perceptions and public discourse, squelching criticism of its repressive domestic policies and discouraging opposition to its expanding international influence.[118]

China may not be actively promoting authoritarianism, at least not yet. But its policies have helped prevent the further spread of democracy, especially in nations around its immediate periphery, and they are contributing to the erosion of liberal norms and institutions in places where these have yet to take firm root. In the near term, the latter group of countries should be the focus of Western efforts, including programmes like those organised by the European Union and the congressionally funded International Republican Institute and the National Democratic Institute that aim to strengthen the rule of law, protect human rights and encourage free elections and multiparty democracy. As always, sunlight is the best disinfectant. Accurate, credible information, preferably provided by independent local journalists, scholars and think tanks, can help to reduce the effectiveness of Chinese influence operations.

Along with its defensive aspects, an effective political-warfare strategy must also have an offensive component. Rather than seeming to accept Beijing's ceaseless happy-talk about win–win cooperation, democratic governments need to find ways to convey the fact that, despite its protestations of benign intent, China is engaged in activities on a massive scale that are aggressive, destabilising, flout international norms, impose disproportionate costs on other societies and threaten their long-term prosperity and security. Notwithstanding the evident growth in its material power, China has numerous social, economic and environmental problems, and its continued rise, to say nothing of its ability eventually to dominate Asia and perhaps the world, are by no means inevitable. Whatever its other accomplishments, the Chinese political system is brutal, repressive and profoundly corrupt. The CCP enriches its own members and their families, even as it denies ordinary Chinese people the right to express their opinions, choose their leaders and worship as they see fit. Fearful of its own people, the CCP regime invests enormous resources in monitoring and controlling their activities. These are realities that the United States and its allies should seek to highlight rather than ignoring them out of a misplaced sense of decorum or in a futile attempt at reassurance.

In order to convince others of the enduring virtues of their system of government, the democracies, starting with the United States, must begin to correct the growing dysfunction that in many cases afflicts their political systems and their societies. If they fail to do so then, in the long run, they will be unable to counter China's political warfare or to compete successfully in the military, diplomatic and economic domains. But, having waited so long to bestir themselves, the democracies do not now have the luxury of time. If they wish to defend their shared interests and common values, they must act soon, and preferably together.

Notes

[1] Kurt M. Campbell and Ely Ratner, 'The China Reckoning: How Beijing Defied American Expectations', *Foreign Affairs*, March/April 2018, p. 70.

[2] 'Worldwide Threats Briefing: 5 Takeaways, From Russia to China', *Wired*, 13 February 2018, https://www.wired.com/story/worldwide-threats-

briefing-russia-election-china/.

3   'How the West Got China Wrong: Decades of Optimism About China's Rise Have Been Discarded', *The Economist*, 1 March 2018.

4   Charles Lane, 'We Got China Wrong. Now What?', *Washington Post*, 28 February 2018.

5   White House, 'National Security Strategy of the United States of America', December 2017 [hereafter NSS 2017], p. 25, https://www.whitehouse.gov/wp-content/uploads/2017/12/NSS-Final-12-18-2017-0905.pdf.

6   US Department of Defense, 'Summary of the 2018 National Defense Strategy of the United States of America' [hereafter Summary of the 2018 NDS], p. 1, https://www.defense.gov/Portals/1/Documents/pubs/2018-National-Defense-Strategy-Summary.pdf.

7   During his November 2017 visit to China, for example, Trump described Xi Jinping as 'a very special man', 'a strong man' with whom he has 'great chemistry'. Andrew Restuccia, 'Trump and Xi Compete to Lay On the Highest Praise in Beijing', *Politico*, 9 November 2017, https://www.politico.com/story/2017/11/09/trump-china-trade-deficit-244728.

8   Summary of the 2018 NDS, p. 4.

9   The word 'China' is used here to refer to the Chinese Communist Party regime, as distinct from the Chinese people.

10   Robert B. Zoellick, 'Whither China: From Membership to Responsibility', 21 September 2005, https://2001-2009.state.gov/s/d/former/zoellick/rem/53682.htm.

11   For a discussion of US strategy during this period, see Aaron L. Friedberg, *A Contest for Supremacy: China, America, and the Struggle for Mastery in Asia* (New York: Norton, 2011), pp. 88–119.

12   See Christopher Walker and Jessica Ludwig, 'From "Soft Power" to "Sharp Power"', in Juan Pablo Cardenal et al. (eds), *Sharp Power: Rising Authoritarian Influence* (Washington DC: National Endowment for Democracy, 2018), pp. 8–25.

13   See, for example, the secret writings of former premier Zhao Ziyang. Zhao Ziyang, *Prisoner of the State: The Secret Journal of Premier Zhao Ziyang* (New York: Simon and Schuster, 2009).

14   For an early entry, see Jude Blanchette, 'Perhaps No One Lost China', CATO Unbound, 16 March 2018, https://www.cato-unbound.org/2018/03/16/jude-blanchette/perhaps-no-one-lost-china.

15   Andrew J. Nathan, 'Authoritarian Resilience', *Journal of Democracy*, vol. 14, no. 1, January 2003, pp. 6–17.

16   This is the theme of Minxin Pei, *China's Trapped Transition: The Limits of Developmental Autocracy* (Cambridge, MA: Harvard University Press, 2006).

17   As argued in a prescient book by James Mann, *The China Fantasy: How Our Leaders Explain Away Chinese Repressions* (New York: Viking, 2007).

18   In 2009, commander of US Pacific Command Admiral Robert F. Willard told reporters that 'in the past decade or so, China has exceeded most of our intelligence estimates of their military capability and capacity every year. They've grown at an unprecedented rate in those capabilities.' 'Intelligence Failures?', *Washington Times*, 2 November 2009, https://www.

washingtontimes.com/news/2009/
nov/2/intelligence-failures/.

19 For a discussion of these tendencies,
see Aaron L. Friedberg, *Beyond Air–Sea
Battle: The Debate Over U.S. Military
Strategy in Asia* (Abingdon: Routledge
for the IISS, 2014), pp. 45–66.

20 See Andrew W. Marshall, Director
of the Office of Net Assessment,
to Secretary of Defense Donald
Rumsfeld, 'Near Term Actions to
Begin Shift of Focus Towards Asia',
memorandum, 2 May 2002, quoted
in Nina Silove, 'The Pivot before the
Pivot: U.S. Strategy to Preserve the
Power Balance in Asia', *International
Security*, vol. 40, no. 4, Spring 2016, p.
55.

21 See, for example, the Bush administration's lack of enthusiasm for an
early version of the US–Australia–
Japan–India 'Quad' and the Obama
administration's seemingly endless
equivocation over freedom-of-navigation operations. Tanvi Madan, 'The
Rise, Fall, and Rebirth of the "Quad"',
War on the Rocks, 16 November 2017,
https://warontherocks.com/2017/11/
rise-fall-rebirth-quad/; and Austin
Wright, Bryan Bender and Philip
Ewing, 'Obama Team, Military at
Odds Over South China Sea', *Politico*,
31 July 2015, https://www.politico.
com/story/2015/07/barack-obama-
administration-navy-pentagon-odds-
south-china-sea-120865.

22 David B. Larter, 'White House
Tells the Pentagon to Quit Talking
About "Competition" with China',
Navy Times, 26 September 2016,
https://www.navytimes.com/news/
your-navy/2016/09/26/white-house-
tells-the-pentagon-to-quit-talking-

about-competition-with-china/.

23 Jerome A. Cohen, 'Xi Jinping
Amends China's Constitution',
Lawfare, 7 March 2018, https://
www.lawfareblog.com/
xi-jinping-amends-chinas-constitution.

24 For a concise overview, see Andrew
J. Nathan and Andrew Scobell, 'How
China Sees America', *Foreign Affairs*,
vol. 91, no. 5, September/October 2012,
pp. 32–47.

25 See Dingding Chen and Jianwei
Wang, 'Lying Low No More? China's
New Thinking on the *Tao Guang Yang
Hui* Strategy', *China: An International
Journal*, vol. 9, no. 2, September 2011,
pp. 195–216.

26 See Aaron L. Friedberg, 'Globalisation
and Chinese Grand Strategy', *Survival*,
vol. 60, no. 1, February–March 2018,
pp. 7–40.

27 For a discussion of the concept of
'comprehensive national power' and
the various ways that it has been
measured by Chinese analysts, see
Michael Pillsbury, *China Debates
the Future Security Environment*
(Washington DC: National Defense
University Press, 2000), pp. 203–58.

28 See Yuhua Wang and Carl Minzner,
'The Rise of the Chinese Security
State', *China Quarterly*, May 2015,
pp. 1–21. On patriotic education, see
Zheng Wang, *Never Forget National
Humiliation: Historical Memory in
Chinese Politics and Foreign Relations*
(New York: Columbia University
Press, 2012).

29 See Jia Qingguo, 'Learning to Live
with the Hegemon: Evolution of
China's Policy Toward the US Since
the End of the Cold War', *Journal of
Contemporary China*, vol. 14, no. 44,

2005, pp. 395–407.

30 See Wang Jisi, 'China's Search for a Grand Strategy: A Rising Power Finds Its Way', *Foreign Affairs*, vol. 90, no. 2, March/April 2011, pp. 68–79.

31 For an overview of the debate on these issues, see Dong Wang and Li Kan, 'Eying the Crippled Hegemon: China's Grand Strategy Thinking in the Wake of the Global Financial Crisis', September 2010, https://papers.ssrn.com/sol3/papers.cfm?abstract_id=1673813.

32 Michael Pettis, 'China's Troubled Transition to a More Balanced Growth Model', New America, 1 March 2011, https://www.newamerica.org/economic-growth/chinas-troubled-transition-to-a-more-balanced-growth-model/. Many of the measures employed to lessen the immediate impact of the global slowdown (especially massive new infrastructure projects carried out by state-owned enterprises) tended to reinforce existing policies, pushing reform even further into the future.

33 Their concerns on this score were further heightened by violent protests in Tibet and Xinjiang, the circulation of a widely publicised human-rights manifesto and, somewhat later, by the toppling of a string of authoritarian governments in the so-called Arab Spring and a scandal that revealed corruption at the highest levels of the Party elite. See 'Is China Fraying?', *The Economist*, 9 July 2009, https://www.economist.com/node/13988479; and Andrew Jacobs and Jonathan Ansfield, 'Well-Oiled Security Apparatus in China Stifles Calls for Change', *New York Times*, 28 February 2011.

34 Several scholars have shown how the regime permitted or encouraged expressions of nationalist sentiment during the various confrontations over maritime disputes. These accounts generally argue that Beijing manipulated public sentiment for the purpose of strengthening its bargaining position in relation to other powers, rather than claiming that it sought out confrontation for the purpose of mobilising nationalism. See Andrew Chubb, 'Propaganda, Not Policy: Explaining the PLA's "Hawkish Faction" (Part Two)', *China Brief*, vol. 13, no. 16, August 2013, pp. 12–16, https://jamestown.org/wp-content/uploads/2013/07/cb_07_26.pdf?x87069; and Jessica Chen Weiss, *Powerful Patriots: Nationalist Protest in China's Foreign Relations* (New York: Oxford University Press, 2014).

35 See Javier C. Hernandez, 'To Inspire Young Communists, China Turns to "Red Army" Schools', *New York Times*, 15 October 2017; and Chris Buckley, 'China Says Its Students, Even Those Abroad, Need More "Patriotic Education"', *New York Times*, 10 February 2016.

36 See Human Rights Watch, 'World Report 2015: China', https://www.hrw.org/world-report/2015/country-chapters/china-and-tibet; Orville Schell, 'Crackdown in China: Worse and Worse', *New York Review of Books*, 21 April 2016, http://www.nybooks.com/articles/2016/04/21/crackdown-in-china-worse-and-worse/; and Simon Denyer, 'China's Scary Lesson to the World: "Censoring" the Internet Works', *Washington Post*, 23 May 2016.

37 For the contents of the so-called

'Communiqué on the Current State of the Ideological Sphere', see 'Document 9: A ChinaFile Translation', ChinaFile, 8 November 2013, https://www.chinafile.com/document-9-chinafile-translation.

38 This phrase appears to have been used for the first time by Xi in an October 2013 speech to a Party conference on China's diplomatic strategy. See Yan Xuetong, 'From Keeping a Low Profile to Striving for Achievement', *Chinese Journal of International Politics*, vol. 7, no. 2, 2014, p. 160.

39 On rejuvenation as 'a restoration of fairness', see Zheng Wang, 'The Chinese Dream: Concept and Context', *Journal of Chinese Politics*, no. 19, 2014, p. 9.

40 Shi Yinhong, 'The Latest Transfer in China's Foreign Strategy: From "Military Strategy" to "Economic Strategy"', *China International Relations*, vol. 25, no. 2, March/April 2015, p. 52. A number of Western observers have reached similar conclusions. According to one former senior CIA analyst, 'the great rejuvenation means that the PRC by 2049 intends to restore itself to a regional positional of primacy'. Christopher K. Johnson, *Decoding China's Emerging 'Great Power' Strategy in Asia* (Washington DC: Center for Strategic and International Studies, May 2014), p. 17.

41 Chris Buckley, 'China Leader Affirms Policy on Islands', *New York Times*, 29 January 2013. See also Timothy Heath, 'The "Holistic Security Concept": The Securitization of Policy and Increasing Risk of Militarized Crisis', *China Issue Brief*, vol. 15, no. 12, 19 June 2015,

http://www.jamestown.org/single/?tx_ttnews%5Btt_news%5D=44061&no_cache=1#.VoMq5Mda7WY.

42 The ADIZ was announced on November 2013 and land-reclamation projects began the following month. See US Department of Defense, 'The Asia-Pacific Maritime Security Strategy: Achieving U.S. National Security Objectives in a Changing Environment', August 2015, p. 15, http://www.defense.gov/Portals/1/Documents/pubs/NDAA%20A-P_Maritime_Security_Strategy-08142015-1300-FINALFORMAT.PDF. According to Bonnie Glaser and Deep Pal, 'Hu Jintao resisted pressure from the PLA to announce the East China Sea ADIZ in his final year in power'. Bonnie S. Glaser and Deep Pal, 'Is China's Charm Offensive Dead?', *China Brief*, vol. 14, no. 15, 31 July 2014, pp. 8–11, https://jamestown.org/wp-content/uploads/2014/07/China_Brief_Vol_14_Issue_15__4_.pdf?x87069.

43 See Nadège Rolland, *China's Eurasian Century? Political and Strategic Implications of China's Belt and Road Initiative* (Seattle, WA: National Bureau of Asian Research, 2017).

44 See Timothy R. Heath, 'China and the U.S. Alliance System', *Diplomat*, 11 June 2014, http://thediplomat.com/2014/06/china-and-the-u-s-alliance-system/.

45 Xi Jinping, 'New Asian Security Concept for New Progress in Security Cooperation', remarks at the Fourth Summit of the Conference on Interaction and Confidence Building Measures in Asia, Shanghai Expo Center, 21 May 2014, http://www.

chinausfocus.com/wp-content/
uploads/2014/07/Xi-01.pdf.

46 On the significance of this phrase,
see Nadège Rolland, 'Beijing's Vision
for a Reshaped Order', *China Brief*,
vol. 18, no. 3, February 2018, https://
jamestown.org/program/beijings-
vision-reshaped-international-order/.

47 See Paul Mancinelli, 'Conceptualizing
"New Type Great Power Relations":
The Sino-Russian Model', *China Brief*,
vol. 14, no. 9, 7 May 2014, pp. 12–16,
https://jamestown.org/program/
conceptualizing-new-type-great-
power-relations-the-sino-russian-
model/.

48 Yuan Peng, 'A New Model of China–
U.S. Relations after Beijing's Second
Reform', *Contemporary International
Relations*, vol. 25, no. 1, January/
February 2015, p. 8.

49 Fu Ying, 'China and the Future
of International Order', Chatham
House, 6 July 2016, https://www.
chathamhouse.org/sites/files/
chathamhouse/events/special/2016-07-
08-China-International-Order_0.pdf.

50 As a leading CCP spokesperson and
theorist explains, 'Earlier than we
expected, the weight of international
responsibilities is falling on Chinese
shoulders'. Fu Ying, 'The US World
Order Is a Suit That No Longer Fits',
Financial Times, 6 January 2016, https://
www.ft.com/content/c09cbcb6-b3cb-
11e5-b147-e5e5bba42e51.

51 Chris Buckley and Keith Bradsher,
'Xi Jinping's Marathon Speech: Five
Takeaways', *New York Times*, 18
October 2017.

52 Thomas Friedman, 'U.S. Vision of
Foreign Policy Reversed', *New York
Times*, 22 September 1993.

53 X [George F. Kennan], 'The Sources of
Soviet Conduct', *Foreign Affairs*, vol.
25, no. 4, 1947, p. 582.

54 For a discussion of the full array of
alternative strategies, see Aaron L.
Friedberg, 'The Debate Over US China
Strategy', *Survival*, vol. 57, no. 3, June–
July 2015, pp. 89–110.

55 See Robert S. Ross, 'The Geography
of the Peace: East Asia in the Twenty-
First Century', *International Security*,
vol. 23, no. 4, Spring 1999, pp. 81–118.

56 See Charles L. Glaser, 'A U.S.–China
Grand Bargain: The Hard Choice
between Military Competition and
Accommodation', *International
Security*, vol. 39, no. 4, Spring 2015, pp.
49–90.

57 'GDP Growth (Annual%)', World
Bank, https://data.worldbank.
org/indicator/NY.GDP.MKTP.
KD.ZG?locations=CN.

58 'Does China Have an Aging
Problem?', ChinaPower Project,
https://chinapower.csis.org/
aging-problem/.

59 Measured in current-dollar terms,
the United States and its major Asian
allies still enjoy a 2.3:1 advantage
in GDP over China (2.5:1 if India is
included). Using purchasing-power
parity, the margin shrinks to 1.3:1, but
it increases to a 1.7:1 edge if India is
included. See World Bank tables for
2016, http://wdi.worldbank.org/table/
WV.1. Derek Scissors argues that net
national wealth is actually a better
measure of what he describes as 'the
resources available to countries to
pursue national interests' than GDP.
By this standard the US remains far
ahead of China and the gap is not
closing. Derek M. Scissors, 'Is China's

Economic Power a Paper Tiger?',
National Interest, 27 November 2017,
http://nationalinterest.org/feature/
chinas-economic-power-paper-
tiger-23326.

60 For a sober assessment, see Andrew
F. Krepinevich, *Preserving the Balance:
A U.S. Eurasia Defense Strategy*
(Washington DC: Center for Strategic
and Budgetary Assessments, 2017),
pp. 59–63.

61 See Samuel P. Huntington, *The Clash of
Civilizations and the Remaking of World
Order* (New York: Simon and Schuster,
1996), pp. 229–38.

62 See Prashanth Parameswaran,
'What's Next for Japan–Vietnam
Defense Ties?', 2 November 2017,
https://thediplomat.com/2017/11/
whats-next-for-japan-vietnam-
defense-ties/; Andrew O'Neil and
David Walton, 'The Australia–Japan
Relationship: Worthy of More
Reflection', *Lowy Interpreter*, 3 October
2017, https://www.lowyinstitute.org/
the-interpreter/australia-japan-rela-
tionship-worthy-more-reflection; Tan
Ming Hui and Nazia Hussain, 'Japan
and India: Deepening Ties in the Age
of Uncertainty', *Diplomat*, 23 February
2017; Ankit Panda, 'India, Australia
Hold First Two-Plus-Two Foreign
and Defense Secretaries Meeting',
Diplomat, 13 December 2017, https://
thediplomat.com/tag/india-australia-
relations/; and Suhasini Haidar, 'India,
Vietnam Lay Stress on Defence Ties',
Hindu, 3 March 2018, http://www.
thehindu.com/news/national/india-
vietnam-lay-stress-on-defence-ties/
article22920441.ece.

63 For this reason, some Chinese observers have been dismissive of the Quad,
saying that Beijing 'does not care
about it' because 'in the short term …
the ability to form a real coalition is
limited'. Shi Yinhong quoted in Jane
Perlez, 'Xi Jinping Extends Power, and
China Braces for a New Cold War',
New York Times, 27 February 2018.

64 For some proposals along these lines,
see Michael J. Green, Kathleen H.
Hicks and Zack Cooper, 'Federated
Defense in Asia', Center for Strategic
and International Studies, December
2014, https://csis-prod.s3.amazonaws.
com/s3fs-public/legacy_files/
files/publication/141120_Green_
FederatedDefenseAsia_Web.pdf.

65 See Ryan Hass and Alex Pascal,
'Trump in Asia: Transatlantic
Cooperation Key for Continued
Leadership', *National Interest*,
8 November 2017, http://
nationalinterest.org/feature/
trump-asia-transatlantic-cooperation-
key-continued-23110?page=2. A
coordinated policy on export controls
and arms sales could also help to
ensure that the activities of European
firms help to strengthen the balance of
power in Asia rather than tending to
undermine it. See Mathieu Duchâtel,
'China Is Building Up Its Military
and European Arms Dealers Could
Start Cashing In', *South China Morning
Post*, 7 February 2018, available at
http://www.businessinsider.com/
china-military-buildup-europe-arms-
dealers-2018-2.

66 See, for example, the account of a
meeting between Australian and
Chinese counterparts shortly following the 2016 presidential election.
Peter Hartcher, 'China's Warning
for Australia: Don't Side Against

Us with Donald Trump', *Sydney Morning Herald*, 28 November 2016, https://www.smh.com.au/opinion/chinas-warning-for-australia-dont-side-against-us-with-donald-trump-20161128-gsyyrq.html.

67   For an optimistic interpretation of administration policy, see Jeff M. Smith, 'Unpacking the Free and Open Indo-Pacific', *War on the Rocks*, 14 March 2018, https://warontherocks.com/2018/03/unpacking-the-free-and-open-indo-pacific/.

68   See, for example, Brahma Chellaney, 'China's Creditor Imperialism', *Japan Times*, 21 December 2017, https://www.japantimes.co.jp/opinion/2017/12/21/commentary/world-commentary/chinas-creditor-imperialism/#.WrUynGaZOWY.

69   China has also invested heavily in an integrated air-defence system and extensive construction of hardened underground facilities to blunt US airstrikes, as well as anti-satellite, cyber and electronic-warfare capabilities whose purpose is to degrade US C4ISR. More recently, Beijing has also turned its attention to developing anti-submarine-warfare capabilities and long-range conventional-strike weapons capable of hitting US targets outside the theatre. For details, see Friedberg, *Beyond Air–Sea Battle*, pp. 15–44.

70   See 'Document: Air Sea Battle Name Change Memo', *U.S. Naval Institute Proceedings*, 20 January 2015, https://news.usni.org/2015/01/20/document-air-sea-battle-name-change-memo. The Third Offset was conceived and directed by then-deputy secretary of defense Robert Work. See

'Remarks by Deputy Secretary Work on Third Offset Strategy', Brussels, 28 April 2016, https://www.defense.gov/News/Speeches/Speech-View/Article/753482/remarks-by-d%20eputy-secretary-work-on-third-offset-strategy/; and Cheryl Pellerin, 'Deputy Secretary: Third Offset Strategy Bolsters America's Military Deterrence', *DoD News*, 31 October 2016, https://www.defense.gov/News/Article/Article/991434/deputy-secretary-third-offset-strategy-bolsters-americas-military-deterrence/.

71   See Kathleen Hicks and Andrew Hunter, 'What Will Replace the Third Offset? Lessons from Past Innovation Strategies', *Defense One*, 17 March 2017, http://www.defenseone.com/ideas/2017/03/what-will-replace-third-offset-lessons-past-innovation-strategies/136260/.

72   Under the terms of its 1987 Intermediate-Range Nuclear Forces treaty with the Soviet Union, the United States cannot develop land-launched ballistic or cruise missiles with ranges between 500 and 5,500 kilometres, but air- and sea-launched missiles are not prohibited. See Eric Sayers, 'The Intermediate-Range Nuclear Forces Treaty and the Future of the Indo-Pacific Military Balance', *PacNet*, no. 21, 15 March 2018, https://www.csis.org/analysis/pacnet-21-intermediate-range-nuclear-forces-treaty-and-future-indo-pacific-military-balance.

73   Developing a mixture of ballistic as well as air-breathing delivery systems could help shift the long-term military competition in more favourable directions by inducing the PLA

to direct some of its scarce resources towards activities that are less directly threatening to the US and its allies, including active and passive defences against air-attack and ballistic-missile defences.

74 For various proposals and critiques of this possibility, see T.X. Hammes, 'Offshore Control: A Proposed Strategy for an Unlikely Conflict', *Strategic Forum*, no. 278, June 2012; Jeffrey E. Kline and Wayne Hughes, Jr, 'Between Peace and Air–Sea Battle: A War at Sea Strategy', *Naval War College Review*, vol. 65, no. 5, Autumn 2012, pp. 35–41; Sean Mirski, 'Stranglehold: The Context, Conduct and Consequences of an American Naval Blockade of China', *Journal of Strategic Studies*, vol. 36, no. 3, June 2013, pp. 385–421; and Evan Braden Montgomery, 'Reconsidering a Naval Blockade of China: A Response to Mirski', *Journal of Strategic Studies*, vol. 36, no. 4, 2013, pp. 615–23.

75 For a thorough overview of these developments and their implications, see Eric Heginbotham et al., *China's Evolving Nuclear Deterrent: Major Drivers and Issues for the United States* (Santa Monica, CA: RAND Corporation, 2017).

76 The Trump administration's recent Nuclear Posture Review makes a number of recommendations along these lines. See Office of the Secretary of Defense, 'Nuclear Posture Review', February 2018, https://media.defense. gov/2018/Feb/02/2001872886/-1/-1/1/2018-NUCLEAR-POSTURE-REVIEW-FINAL-REPORT.PDF. For an elaboration of the argument in favour of limited nuclear options, see

an essay by current Deputy Assistant Secretary of Defense for Strategy and Force Development Elbridge Colby, 'The Need for Limited Nuclear Options', in David Ochmanek and Michael Sulmeyer (eds), *Challenges in U.S. National Security Policy: A Festschrift Honoring Edward L. (Ted) Warner* (Santa Monica, CA: RAND Corporation, 2014), pp. 141–68.

77 For an overview of the various possible approaches to the problem, see Hal Brands and Zack Cooper, 'Getting Serious About Strategy in the South China Sea', *U.S. Naval War College Review*, vol. 71, no. 1, Winter 2018, pp. 13–32.

78 The Trump administration's evident willingness to step up freedom-of-navigation operations, without either the agonising or the public fanfare that accompanied the actions of its predecessor, is a hopeful sign, as are recent cruises by the French and British navies. See Shashank Joshi and Euan Graham, '"Global Britain" on the Line in the South China Sea', *Lowy Interpreter*, 22 February 2018, https://www. lowyinstitute.org/the-interpreter/ global-britain-line-south-china-sea.

79 Japan has already taken significant steps of its own by making preparations to deploy anti-ship and anti-aircraft missile batteries on islands in the East China Sea. See Tim Kelly and Nobuhiro Kubo, 'Exclusive: Japan's Far-Flung Island Defense Plan Seeks to Turn Tables on China', Reuters, 17 December 2015; and Toshi Yoshihara, 'Going Anti-Access at Sea: How Japan Can Turn the Tables on China', Center for a New

American Security, September 2014,
https://s3.amazonaws.com/files.cnas.
org/documents/CNAS-Maritime2_
Yoshihara.pdf. For a detailed proposal
along these lines, see Michael Beckley,
'The Emerging Military Balance in
East Asia: How China's Neighbors
Can Check Chinese Naval Expansion',
International Security, vol. 42, no. 2,
Fall 2017, pp. 78–119.

80 See, for example, accounts of Premier
Li Keqiang's 2017 visit to Australia.
Sam Roggeveen, 'China Versus the US:
Australia's Increasingly Hard Choice',
CNN, 24 March 2017, https://www.
cnn.com/2017/03/24/opinions/premier-
li-keqiang-visit-australia-china/index.
html.

81 Even less subtle are an assortment
of recent cases in which the Chinese
government demanded and quickly
received apologies from Western companies whose websites listed Taiwan,
Hong Kong, Tibet and Macau as separate countries or, in one case, had a
US-based employee who 'liked' a tweet
favouring Tibetan independence. Abha
Bhattarai and Steven Mufson, 'Marriott
and Other Firms Bow to China to
Protect Business Interests', *Washington
Post*, 19 January 2018.

82 Thus, despite being imposed for a
relatively brief period, China's unof-
ficial sanctions reportedly shaved a
non-trivial 0.3% off South Korea's
GDP growth for 2017. James Mayger
and Jiyeun Lee, 'China's Missile
Sanctions Are Taking a Heavy Toll
on Both Koreas', Bloomberg, 29
August 2017, https://www.bloomb-
erg.com/news/articles/2017-08-29/
china-s-missile-sanctions-are-taking-a-
heavy-toll-on-both-koreas.

83 The term 'co-prosperity sphere' refers
to the Japanese concept for an integrated pan-Asian regional economy
promulgated during the 1930s.

84 In 2016, the countries in the CPTPP
comprised 13.5% of global GDP, with
Japan alone accounting for 6.5% of
global GDP. Adding the US would
bring the total to 38.2%. Andrew
Small, 'Rival Economic Orders', in
Janka Ortel, Andrew Small and Amy
Studdart, *Liberal Order in the Indo-
Pacific* (Washington DC: German
Marshall Fund, March 2018), p.
8. Meanwhile, Japan and the EU
together account for 28.3% of world
output. Although prospects for such
arrangements appear remote at
present, a US–EU agreement would
make up 46.5%, and a grouping that
included Japan, the US, the EU and
the other ten CPTPP members would
comprise 60% of global GDP. By
comparison, in 2016 China accounted
for just under 15% of world GDP. See
Japanese Ministry of Foreign Affairs,
'Benefits of the Japan–EU EPA', 21
November 2017, http://www.mofa.
go.jp/files/000013835.pdf.

85 The Chinese government now reportedly offers 10,000 scholarships each
year to students from Belt and Road
countries. This figure likely does
not include training and education
programmes for military, police and
intelligence officers. Chi Dehua, 'Belt
and Road Initiative Now Extends to
Education', *Global Times*, 23 May 2017,
https://gbtimes.com/belt-and-road-
initiative-now-extends-education.
As part of the 'digital Silk Road',
Chinese companies are also building
telecommunications infrastructure in

Belt and Road countries. In addition to expanding markets and acquiring commercially useful data, these projects will enable Beijing to help friendly repressive governments monitor and control their populations, even as it conducts its own surveillance. See Nadège Rolland, 'A Fiber-Optic Silk Road', *Diplomat*, 2 April 2015, https://thediplomat.com/2015/04/a-fiber-optic-silk-road/.

86 See Kiran Stacey, 'China Signs 99-Year Lease on Sri Lanka's Hambantota Port', *Financial Times*, 11 December 2017. Other countries potentially at risk include Mongolia, Djibouti, Pakistan, the Maldives and Tajikistan. See John Hurley, Scott Morris and Gailyn Portelance, 'Examining the Debt Implications of the Belt and Road Initiative from a Policy Perspective', Center for Global Development, March 2018, https://www.cgdev.org/sites/default/files/examining-debt-implications-belt-and-road-initiative-policy-perspective.pdf.

87 On the strategic motivations underpinning the Belt and Road Initiative, see Rolland, *China's Eurasian Century?*, pp. 109–19.

88 See Andrew Small, 'The Backlash to Belt and Road', *Foreign Affairs*, 16 February 2018, https://www.foreignaffairs.com/articles/china/2018-02-16/backlash-belt-and-road.

89 Japan and India have taken the lead in this regard. See Wade Shepard, 'India and Japan Join Forces to Counter China and Build Their Own New Silk Road', *Forbes*, 31 July 2017, https://www.forbes.com/sites/wadeshepard/2017/07/31/

india-and-japan-join-forces-to-counter-china-and-build-their-own-new-silk-road/#40dcc4ff4982; and 'Australia, U.S., India and Japan in Talks to Establish Belt and Road Alternative: Report', Reuters, 18 February 2018.

90 See the recommendations in Nadège Rolland, 'China's Belt and Road Initiative: Five Years Later', testimony before the US–China Economic and Security Review Commission, 25 January 2018, http://www.nbr.org/research/activity.aspx?id=837. Controversy aroused by recent reporting on China's activities in Vanuatu provides one example of the possible benefits of 'sunlight'. See David Wroe, 'China Eyes Vanuatu Military Base in Plan with Global Ramifications', *Sydney Morning Herald*, 9 April 2018, https://www.smh.com.au/politics/federal/china-eyes-vanuatu-military-base-in-plan-with-global-ramifications-20180409-p4z8j9.html.

91 See, for example, Daniel H. Rosen, 'A Post-Engagement US–China Relationship?', Rhodium Group, 19 January 2018, https://rhg.com/research/post-engagement-us-china-relationship/.

92 For assessments of the best-known of China's recent plans, see Jost Wubbeke et al., 'Made in China 2025: The Making of a High-Tech Superpower and Consequences for Industrial Countries', Mercator Institute, December 2016; and 'Made in China 2025: Global Ambitions Built on Local Protections', US Chamber of Commerce, 2017.

93 Many of these practices are described

in great detail in Office of the United States Trade Representative, 'Findings of the Investigation into China's Acts, Politics, and Practices Related to Technology Transfer, Intellectual Property, and Innovation Under Section 301 of the Trade Act of 1974', 22 March 2018, https://ustr.gov/sites/default/files/Section%20301%20FINAL.PDF. For a study initiated by the Obama administration, see also Michael Brown and Pavneet Singh, 'China's Technology Transfer Strategy', Defense Innovation Unit Experimental, February 2017, https://new.reorg-research.com/data/documents/20170928/59ccf7de70c2f.pdf. First to sound the alarm over the full extent of China's theft of intellectual property was a report prepared by the National Bureau of Asian Research: 'The Report of the Commission on the Theft of American Intellectual Property', National Bureau of Asian Research, 2013, http://www.ipcommission.org/report/IP_Commission_Report_052213.pdf.

94 Wubbeke et al., 'Made in China 2025', pp. 201–21.

95 Brown and Singh, 'China's Technology Transfer Strategy', p. 11.

96 One area of concern is quantum computing, where the side that achieves the initial breakthroughs could gain a decisive edge in securing its own communication while being able to break even the most sophisticated cryptographic systems. See Elsa Kania, 'Is China Seeking "Quantum Surprise"?', *Bulletin of the Atomic Scientists*, 1 March 2018, https://thebulletin.org/china-seeking-"quantum-surprise"11552.

97 Brown and Singh, 'China's Technology Transfer Strategy', p. 8.

98 On the dangers of such a pyrrhic victory, see Matt Sheehan, 'Trump's Trade War Isn't About Trade. It's About Technology', MacroPolo, 3 April 2018, https://macropolo.org/trumps-trade-war-isnt-trade-technology/.

99 For a top-ten list of changes the US should demand, see Scott Kennedy, 'Surviving March Madness in U.S.–China Trade Relations', CSIS, 27 March 2018, https://www.csis.org/analysis/surviving-march-madness-us-china-trade-relations.

100 See Keith Zhai, 'China Talks Stalled Over Trump's Demands on High-Tech Industries, Source Says', Bloomberg, 10 April 2018, https://www.bloomberg.com/news/articles/2018-04-10/u-s-china-talks-said-to-have-stalled-over-high-tech-industry.

101 Claire Reade, 'Finding the Right Off-Ramp from the Trade War', CSIS, 27 March 2018, https://www.csis.org/analysis/finding-right-ramp-trade-war.

102 *Ibid.*

103 Jane Cai, 'China Steps Up Scrutiny of IP Transfers to Foreign Firms on National Security Grounds', *South China Morning Post*, 20 March 2018, http://www.scmp.com/news/china/economy/article/2139713/china-steps-scrutiny-ip-transfers-foreign-firms-national-security.

104 See Robert D. Williams, 'CFIUS Reform and U.S. Government Concern Over Chinese Investment: A Primer', Lawfare, 13 November 2017, https://www.lawfareblog.com/cfius-reform-and-us-government-concerns-over-chinese-investment-primer.

Chinese Culture and Soft Power

Nigel Inkster

In late 2011, the then-Secretary-General of the Chinese Communist Party Hu Jintao made a speech on the subject of Chinese soft power, the text of which was subsequently published in the Communist Party's theoretical journal *Qiu Shi* (an august publication read by virtually no-one in China).[1] Hu bemoaned the dismal quality of Chinese popular culture, in particular the plethora of television programmes with titles such as *Fei Cheng Wu Rao* (*If You Are the One*): imitations of Western dating and reality TV shows that then dominated the ratings.

Such shows, if anything more vacuous even than their Western counterparts, had been widely criticised as promoting a consumerist culture devoid of civic values, a perception epitomised by the statement of one young female contestant that she would rather be weeping in a BMW than laughing on a bicycle.

How, Hu asked, could China possibly hope to project soft power when its own culture risked being submerged by this tide of Western commercialism? The development and promotion of a strong and healthy Chinese culture to counter this trend was an urgent imperative.

This focus on soft power has since been taken up by his successor Xi Jinping who, at the beginning of 2014, delivered a speech on the importance of promoting China's cultural soft power by disseminating modern Chinese values. China, Xi said, should be presented as a civilised country with a

Nigel Inkster is a Senior Adviser to the IISS. A version of this article previously appeared on the IISS Voices blog.

Survival | vol. 60 no. 3 | June–July 2018 | pp. 65–70   DOI 10.1080/00396338.2018.1470759

rich history, ethnic unity and cultural diversity. He spoke of the need to promote advanced socialist culture in order to increase China's overall cultural strength and creativity, and of the need to integrate traditional Chinese culture with modern international trends.[2]

Assault on traditional values

The challenge of defining and promoting Chinese culture was at odds with the situation prevailing throughout most of China's history, when its material and intellectual culture was eagerly embraced by the states on its periphery, notably Japan and Korea. Until the nineteenth century, foreign invaders were invariably 'Sinicised', as happened with the Yuan (Mongol) and Qing (Manchu) dynasties. Meanwhile, Western intellectuals of the Enlightenment saw China's system of government by an educated caste of atheistic civil servants as an ideal to be emulated. And the European fashion for chinoiserie gave rise to a substantial Chinese export sector.

The shock China endured in the mid-nineteenth century at the hands of the industrialised Western powers was unprecedented. These powers, though in Chinese eyes largely devoid of civilised values, had clearly leap-frogged China in science and technology, and this realisation gave rise to massive intellectual turmoil and soul-searching. Responses ranged from a doubling-down on traditional Chinese values to their wholesale rejection, as promoted by early twentieth-century intellectuals such as Hu Shi. A hybrid response also emerged, epitomised by the Self-Strengthening Movement and its guiding principle of 'Chinese learning for substance, Western learning for utility'.

China's turmoil was made all the worse by the recognition that Japan, hitherto seen as a vassal state of no consequence, had successfully embraced Western modernity. Indeed, it was Japanese scholars, drawing on a shared classical Chinese linguistic heritage just as their Western counterparts had done with Latin and Greek, who developed much of China's modern scientific and technical lexicography.

The question of what actually constituted the Chinese value system was further complicated when the Chinese Communist Party took power in 1949. The promotion of 'progressive' ideas at the expense of traditional 'feudal' values led to the suppression of many aspects of traditional Chinese culture. The collectivisation of agriculture in the 1950s aimed to erode traditional family structures with such measures as communal refectories replacing the family dining table.

The Cultural Revolution, unleashed in 1966 and lasting for a decade, resulted in an iconoclastic assault on traditional Chinese culture leading to the wholesale destruction of religious and historical monuments and artefacts, books and paintings. In the performing arts, traditional operas were suppressed and replaced with a handful of 'model' operas or *yangban xi* – such as *The Red Detachment of Women* – of debatable artistic merit or entertainment value.

Defining modern Chinese values

Following the end of the Cultural Revolution, the imperative to pursue economic modernisation initially sidelined concerns about culture and values. But the Chinese Communist Party, aware that much of the population had been alienated and rendered cynical by the Cultural Revolution and the violent suppression of the Democracy Movement on 4 June 1989, began to resurrect aspects of traditional Chinese culture while simultaneously seeking to stoke a sense of national pride through a mandatory patriotic-education programme highlighting the wrongs suffered by China at the hands of foreign powers.

This resurrection has taken the form of a partial and selective cherry-picking exercise, focusing on Confucian concepts of hierarchy – the idea that each person in society has their place – and social harmony, requiring the interests of the individual to be subordinated to those of the collective. The name of Confucius has been invoked in support of the Party's efforts to promote their version of Chinese culture through a global network of Confucius Institutes. The ostensible purpose of such institutes is to promote the teaching of the Chinese language, but a large part of their remit is to discourage the teaching and dissemination of 'incorrect' ideas about China.

To date there has been relatively little specificity about what Chinese culture and values should be. But as China increasingly seeks to differentiate itself internationally, so the need for greater definition has become evident.

Cultural self-confidence

A recent article in the People's Liberation Army newspaper *Liberation Army Daily*, entitled 'Draw on Cultural Self-Confidence to Unleash Spiritual Modernisation',[3] offers some useful insights into what the Party is aiming for.

The article starts, as all such articles now must, by citing Xi Jinping's remarks to the 19th Party Congress in which he observed that 'culture is the soul of a country and a people'. Xi spoke of the need to 'dig deeply into the thought and concepts, humanistic culture and ethical norms to be found in China's excellent traditional culture, link continuity and creativity in line with the demands of the era and permit Chinese culture to demonstrate its eternal attraction and contemporary charisma'. The article goes on to cite quotations from classical Chinese texts that are obscure to the point of meaninglessness to non-Chinese readers but familiar to any Chinese high-school graduate, illustrating what Chinese culture is meant to consist of.

These quotations draw principally from the Confucian classics (the *Analects*, the *Book of Rites*, the *Classic of Changes*, *Mencius*); the principal text of Daoism, the *Daodejing*; and assorted quotations from the Tang poet Li Po, the historian Sima Qian and the Song-dynasty statesman Wen Tianxiang.

The values they highlight include benevolence, righteousness, honesty, integrity and social harmony, the latter with reference to the Confucian concept of an ideal state in which all mankind lives in peace and harmony with nature, known as the Great Unity or *Datong*. (It is supposed to be preceded by an era of moderate prosperity – *xiaokang*. China's leadership has committed itself to delivering a moderately prosperous society – *xiaokang shehui* – by 2021.) Other values highlighted include a selfless dedication to public service; a readiness to sacrifice oneself for the nation; an awareness of the need for self-improvement; and an awareness of the need to prepare for the unexpected.

The article goes on to assert the Party's claim to be the inheritor and custodian of these traditional values. In the words of the author, 'today Communist ideology and the common ideology of socialism with Chinese characteristics exemplify the search for values imparted and inherited by the Chinese people over the ages: the process of Sinification of Marxism

involves fusion with the essence of China's traditional culture and alignment with China's concrete realities'.

This attempt to reconcile diverse ideas and philosophies is very much
in line with Chinese intellectual traditions. One need only look at how the
austere and ascetic figures of Indian (Hinayana) Buddhism morphed into
the fat jolly Buddhas portrayed in Chinese (Mahayana) Buddhism, and the
way the latter incorporated multiple aspects of Chinese folk religion, to
appreciate how this process has worked.

It remains to be seen whether this approach will satisfy what the Party
recognises as a need for greater spiritual fulfilment and clearly articulated
values. The country's spiritual gap has to date largely been met by a combination of Christianity, followed by tens of millions, and traditional Chinese
belief systems based around martial arts and meditation practices such as
the banned Falun Gong movement.

Both present challenges to an increasingly controlling Communist Party.
Beijing has borne down on Protestant 'house' churches operating outside
the state-controlled Three-Self movement, and negotiated an agreement –
not yet finalised – with the Vatican whereby it has a decisive voice in the
appointment of Catholic bishops.

Harking back to values deeply embedded in China's cultural and
political DNA has obvious attractions. But such an approach could prove
counterproductive, leading to the imposition of a rigid culture of conform-
ity policed by severe sanctions for those citizens perceived as defecting from
state-imposed values.

Exporting a new value system
A far bigger challenge will be to market the new value system outside
China. These values are characteristic of a unique and until recently largely
self-contained culture, and do not always align well with some of the values
of Western liberal democracy, in particular the Chinese concept of a natural
hierarchical order and the subordination of individual rights to the interests
of the collective.

But liberal democracy is something to which many states, particularly in
the developing world, pay only lip service. A Chinese model that presents

the country as an exemplar of rational modernity, technological advancement, economic progress and social stability, anchored by a set of values that in the past have proven both meaningful and durable, seems likely to exercise wider attraction. For many states, the need to pay public deference to China's primacy may be an acceptable price to pay for access to the economic benefits that a resurgent China can provide.

Whether China wishes to or can displace the predominant global value system with its own, and what the consequences of that might be, remains to be determined. What is clear is that the continuation of the current global order cannot be taken for granted.

Notes

1   For an English translation of the article together with the Chinese original, see 'Hu Jintao's Article in Qiushi Magazine – translated', China Copyright and Media, 4 January 2012, https://chinacopyrightandmedia.-wordpress.com/2012/01/04/hu-jintaos-article-in-qiushi-magazine-translated/.

2   'China to Promote Cultural Soft Power', *China Daily*, 1 January 2014, http://www.chinadaily.com.cn/china/2014-01-01/content_17208354.htm.

3   Sun Zhongyi, 'Yi wenhua zixin ji fa jingshen dongli', *Jiefangjun Bao* [Liberation Army Daily], 26 December 2017, http://www.81.cn/jfjbmap/content/2017-12/26content_195480.htm.

China's Innovation Trajectories

Andrew B. Kennedy

For more than half a century, US leadership in technological innovation has sustained the United States' economic and military power. For many observers, it is difficult to imagine a world in which the United States is not the undisputed innovation leader. In recent years, however, China's rising profile in innovation has stoked anxieties about the future of US technological leadership. In 2017, China's national research and development (R&D) spending reached RMB1.76 trillion (roughly $279 billion), and it is now poised to overtake that of the United States within the next decade.[1] China has also made headlines with showy accomplishments in areas ranging from supercomputers to space exploration. Some analysts, meanwhile, worry that cyber espionage provides Chinese companies with the means to catch up and compete with traditional industry leaders on the cheap. Is China rapidly becoming a world leader in science and technology?

This question has received a great deal of attention, but there is remarkably little consensus as to what the answer is. Focusing on China's rapid progress, some observers see a country with the potential to surprise the world with its technological prowess in years to come. Others are sceptical, and sometimes even dismissive, of this possibility, citing serious weaknesses in China's national innovation system, among other problems. Still others remain more or less undecided about China's technological trajectory.[2]

Andrew B. Kennedy is senior lecturer in policy and governance at the Crawford School of Public Policy at the Australian National University. He is the author of *The Conflicted Superpower: America's Collaboration with China and India in Global Innovation* (Columbia University Press, 2018).

Survival | vol. 60 no. 3 | June–July 2018 | pp. 71–86   DOI 10.1080/00396338.2018.1470756

This article suggests that the question must be rethought. Chinese development is not following a single path; different parts of the country are on very different trajectories. Critical features of China's innovation landscape, particularly Chinese firms, remain relatively weak. In other respects, China is developing with remarkable speed. The R&D activity of foreign firms in China, and the research and international collaboration being carried out by top Chinese scientists, are impressive in a number of ways.

China's points of weakness, combined with the increasingly global nature of innovation, mean that the country will continue to need collaboration with more developed countries in some areas for years to come. China's emerging strengths, in turn, make it an increasingly attractive partner for foreign companies and universities, even as tensions have mounted between Beijing and foreign technology firms in recent years. At the same time, China's changing profile poses important challenges for the outside world, both military and economic, that the US and its allies must address.

The weakest link: Chinese firms

Chinese firms are investing in innovation like never before. Since 2009, China has invested more in R&D than any country save the United States, and business has typically accounted for around three-quarters of China's R&D spending.[3] The vast majority of this investment comes from Chinese firms; the foreign share is quite small. China's surging R&D is impressive, but spending money is not an end in itself. What is China getting for all this investment?

Not nearly as much as China's leaders would prefer. Generally speaking, the efficiency with which Chinese companies translate investment into valuable patents and competitive new products is quite low.[4] Although the number of patents granted within China has skyrocketed, the standards for Chinese patents are low, and many of those granted to Chinese firms are of dubious value. Even the state-controlled media derides China's patent boom as 'high quantity, low quality'.[5] China-based inventors have recorded a growing number of patents in the United States and Europe as well, but a large share of these belong to foreign multinationals.[6] Chinese firms also lag behind in introducing new products. In 2015, domestic firms in China derived 12% of their revenue from new products, while foreign-funded firms derived 19%.[7] More generally, China's share of the world's top 100 companies (in terms of market capitalisation) remained stuck at 11% from 2009 to 2017, even as the US share rose from 42% to 55%.[8]

The struggles of Chinese firms are not surprising, given that the Chinese government often intervenes in the country's economy and society in ways that degrade the efficiency of the innovation system. State banks and government-sponsored initiatives have long privileged state-owned enterprises, for example, but these are hardly China's most innovative firms.[9] More recently, the government's 13th five-year plan included remarkably detailed technology initiatives, which could conflict with the investment plans of Chinese companies.[10] Various levels of the government are also heavily involved in the country's booming venture-capital industry, creating distortions in the market and sometimes placing conditions on entrepreneurs.[11] In other respects, it is the inactivity of the Chinese government that is problematic. Weak protection of intellectual property (IP) poses a particular challenge for would-be innovators in China, who must contend with competition from a wide array of imitators.[12]

China does have success stories, of course. The country is well known for 'efficiency-based' innovation – improving production processes, product design and supply-chain management to reduce cost and time to market.[13] Some Chinese firms excel at 'customer-based' innovation, showing heightened sensitivity to customer needs, as evidenced by the country's rapid development of financial technology ('fintech'). And while Chinese firms are weaker in engineering- and science-based innovation, there are important exceptions. Huawei stands out in this regard: a global success story, the firm not only ranks among the world leaders in terms of total R&D spending, but also typically devotes a sizeable portion (20–30%) to more ambitious 'research and innovation' projects.[14] In addition, some China-based but foreign-financed 'hybrid firms', such as Alibaba, have succeeded in part because of the discipline imposed by their foreign financing.[15] In the long term, China could conceivably develop leading firms in sectors ranging from semiconductors to biotech, as envisioned in the 'Made in China 2025' plan, though this is hardly guaranteed.[16] For now, however, China's firms remain a relatively weak link in the country's innovation system.

Can Chinese firms make up for their weaknesses through illicit means? Some have certainly tried. But how much Chinese firms can gain from stolen technology is unclear. Some argue that, as American cyber-security firm Mandiant put it, 'stolen information can be used to obvious advantage by the PRC [People's Republic of China] and Chinese state-owned enterprises'.[17] This has clearly been the case in some instances. Yet recent scholarship has demonstrated that the challenges of stealing, assimilating and applying valuable information can be formidable.[18] The most valuable information can be difficult to locate, and crucial knowledge needed to apply it may not be written down, existing instead in the form of tacit knowledge or organisational routines.[19] Relying on stolen technology also risks creating organisations that are optimised for imitation rather than innovation.[20] The extent and nature of China's reliance on economic espionage may be changing as well. There is evidence that the scale of Chinese cyber espionage against private companies has declined in recent years, following domestic reforms in China, public exposure and actions by the US government.[21] While China's activity continues – some have even suggested that it increased in the second half of 2017 – US officials believe it has become more targeted and calculating.[22] Taking all these points together, it is unclear just how much economic espionage will benefit Chinese firms going forward.

Foreign R&D

Foreign firms' R&D investment in China has grown rapidly over the past two decades. Indeed, according to one estimate, China attracted more than twice as much new foreign R&D investment (in terms of value) as the United States from 2010 to 2014.[23] In general, US firms have led the way in making R&D investments in China. From 2005 to 2013, for example, US companies spent 2.7 times more than Japanese companies did on R&D in China.[24] The list of companies making investments includes top information- and communication-technology firms such as Microsoft and Intel and, more recently, pharmaceutical giants such as Pfizer and Amgen. Microsoft has been a particularly noteworthy player. Microsoft Research Asia was established in Beijing in 1998 and has become the company's second-largest research organisation, after its counterpart in the United States. The centre's international collaboration is extensive. The emerging Skype Translator feature, for example, was created by a long-term collaborative effort between dozens of Microsoft researchers in the United States and China.[25]

Microsoft is hardly the only example. Between 1981 and 2012, the US Patent and Trademark Office granted 13,308 patents to non-Chinese multinationals with at least one inventor residing in China – with most of this activity taking place after 2005.[26] Besides Microsoft, other leaders in this activity include Intel, IBM and Taiwan's Hon Hai (also known as Foxconn). A slight majority of these patents (53%) were granted to transnational teams of inventors that included individuals both inside and outside of China. The quality of these 'co-invention' patents, in turn, is generally quite high: within a given firm, the quality of its co-invention patents involving China is indistinguishable from those granted to inventors based in the multinational's home country, judging by how often they are cited by subsequent patents. In contrast, patents granted to foreign multinationals that only included individuals within China were initially of lower quality. Over time, however, they too have become comparable to patents granted to inventor teams in the firm's home country.[27]

The extent and significance of foreign R&D in China should not be overstated, however. For one, multinational firms still tend to conduct core R&D in their home countries. In 2014, for example, total R&D spending by US foreign affiliates worldwide was only 19% of what their parent companies spent in the United States.[28] This is partly due to the embeddedness of multinationals in their home countries and the challenges of managing global R&D networks. In addition, a variety of barriers inhibit foreign firms' innovation activity in China. In 2017, a survey of US firms in China found that these included insufficient IP protection, insufficient talent, more restrictive data-security-related policies, requirements to comply with unique Chinese standards and indigenous innovation policies that discriminate against foreign firms.[29]

There are also questions about the future of foreign R&D in China. Recent disclosures regarding US cyber surveillance overseas have intensified suspicions of US technology firms within China, causing the regulatory environment those firms are facing to become quite challenging. In 2016, only 10% of US technology firms in China were 'optimistic' or 'slightly optimistic' about the future of China's regulatory environment, while 57% were 'pessimistic' or 'slightly pessimistic'.[30] Even so, leading firms are persevering. In 2015, Cisco announced it would invest $10bn in China over the next few years – a clear effort to get back in Beijing's good graces. Chipmakers Qualcomm and Intel have battled for market share through new investments and partnerships with Chinese firms. Apple is developing a series of R&D centres in China, and Google plans to open an artificial-intelligence centre in Beijing. As James McGregor of APCO Worldwide put it, 'People are adapting the best they can because the market matters so much'.[31]

Even so, it is clear that enthusiasm for China as an investment destination more broadly has cooled. From 2012 to 2016, the share of US firms in China listing the country as their top or a top-three investment destination fell from 78% to 56%.[32] For European firms, meanwhile, the share reporting China as a top-three investment destination fell from 72% to 61% between 2012 and 2017.[33] In addition, the share of European firms likely to increase R&D investments or operations in China in the near future fell from 85% in 2015 to 69% in 2017.[34] If these trends continue, they will constrain the pace of China's integration into global innovation networks.

The rise of Chinese science

The development of Chinese science in recent years has been remarkable. While critics often point to China's lack of Nobel laureates, such prizes are often awarded long after recipients' groundbreaking research was carried out, making them a lagging indicator of achievement. The first citizen of the People's Republic of China to win a Nobel Prize in the natural sciences, Tu Youyou, did so in 2015 for research performed in the 1970s. A more useful indicator is China's performance in the Nature Index, which tracks the affiliations of articles published in 68 top scientific journals. While the United States remains the clear leader, China now ranks second, with its score in the index jumping from 24% to 40% of the US figure from 2012 to 2016.[35] China is particularly strong in chemistry, but has been improving its performance in the physical and life sciences as well.

China has also become far and away the leading source of foreign collaborators for American scientists. Chinese scientists and engineers published nearly 44,000 articles with US counterparts in 2016 – a dramatic increase from just 5,406 in 2003.[36] China's total in 2016 nearly equalled the figures for the next two leading partners – the United Kingdom and Germany – put together. Popular fields of collaboration have included materials science, electrical engineering, biochemistry, chemistry and multidisciplinary science.

The growing collaboration between American and Chinese scientists is not surprising. China's top scientists are often educated overseas, frequently in the United States, or hold post-doctoral fellowships abroad. Peking University's chemistry department, for example, includes graduates of Harvard, MIT, California Institute of Technology, Columbia, Berkeley, the University of Pennsylvania and the University of Chicago, among other US universities. Overall, 92% of the department's faculty had either received a PhD or held a post-doctoral position abroad as of mid-2016. The corresponding figure for Tsinghua University's chemistry department was 77%.[37] Moreover, some Chinese scientists are receiving international acclaim for their laboratories' accomplishments. In 2015, the London-based *Physics World* awarded its 'Breakthrough of the Year' award to Pan Jianwei and Lu Chaoyang at the University of Science and Technology in Anhui for their work in quantum teleportation. Another Chinese team was among the top ten contenders for the award.[38]

Collaboration with foreign scientists is part of the explanation for China's increasing prowess in scientific publishing. This is particularly evident in the top journals. In 2014 and 2015, nearly 80% of the articles published in *Cell* featuring a China-based author also featured a US-based one (see Figure 1 below). The figures for *Nature* and *Science* were also high. In some of the less luminary Nature Index journals, however, the rate of co-authorship between Chinese and US scientists is much lower. In *Analytical Chemistry*, for example, the figure is a mere 12%.[39]

In short, China's elite scientists, if not the average Chinese researcher, are gaining in international prominence. This accomplishment is all the more noteworthy given that the Chinese government has not traditionally

Figure 1. **Percentage of articles featuring a China-based author with a US co-author (2014–15)**

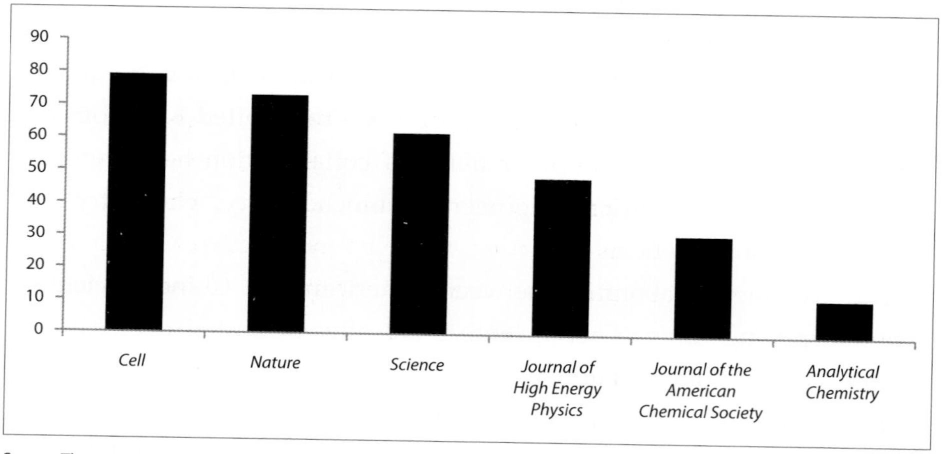

Source: Thomson Reuters Web of Science

prioritised basic science funding. In 2016, China invested RMB82bn (roughly $11.9bn) in basic research, representing just 5% of national R&D spending, while 84% was devoted to development.[40] For more developed countries, the share of basic research is typically higher. In 2015, for example, it was 12% in Japan and a striking 17% in the United States, the United Kingdom and South Korea.[41] China's neglect of basic science is starting to change, however: the government's latest five-year plan aims to increase basic science funding to 10% of national R&D.[42]

To be sure, many problems continue to plague Chinese science. The funding system has long suffered from a range of shortcomings, including fragmentation, inflexibility and inadequate oversight. Personal connections still play too large a role in the allocation of government funding. Chinese scientists are also heavily rewarded for publishing in highly ranked journals, and the preoccupation with this particular indicator of achievement has the potential to distort the research and promotion process.[43] They also face pressure to demonstrate productivity on relatively short timetables, which reduces the incentive to take risks and promotes academic misconduct, including plagiarism and fraud.[44] One study found that China's 'retraction index' – the rate at which published articles have to be withdrawn – was more than twice as high as that of the United States.[45] Not surprisingly, a

2015 survey found that 91% of Chinese scientists felt that more should be done to detect, prevent and punish misconduct.[46]

Even so, serious efforts to address some of these problems are being made. The last few years have seen the government overhaul the research-funding system, which has included the elimination of long-standing programmes and the consolidation of funding into five major streams. The government is also setting up a range of professional scientific associations (*zhuanye jigou*) to administer these streams and improve project management. The massive Chinese Academy of Sciences is undergoing a range of reforms, and new national laboratories are being established to promote interdisciplinary research. Top institutions are also experimenting with more nuanced and flexible means of performance evaluation. These reforms are still a work in progress, and it remains to be seen just how successful they will be, but it is clear that Chinese science is not standing still.[47]

For all its problems, then, basic scientific research is developing in a more impressive fashion than is Chinese corporate R&D. Top Chinese scientists are well connected abroad and collaborate frequently with counterparts in more developed countries. They can also point to a rapidly growing list of accomplishments, even though funding for basic science has not been the Chinese government's priority. Although many problems remain, there are also concerted efforts being made to address them.

Implications, opportunities and challenges

China's multiple-track trajectory has a range of implications – not only for the United States but also for many of its allies in the developed world. Firstly, China's weaknesses mean that the country will have good reason to work with more developed countries for years to come, not only by allowing foreign R&D but also by remaining at least somewhat open to foreign products. Indeed, while China has tried to increase its reliance on indigenous technology, there are serious drawbacks to this approach, particularly when most Chinese companies cannot provide top-tier products. As Huawei executive Eric Xu noted in 2015, 'if we're not open, if we don't bring in the world's best technology, we'll never have true information security'. He went on to underscore the gap between Chinese firms and their foreign counterparts, saying, 'Even if you localize, make your own CPUs [central processing units], make your own operating systems, make your own database software, it would still be at a grade school level [with] your [security measures] transparent to ... college students'.[48]

The downside of China's weakness in this regard is that the country's efforts to acquire foreign technology through unwelcome channels will continue. Pressure on foreign firms to transfer technology to local partners, for example, will likely persist in one form or another. While economic espionage may have abated in some areas, it is difficult to monitor, and it is apparent that some efforts continue. China's fear of foreign technological domination will also mean that the government will continue to worry about foreign firms' market share in the country. The danger for China is that these tendencies will alienate other governments that are economic partners (as is already happening with the United States), or that foreign firms will become less interested in the country as an R&D platform.

Secondly, China's emerging strengths represent important opportunities for innovators in more developed countries. Sophisticated foreign R&D centres help facilitate access to China's varied and changing market through what China analyst Nick Marro has called the 'in China, for China' approach.[49] They also allow foreign firms to tap China's talented and growing supply of human capital for more globally oriented projects, at least when IP concerns do not deter such collaboration. China's top universities are generating knowledge and collaborators for scientists and engineers in other countries. They are also emerging as partners for foreign companies in recruiting, research and branding. And while many Chinese firms are still lagging, there are also cases where collaboration between Chinese and foreign firms has been productive.

Yet China's rising profile also poses a range of serious challenges for developed countries. Firstly, China's growing capacity for innovation has implications for the country's military power. In recent years, China's leaders have pursued 'military–civil fusion' (*junmin ronghe*) in an intensified effort to leverage both military and civilian resources as they modernise the country's armed forces.[50] As part of this effort, China's military now works more closely with the country's universities and civilian firms investing in dual-use technologies, in areas ranging from robotics to cutting-edge materials. By March 2016, more than 1,000 civilian Chinese firms had been approved to research, develop and produce equipment for China's military – a total that constituted roughly 40% of all Chinese defence contractors.[51]

For China's rivals, this trend poses a clear challenge, particularly as well-heeled Chinese firms have increased their investments in foreign technology assets and their collaboration with foreign partners. The natural response is to conduct more expansive reviews of incoming foreign investments and foreign collaborations, as is currently being considered in the United States. While this is important, 'playing defence' will always be an imperfect solution, given the difficulty of evaluating emerging technologies, the limits of government capacity and the increasingly transnational character of innovation. The more fundamental requirement is to maintain robust innovation ecosystems at home that support continuing technological leadership. The United States is stumbling in this regard, even as worries about China's technological trajectory increase. President Donald Trump in particular has been described as 'apathetic' and even 'hostile' to science and technology, although Congress has thwarted his proposed cuts to scientific research.[52] In addition, the recent repeal of 'net neutrality' – the idea that internet service providers should treat all online traffic equally – in the United States will make it more difficult for many start-up firms to compete with established incumbents.[53] In short, while greater scrutiny of foreign partners is appropriate, it must be accompanied by more enthusiastic support for innovation at home.

The United States is stumbling

In addition, China's rising profile has clearly strengthened its ability to compete with other countries for the most crucial ingredient in innovation: brainpower. The number of students returning to China after completing their studies has approached 80% of the number of students going abroad – up from just 31% in 2007.[54] Some developed countries have made concerted efforts to compete for this sizeable pool of human capital. Canada, for example, introduced a 'Global Skills Strategy' in June 2017 through which skilled immigrants can acquire work visas in as little as two weeks. Australia, in contrast, appears torn. The government moved to restrict immigration in 2017 but, following criticism from technology companies, introduced a new 'Global Talent Scheme' on a trial basis shortly thereafter.[55] The United States, meanwhile, is simply shooting itself in the foot. While it educates more foreign students than any other country, the US offers foreign graduates some opportunity for temporary employment but then imposes per country caps that make it hard for those from China and India to receive permanent residency – effectively encouraging them to go elsewhere.[56] The Trump administration has vowed to improve some aspects of the system, but so far has mainly made it more difficult to hire foreign workers.[57] In short, the developed world could clearly compete more effectively for the growing pool of Chinese talent.

Lastly, while China's firms in general remain a weak link, the support some receive from the government has allowed them to compete on the cheap and increase their market share, particularly in China but also in other countries.[58] Over time, this trend may put pressure on the revenues of more innovative industry leaders, compromising their ability to invest in R&D and stifling the pace of high-tech innovation. As one recent report puts it, 'China could do to semiconductors, artificial intelligence, and pharmaceuticals what it has done to steel and aluminum'.[59] In response, the Trump administration has taken unilateral actions in an effort to curtail discriminatory measures and level the playing field within China. But while unilateral pressure may get Beijing's attention, the United States must invest much more actively in bilateral and multilateral solutions as well. Negotiations for a bilateral investment treaty with China began in 2008, but talks have languished since President Trump took office. More broadly, the Trump administration has made an ill-advised retreat from multilateral economic diplomacy in Asia. Washington needs to re-engage in an effort to steer the emerging economic order in Asia away from China's state-capitalist model.

*   *   *

While unequivocal proclamations about China's rise – or failure to rise – in innovation can make for enjoyable reading, they are not a firm basis for sound policy. Recent assessments that imply China is on the verge of becoming the world's innovation leader ignore serious weaknesses in the country's innovation system. They also overstate China's potential for self-reliance. Recent assessments that have dismissed China's prospects, in contrast, miss important advances that the country has made. In doing so, these assessments understate China's potential both as a partner and as a challenger for other countries.

Recognising that China is developing along multiple trajectories is only the first step to sound policymaking. The second step is to make changes to policy where changes are needed. The United States in particular, as the world's innovation leader, needs to change course – if not under its current president then under the next one.

Acknowledgements

The author would like to thank Tai Ming Cheung for feedback on an earlier version of this article. He also wishes to thank Rongfang Pan and Nan Liu for excellent research assistance. The standard caveats apply.

Notes

1   'China's Spending on R&D Jumps 14pc in 2017 to US$279 Billion', *South China Morning Post*, 27 February 2018, http://www.scmp.com/news/china/policies-politics/article/2134895/chinas-spending-research-and-development-14pc-2017.

2   Andrew B. Kennedy, 'Powerhouses or Pretenders? Debating China's and India's Emergence as Technological Powers', *Pacific Review*, vol. 28, no. 2, 2015, pp. 281–302.

3   Andrew B. Kennedy, 'Slouching Tiger, Roaring Dragon: Comparing India and China as Late Innovators', *Review of International Political Economy*, vol. 23, no. 2, 2016, pp. 71–2.

4   Scott Kennedy, *The Fat Tech Dragon: Benchmarking China's Innovation Drive* (Washington DC: Center for Strategic and International Studies, 2017), p. 39.

5   'High Quantity, Low Quality: China's Patent Boom', *China Daily*, 23 June 2014, http://www.chinadaily.com.cn/business/2014-06/23/content_17609675.htm.

6   Lee Branstetter, Guangwei Lee and Francisco Veloso, 'The Rise of International Coinvention', in Adam B. Jaffe and Benjamin F. Jones (eds), *The Changing Frontier: Rethinking Science and Innovation Policy* (Chicago, IL: University of Chicago Press, 2015), p. 140.

7   China State Statistical Bureau, *Zhongguo Keji Tongji Nianjian 2016* [China Statistical Yearbook on Science and Technology 2016] (Beijing:

Zhongguo Tongji Chubanshe, 2016), p. 31.

8 PricewaterhouseCoopers, 'Global Top 100 Companies by Market Capitalization', 31 March 2017, p. 9, https://www.pwc.com/gx/en/audit-services/assets/pdf/global-top-100-companies-2017-final.pdf.

9 Kennedy, 'Slouching Tiger, Roaring Dragon', p. 81.

10 On the initiatives, see Scott Kennedy and Christopher K. Johnson, *Perfecting China, Inc.: The 13th Five-Year Plan* (Washington DC: Center for Strategic and International Studies, 2016), pp. 27–8.

11 Douglas Fuller, 'The Critical and Contested Foreign Links for China's High-Tech Entrepreneurship', China Policy Institute: Analysis, 9 May 2017, https://cpianalysis.org/2017/05/09/the-critical-and-contested-foreign-links-for-chinas-high-tech-entre-preneurship; Chinese entrepreneur, interview by author, Beijing, 29 May 2015.

12 Samm Sacks, *Disruptors, Innovators, and Thieves: Assessing Innovation in China's Digital Economy* (Washington DC: Center for Strategic and International Studies, 2018), p. 18.

13 Jonathan Woetzel et al., 'The China Effect on Global Innovation', McKinsey Global Institute, October 2015, pp. 41–102.

14 'Huawei Ren Zhengfei Zai Quanguo Keji Chuangxin Dahuishang de Huibao' [Report on Speech by Huawei's Ren Zhengfei at the National Science and Technology Innovation Conference], 6 June 2016, http://ql1d.com/news/show/id/162751.html.

15 Douglas B. Fuller, *Paper Tigers, Hidden Dragons: Firms and the Political Economy of China's Technological Development* (Oxford: Oxford University Press, 2016).

16 Tai Ming Cheung et al., *Planning for Innovation: Understanding China's Plans for Technological, Energy, Industrial, and Defense Development*, Report Prepared for the US–China Economic and Security Review Commission (San Diego, CA: University of California at San Diego Institute for Global Conflict and Cooperation, 2016), pp. 45–51.

17 Mandiant, 'APT1: Exposing One of China's Cyber Espionage Units', 2013, p. 25, https://www.fireeye.com/content/dam/fireeye-www/services/pdfs/mandiant-apt1-report.pdf.

18 Jon R. Lindsay and Tai Ming Cheung, 'From Exploitation to Innovation: Acquisition, Absorption, and Application', in Jon R. Lindsay, Tai Ming Cheung and Derek S. Reveron (eds), *China and Cybersecurity: Espionage, Strategy, and Politics in the Digital Domain* (Oxford: Oxford University Press, 2015), pp. 51–86.

19 Adam Segal, *The Hacked World Order: How Nations Fight, Trade, Maneuver, and Manipulate in the Digital Age* (New York: PublicAffairs, 2016), p. 130.

20 Lindsay and Cheung, 'From Exploitation to Innovation', p. 79.

21 FireEye, 'Redline Drawn: China Recalculates Its Use of Cyber Espionage', June 2016, https://www.fireeye.com/content/dam/fireeye-www/current-threats/pdfs/rpt-china-espionage.pdf.

22 See Adam Segal, 'The US–China Cyber Espionage Deal One Year Later', Council on Foreign Relations, 28

September 2016, https://www.cfr.org/blog/us-china-cyber-espionage-deal-one-year-later; and Andy Greenberg, 'China Tests the Limits of Its US Hacking Truce', *Wired*, 31 October 2017, https://www.wired.com/story/china-tests-limits-of-us-hacking-truce/.

23 Courtney Fingar, 'China Passes US in Race for FDI in Research and Development', *Financial Times*, 22 July 2015, http://www.ft.com/intl/cms/s/3/241d9366-3058-11e5-91ac-a5e17d9b4cff.html#axzz4BVjRStWH.

24 Andrew B. Kennedy, 'Innovation, Interdependence, and Power: China, India, and the United States in the Globalization of R&D', *Political Science Quarterly*, vol. 132, no. 1, 2017, pp. 63–86.

25 Personal communication from Joy Ann Lo, Senior Communications Manager at Microsoft Research Asia (2011–14), 22 September 2015.

26 Lee Branstetter, Guangwei Li and Francisco Veloso, 'Bridge to Excellence? The Impacts of International Coinvention on Multinational R&D in China' (Pittsburgh, PA: Carnegie Mellon University, 2016), p. 10, https://www.andrew.cmu.edu/user/guangwei/Research.html.

27 *Ibid.*, p. 21.

28 US National Science Foundation, *Science and Engineering Indicators 2018* (Arlington, VA: National Science Foundation, 2018), pp. 4–72.

29 AmCham China, *2017 China Business Climate Survey Report* (Beijing: AmCham China, 2017), p. 45.

30 *Ibid.*, p. 32.

31 Quoted in Shai Oster and Danielle Muoio, 'Cisco Pledges $10 Billion China Investment to Regain Ground', Bloomberg, 19 June 2015, http://www.bloomberg.com/news/articles/2015-06-17/cisco-to-invest-10-billion-in-china-to-create-jobs-promote-r-d.

32 AmCham China, *2017 China Business Climate Survey Report*, p. 24.

33 European Chamber of Commerce in China, *European Business in China: Business Confidence Survey 2017* (Beijing: European Chamber of Commerce in China, 2017), p. 34.

34 *Ibid.*, p. 48.

35 Nature Group, 'Nature Index', http://www.natureindex.com/.

36 US National Science Foundation, *Science and Engineering Indicators 2018*, appendix table 5–44.

37 Author's calculations from departmental websites.

38 Tushna Commissariat and Hamish Johnston, 'Double Quantum-Teleportation Milestone Is Physics World 2015 Breakthrough of the Year', *Physics World*, 11 December 2015, http://physicsworld.com/cws/article/news/2015/dec/11/double-quantum-teleportation-milestone-is-physics-world-2015-breakthrough-of-the-year.

39 Author's calculations from Thomson Reuters 'Web of Science' database.

40 National Bureau of Statistics of China, 'National Data: Science and Technology', http://data.stats.gov.cn/english/easyquery.htm?cn=C01.

41 US National Science Foundation, *Science and Engineering Indicators 2016*, pp. 4–47.

42 Hao Xin, 'Five-Year Plan Boosts Basic Research Funding', *Science*, vol. 351, no. 6,280, 25 March 2016, p. 1,382.

43 On this point, I am indebted to a con-

versation with an expatriate scientist who has worked in China.

44 Jane Qiu, 'China Goes Back to Basics on Research Funding', *Nature*, vol. 507, no. 7,491, 13 March 2014, pp. 148–9; 'Fraud in Academia Is Killing China's Nobel Dream', *South China Morning Post*, 10 February 2014, http://www.scmp.com/comment/insight-opinion/article/1424571/fraud-academia-killing-chinas-nobel-dream.

45 Tianwei He, 'Retraction of Global Scientific Publications from 2001 to 2010', *Scientometrics*, vol. 96, no. 2, August 2013, pp. 555–61.

46 Charlotte Liu et al., *Turning Point: Chinese Science in Transition* (London and Shanghai: Nature Publishing Group, November 2015), p. 14, http://www.nature.com/press_releases/turning_point.pdf.

47 On these reforms, see Yingying Zhou, 'The Rapid Rise of a Research Nation', *Nature*, vol. 528, no. 7,582, 17 December 2015, pp. S170–73; and Cong Cao and Richard P. Suttmeier, 'Challenges of S&T System Reform in China', *Science*, vol. 355, no. 6,329, 2017, pp. 1,019–21.

48 Quoted in Gerry Shih, 'Exclusive: Huawei CEO Says Chinese Cybersecurity Rules Could Backfire', Reuters, 21 April 2015, http://www.reuters.com/article/us-huawei-cyber-security-idUSKBN0NC1G920150421.

49 Nick Marro, 'Foreign Company R&D: In China, For China', *China Business Review*, 1 June 2015.

50 Greg Levesque and Mark Stokes, *Blurred Lines: Military–Civil Fusion and the 'Going Out' of China's Defense Industry* (Washington DC: Pointe Bello, 2016), pp. 8–9.

51 *Ibid.*, p. 23.

52 Tanya Lewis, 'How Trump Shaped Science in 2017', *Scientific American*, 14 December 2017, https://www.scientificamerican.com/article/how-trump-shaped-science-in-2017/.

53 Ryan Singel, 'If the FCC Kills Net Neutrality, Expect Fewer Great Startups', *Wired*, 12 December 2017.

54 China Scholarship Council, 'Chuguo Liuxue Fazhan Zhuangkuang Diaocha Baogao' [Report on an Investigation of the Study Abroad Situation] (Beijing: Chinese Education Online and Best Choice for Education, 2015), http://www.gol.edu.cn/zt/report/; and Andrew B. Kennedy, *The Conflicted Superpower: America's Collaboration with China and India in Global Innovation* (New York: Columbia University Press, 2018), pp. 32–3.

55 Chris Pash, 'Australian Startups Say They Are Being Choked by New Visa Rules', *Business Insider*, 30 November 2017, https://www.businessinsider.com.au/australia-startups-457-visa-rules-2017-11.

56 Kennedy, *The Conflicted Superpower*, pp. 78–9.

57 Laura Meckler, 'Trump Administration Tightens Scrutiny of Skilled Worker Visa Applicants', *Wall Street Journal*, 19 November 2017, https://www.wsj.com/articles/trump-administration-tightens-scrutiny-of-skilled-worker-visa-applicants-1511114338.

58 Kennedy, *The Fat Tech Dragon*, pp. 2–3.

59 *Ibid.*, p. 3.

China and the Vatican

Lanxin Xiang

China and the Vatican seem finally on the verge of a historic breakthrough in diplomatic talks that have dragged on for years. The question at issue is who should appoint bishops. It is apparent, after an arduous negotiation process, that the Vatican has made a historic compromise, allowing the Chinese government to have a strong voice in episcopal appointments. This has produced an outcry in the Western media, as though Pope Francis had agreed to sell millions of Chinese Catholics down the river to satisfy the needs of a brutal communist dictatorship. But this narrative is misleading.

To begin with, the Vatican has already set a precedent in compromising with a communist regime over episcopal appointments. Under the so-called Vietnamese model, the Vatican prepares a shortlist of candidates to the bishopric which is submitted to the government for approval. If approval is forthcoming, the Holy See officially appoints the new bishop. If the government refuses, the Vatican presents another name, and so on until a consensus is reached. From the very beginning, this process has emphasised pragmatic bargaining.

Unlike the Catholic Church in Vietnam, however, the Catholic Church in China has long been divided into two distinct parts: an ever-growing 'underground Church' loyal to the Pope and oppressed by Chinese authorities, and an 'official Church' led by the Chinese Catholic Patriotic Association (CCPA), a state organ loyal to the authorities. (Vietnam, by contrast, has no

Lanxin Xiang is Professor of International History and Politics at the Graduate Institute, Geneva, and a Contributing Editor to *Survival*.

Survival | vol. 60 no. 3 | June–July 2018 | pp. 87–94   DOI 10.1080/00396338.2018.1470757

official Church whose bishops are appointed by an atheist political regime.) Thus, any significant breakthrough in the Chinese case would require both the Chinese government and the Vatican to make substantial concessions.

There are practical reasons why both the Vatican and China would like to reach a compromise. The Catholic Church wishes to further its project of global expansion, while the Chinese government seeks to maintain social stability. Neither side is inclined to sabotage the political legitimacy of the other. In contrast to many Western political leaders, the Catholic hierarchy does not harbour a 'regime change' agenda. This benign stance could become a political asset for Beijing in dealing with increasingly restless 'underground' Catholics in China who might otherwise become a formidable source of political opposition to the regime.

The Chinese Rites Controversy

Another point of commonality, often neglected by the media, is the fact that both the Church and the Chinese government are heirs to the unique but vicious ecclesiastical dispute known as the Chinese Rites Controversy, which played out between 1645 and 1742. The controversy emerged at a time when both China and the Church were confronted with the implications of significant political and philosophical change in Europe.

The first Western discussion about the Chinese system took place more than 400 years ago, during the final stage of the Ming Dynasty (1368–1644). Because democratic ideology had not yet become widespread in Europe, the question of whether the Chinese way of governance was legitimate was not seen as relevant at that time. Beginning in the eighteenth century, however, the increasing dominance of European Enlightenment thinking posed a challenge, sometimes implicit, sometimes explicit, both to the Vatican and to non-Western cultures such as China. The question of how best to make room for alternatives to this deeply entrenched hegemony is a question that has preoccupied both China and the Vatican for some time.

Today, pre-modern Europe's rich interactions with the non-Western world are often dismissed, if not deliberately ignored, by Eurocentric historians. Yet the most genuine attempt by Europeans to understand China and its statecraft occurred at the beginning of the seventeenth century, at a time when the Christian church in Europe was wracked by civil war. The Catholic Church had suffered heavily under the explosive intellectual rebellion of the Protestant Reformation, mounting a Counter-Reformation in response. Much of the hard work in battling Protestantism was to be done by the Society of Jesus (whose members are known as Jesuits), which was founded in 1540 by Ignatius of Loyola (1491–1556). From the beginning, the Jesuits were meant to be the vanguard of a revived Catholic Christianity and reformers of Europe's far-flung networks of settlers. Yet as the order began its work among the various cultural traditions of the non-Western world, the Jesuits recognised the vast potential for expanding the Christian community beyond Europe and its diaspora. Through rigorous training and sheer strength of will, the Jesuits managed to learn the customs, languages, religious habits and thought patterns of the many societies in which they were operating. More remarkably, they were soon in a position to restructure Christian theology so as to incorporate its basic tenets into local value systems. Thus unified under the common label of *accommodatio*, the Jesuits launched a major incursion into the non-Christian world, thereby prompting a rapid expansion of the Church.

Given that the Jesuits regarded the prevailing political pattern in Europe itself to be corrupt and illegitimate, their practice of cultural accommodation harboured no strong desire to downgrade other cultures by delegitimising their existing systems of governance. When the Jesuits arrived in China at the end of the sixteenth century, the typically 'modern' pairing of discourse on political legitimacy with attempts to discredit other political systems did not yet exist. This rhetorical pattern was to become commonplace only after the European Enlightenment. The Jesuits, therefore, merely tried to work out whether Chinese 'native religion' was compatible with the fundamental tenets of Christianity as they defined them. Their dealings with Chinese civilisation did not rely upon any sense of Western cultural superiority, not least because the Confucian state they found in China, though not a religious authority, seemed to match their conception of a virtuous *res publica perfecta* (perfect commonweatlh). Even more importantly, the idea that the Chinese people belonged to an inferior 'yellow' (or 'Mongoloid') race would not be accepted as scientific 'fact' until two centuries later.[1]

Theologically, the Jesuits were far more frustrated in Europe, where vague distinctions between spiritual and secular matters among the European monarchies often led to war. They wondered why Chinese rulers did not seem to have this problem, and why Chinese citizens seemed to co-exist with religion and the state in relative harmony. To their great delight, they eventually discovered a unique Chinese 'secret of statecraft' (*arcana imperii*), according to which the state acquired its legitimacy only through constant moral attention and behavioural adjustment to nature and the world unknown (*Tian*, or 'heaven'), which the Jesuits preferred to identify as the Christian God, whose name they translated into the Chinese language as 'Lord of Heaven' (天主).[2] In this way, Jesuit missionaries in China initiated the first real cultural interaction between China and the West. Sadly, their promising efforts were to come to an end with the suppression of their order by Pope Clement XIII in 1773.

The so-called Chinese Rites Controversy was to deal another blow not just to the Catholic Church in China, but to the health of the interaction between China and the West in ways that continue to fuel misunderstandings today. The controversy had to do with the rites, terms and sites of Christian worship in China – specifically, whether Chinese converts to Christianity could be allowed to continue performing traditional rites in honour of their ancestors and Confucius; how to accurately render basic Christian terms, especially 'God' (*Deus*), in the Chinese language; and whether members of the Mandarin class (China's scholar-gentry elite) who had accepted the principles of Christianity should be allowed to continue performing official rituals as part of their regular state duties at temples honouring Confucius. The arrogant demand that Chinese converts abandon Confucianism meant that no scholar in any official position – including schoolteachers – could become a Christian without renouncing his cultural heritage, and hence that no Christian could become a government official of any sort. This dogma was seen to pose a direct threat to the peace and stability of the Chinese state and society.

Ironically, the Church's demand that Christianised Mandarins not go to Buddhist or Taoist temples to worship had never posed a problem for Chinese elites, given that China had no history of conscious religious discrimination. Buddhism, Taoism and Confucianism generally coexisted in harmony. The more important question, which was mostly ignored, was whether the Confucian tradition should be considered a *religion* along with Buddhism and Taoism. In *The Meaning and End of Religion*, Wilfred Cantwell Smith contends that 'religion' is a peculiarly European concept of recent origin. Practitioners of any given faith do not regard what they do as 'religion' until they have formed a collective perspective towards outsiders. Religion, in the modern sense of the word, is a product of identity politics:

> One's own 'religion' may be piety & faith, obedience, worship & a vision of god. An alien 'religion' is a system of beliefs or rituals, an abstract & impersonal pattern of observables ... Religion as a systematic entity, as it emerged in the 17th & 18th centuries, is a concept of polemics & apologetics.[3]

China has never had a religion in the Western sense, because it has no *spiritual* need for a collective identity. Confucianism, far from being a religion, is a secular, political body of thought. Therefore, whether or not Confucianism is a religion is a question the Western mind will never be in a position to answer, and the Chinese mind never in a position to ask.

Ultimately, the Rites Controversy had less to do with Chinese civilisation than with religious rivalries in Europe, with China getting caught in the middle of a civil war between Protestantism and Catholicism. Since this episode is largely forgotten today, it is difficult to imagine the extraordinary viciousness the controversy engendered between China and the Christian world. Although it began as a harmless debate among theologians, it would eventually drag in three popes, two Chinese (Manchu) emperors, hundreds of Christian missionaries and the entire theological faculty at the Sorbonne, the intellectual citadel of the Counter-Reformation. Philosophers and scholars throughout Europe, including some of the continent's greatest minds (Leibniz, Kant, Goethe, Rousseau, Voltaire and Montesquieu, as well as political economists Francois Quesnay and Adam Smith), were engaged in or stimulated by this debate.

Also pitted against each other were the Renaissance humanists, represented by many Jesuit missionaries in China, and their arch-enemies, the conservative theologians of various sub-cultures within the Catholic Church. The Jesuits and their immediate followers, including some secular humanists during the early stages of the Enlightenment, chose China and Confucianism as their preferred foil to highlight the backward, feudal, morally corrupt social and political elite in Europe. By the second half of the eighteenth century, however, the prevailing political ideology produced by the Enlightenment was becoming drastically anti-Chinese in character, with the Jesuit model of virtuous governance, encompassing the philosopher-king of the Confucian state, becoming a symbol of wickedness.

An old debate made new

From the Chinese perspective, today's Western debate on China seems broadly similar, but also far inferior, to the original Rites Controversy. Because the parameters of Europe's early encounters with China have long since been forgotten or dismissed as irrelevant to contemporary discussions on topics such as democracy and human rights, these discussions have become a one-way street. Deeply entrenched cultural and racial prejudices have produced a belief among Westerners that traditional Chinese concepts have no place in conversations about democracy, a Western invention. Hence, China must be judged by Western values within a Western conceptual framework.

Yet if we replace the keywords of the seventeenth-century debate with post-Enlightenment concepts such as 'inalienable rights', 'individualism', 'personal freedom' and 'social contract', the similarities between the Rites Controversy and contemporary debates quickly become apparent. Today, Westerners are seeking to determine whether China could ever succeed in promoting the welfare of its citizens without adopting the Western rituals of governance; how to render terms such as 'human rights' and 'freedom' – supposedly 'universal' values – accurately into the Chinese language given that the Chinese tradition resists any concept of universality; and whether the Chinese system should be seen as an alternative to democratic forms of government, provided it successfully serves the people's interest by delivering personal well-being and national security.

So far, the Western answer to these questions has been decidedly negative, with no sign of any willingness to adopt a new accommodationist approach – with the possible exception of the evolving stance of the Catholic Church. In 1939, a few weeks after his election to the papacy, Pope Pius XII ordered the Congregation for the Evangelization of Peoples to relax certain aspects of past papal decrees such that Chinese rites and customs were no longer considered superstitious, but rather as an honourable way of esteeming one's ancestors. Confucianism was also recognised as a philosophy and an integral part of Chinese culture rather than a heathen religion in conflict with Catholicism. This changed the ecclesiastical situation in China in an almost revolutionary way. As the Chinese church began to flourish, Pius XII established a local clerical hierarchy and, in 1946, appointed the first Chinese national (Archbishop Thomas Tian Gengxin) to the College of Cardinals.

The Catholic Church was courageous in correcting its historical mistakes, something that the West's secular governments still seem incapable or unwilling to do. Unlike the Jesuits 400 years ago, Western elites perceive the Chinese political system as nothing more than oriental despotism, leaving little room for discussion, let alone accommodation. This perception has been built upon a post-Enlightenment, teleological view of human history that presupposes the ultimate triumph of Western civilisation. Western superiority is justified by the two alleged advantages of European culture: its superior Christian ethics, and its exceptional talent for economic growth. Most Western scholars assume that democratic modernisation and the accompanying economic progress can only take place within a Christian cultural context (or more precisely, for Max Weber, a Protestant ethical context[4]). However, the re-emergence of 'traditional states' such as China, which increasingly reject any form of cultural tutelage from the West, presents a challenge to this assumption.

The Catholic Church appears to be the only Western actor able to grasp the meaning of China's self-restoration. As a knowledgeable and experienced actor in global politics and diplomacy – and as the Western institution with the longest history of interacting with China – the Vatican's long-term vision usually sets itself apart from the ephemeral and short-sighted vision of national governments. Unlike its Western counterparts, the Vatican has recently embarked on a process of deep reflection and soul-searching over its historical experience with China. Although little noticed by the mainstream media, Pope John Paul II made a speech on 24 October 2001 in which he apologised for any 'errors' made by the Church's missionaries in the past. 'I feel deep sadness for those errors', he said, 'and I regret that in many people these failings may have given the impression of a lack of respect and esteem for the Chinese people on the part of the Catholic Church.' The speech was made at an international convention in Rome being held to commemorate the arrival in China of the first Jesuit missionary, Father Matteo Ricci, more than 400 years ago.[5]

The Society of Jesus once displayed an admirable open-mindedness toward Chinese culture that seems to have all but disappeared among Western governments. Now that a Jesuit has ascended to the papacy for the first time, it seems like the ideal moment for the Vatican and China to resume the healthy cultural dialogue that was so brutally broken off in 1742.

Notes

[1] For a brilliant recent study on how the Chinese came to be classified as 'yellow' and eventually as a 'peril' to Western civilisation, see Michael Keevak, *Becoming Yellow: A Short History of Racial Thinking* (Princeton, NJ: Princeton University Press, 2011).

[2] The Chinese term for Catholicism is derived from Jesuit nomenclature.

[3] Wilfred Cantwell Smith, *The Meaning and End of Religion* (Minneapolis, MN: Fortress Press, 1991), p. 43.

[4] Max Weber, translated by Peter Baehr and Gordon C. Wells, *The Protestant Ethic and the Spirit of Capitalism* (New York: Penguin Books, 2002).

[5] For the text of Pope John Paul II's speech, see http://w2.vatican.va/content/john-paul-ii/en/speeches/2001/october/documents/hf_jp-ii_spe_20011024_matteo-ricci.html.

Conflict and Realignment in the Middle East

Volker Perthes

The political geometry of the Middle East underwent significant shifts in 2017, not unlike in 2011, when a series of popular protests and rebellions spread through the region, unsettling most of its ruling elites (and unseating a few of them), and bringing about significant regional realignments. This rebellious moment ended in most of the Arab states with the re-establishment of authoritarian elites possessing a somewhat – but only somewhat – heightened consideration of public opinion. State breakdown and war, and an upsurge of terrorist violence, were also experienced in many places. Sudden shifts like these have demonstrated that coalitions and alliances in the Middle Eastern state system tend to be temporary in nature, largely subject to considerations of regime security and to the personal hold on power of ruling elites. This accounts to some extent for the lack of a stable balance of power and the absence of even basic regional security arrangements.

Popular explanations for patterns of regional alignment and conflict in the Middle East tend to focus on religious or sectarian divisions (the 'Sunni–Shia divide'), on the form of government (monarchies versus republics), or on the international orientation of states and regimes (pro- or anti-Western). While these dichotomies do sometimes emerge, they are mostly misleading. Consider the confrontation between Qatar and the other members of the

Volker Perthes is the Director of Stiftung Wissenschaft und Politik (German Institute for International and Security Affairs) in Berlin. An earlier and shorter version of this commentary was published in the *Security Times* prepared for the Munich Security Conference 2018.

Survival | vol. 60 no. 3 | June–July 2018 | pp. 95–104   DOI 10.1080/00396338.2018.1470760

Gulf Cooperation Council, which entered an exceptionally hostile period in 2017. This confrontation defies not only the notion of unity among the monarchies, at least on the Arabian Peninsula, but also that of a Persian Gulf conflict pitting the Sunni Arab countries against Shia Iran. Moreover, the crisis has demonstrated that international ties do not necessarily suffice to create or maintain co-directional regional bonds. After all, Saudi Arabia and the United Arab Emirates (UAE) on the one hand, and Qatar on the other, all count among the most important US allies in the region.

We cannot predict the events that are likely to shape regional dynamics, but we can reasonably assume that regional leaders will often try to deal with and shape geopolitical developments in a way that is neither irrational nor ideological, but pragmatic, and underpinned by the logic of domestic power. Three issues are likely to determine the regional agenda in the next year or two: ongoing efforts to wind down the war in Syria, the Saudi–Iranian rivalry and, of course, the positioning and policies of Russia and the US. Other unresolved conflicts – the war in Yemen and the Israeli–Palestinian conflict in particular – will continue to be of enormous consequence to the people affected by them, but can be expected to have a lesser impact on the overall political geometry of the region.

Syria and Iran

In Syria, as well as in neighbouring Iraq, the war against the Islamic State is almost over, at least to the extent that the group's territorially based, jihadist state-building project, or self-styled caliphate, has been largely overcome. The civilian population and the original parties to the wider civil war (mainly government and opposition or rebel forces) have all suffered enormous losses. In Syria, the government of President Bashar al-Assad has re-established control over some two-thirds of the country. It is much weaker today than it was in 2011, however, given its ongoing reliance on the intensive support of Russia, Iran and Iranian-sponsored forces to regain and hold territory previously lost either to oppositional forces or to the Islamic State. If any party has won the war, it is not the Syrian government and certainly not the rebels, but rather Russia. The opposition (meaning those political and armed anti-regime groups that seek, or at least do not reject, a negotiated, national, political solution to the conflict) has not been totally defeated, but it has certainly lost the war: armed opposition groups have been largely relegated to so-called 'de-escalation areas', of which there were initially four. One of these is under Turkish protection, while the rest have been defined by Russia in cooperation with Turkey, Iran and, in one case, the United States. Altogether, opposition-held territory accounts for less than 10% of Syrian territory. In addition, about one-fifth of Syrian land remains under the control of the Kurdish Party of Democratic Union (PYD), which is less interested in who rules Damascus than in how much autonomy it can achieve for Syria's majority-Kurdish areas in the north.

The creation of the de-escalation zones had initially led to a significant reduction in military violence between government and opposition forces. Since late 2017, however, these zones have become the main focus of escalation. The Northern and Southern de-escalation zones have shrunk under fire; and the so-called Eastern Ghouta Zone, just outside Damascus, had returned to government control after heavy fighting and the eventual capitulation of the local armed groups by April 2018.

In contrast to much of the past seven years, most of the relevant regional and international players now tend to agree that the end of the war against the Islamic State provides an opportunity to reach a negotiated settlement between government and opposition that takes the actual balance of forces into account. They also agree, to some extent at least, that without a negotiated settlement providing a modicum of political 'transition', any government will find it impossible to stabilise and rebuild the country. Moreover, almost all interested actors recognise that any failure to reach a basic settlement risks the continued fragmentation of the country and even the emergence of an 'Islamic State 2.0'.

All this is not to say that the principal external players agree on the best way to settle the conflict. It remains to be seen, for example, whether Russia will use its influence in Syria to enforce a pacification process involving only limited constitutional changes that basically preserve the current political system while co-opting opposition leaders – or using force to subdue them if co-option fails. Alternatively, UN efforts to engage the parties in real peace negotiations might eventually lead to a more genuine form of power-sharing, new constitutional arrangements, significant guarantees for political and human rights, and credible, UN-supervised presidential and legislative elections. Given current patterns of influence and leverage in Syria, the former scenario seems more achievable than the latter, but also more brittle. Moreover, the latter could only succeed if regional and international forces, including Russia, the US and the EU – as well as Iran, Saudi Arabia, Turkey and smaller but more aggressive players like Qatar – were actively to support it.

In this way, the Syria conflict is still linked to the ongoing Saudi–Iranian struggle for regional hegemony. Both Riyadh and Tehran tend to see each other as their main rival for regional leadership, and hence as a threat. Both are also taking aggressive steps to impose their respective perceptions on the entire region. Saudi Arabia remains the main sponsor of the Syrian opposition, while Iran is the main regional backer of Assad.

Tehran is unlikely to give up its enormous political investment in Syria, or the geopolitical gains it has made, such as its strong influence on the government and security apparatus in Damascus, the considerable economic opportunities that have presented themselves in Syria, and what basically constitutes a secure land connection from Iran through Iraq and Syria to Lebanon. Advisers from the Islamic Revolutionary Guard Corps, friendly governments and loyal militias have helped Iran to acquire more influence in the Levant than any other power. In contrast to Russia, however, Iran has allies and clients in Syria, but no friends, and it may at some point overreach, particularly if the differences between Tehran and Moscow, or between Iranian operatives and a Syrian government that no longer felt existentially threatened, were to grow more salient. There is also some question about whether domestic actors can or will push the Iranian leadership to adopt a less confrontational regional and international posture, and to concentrate more on implementing economic reforms and building constructive relations with other powers. There are certainly political actors in Iran who would favour such an adjustment, but also those who would prefer to compensate for any sign of domestic weakness by assuming a more aggressive foreign-policy stance.

In the recent past, Iran has more than once been able to capitalise on the weaknesses or mistakes of others, not least by filling the void that was left by the absence of an effective Iraqi force to counter the Islamic State from 2014, or by stabilising the Assad government in Syria. It has also been able to strengthen its relations with Turkey. Ankara and Tehran may have different perspectives on global affairs, but they do share similar threat perceptions. Both have fallen in line with the Russian approach to conflict resolution in Syria; and it should come as no surprise if Ankara eventually re-establishes official links with Damascus. Neither Turkey nor Iran, however, wants to be seen as a mere junior partner in a Russian-planned and -managed settlement of the Syrian conflict. They also want to limit Kurdish independence aspirations in Iraq and Syria. Turkey further wishes to prevent the emergence of a PYD-dominated zone along the Syrian–Turkish border. Add to this Ankara's increasing lack of trust in the United States, particularly since Washington made the PYD (the sister organisation of the Kurdish Workers Party or PKK, which is banned in Turkey) its main military partner in Syria, despite and against all warnings and protests by its Turkish NATO ally. With Turkey's recent military incursion into the northern Syrian district of Afrin, Ankara has come a long way toward weakening the PYD and establishing a Turkish-controlled protectorate along the western parts of the Turkish–Syrian border.

Saudi Arabia

The confrontation between Saudi Arabia and Iran has mostly played itself out in Syria over the past seven years, but the two countries have been geopolitical rivals for much longer, even before Iran became the Islamic Republic. Yet their rivalry is not an immutable fact that cannot be at least partially set aside on the basis of shared political or economic interests. Consider, to give but two examples, the countries' common opposition to the Iraqi takeover of Kuwait in 1990, or their somewhat uneasy but still successful cooperation to settle the Lebanese civil war in the early 1990s.

As regards Syria, Saudi Arabia no longer opposes a settlement that would leave Assad in power, but wishes to block what it would regard as an Iranian takeover. Although there is room for compromise, Riyadh has done little to encourage this. Since his elevation to minister of defence in 2015 and Crown Prince in 2017, Mohammed bin Salman has been the driving force behind a highly assertive and strongly anti-Iranian regional policy. This includes an appallingly destructive war in Yemen that does not seem to be close to either a military decision or a negotiated settlement, and which may have fostered the very Iranian presence and influence there that the Saudi leadership claims to be fighting. Similarly, Riyadh may have helped Iran to strengthen its reputation in Lebanon by trying to force the country's prime minister, Saad Hariri, to resign under murky circumstances from a TV studio in the Kingdom.

The Qatar crisis that emerged in 2017 was a poorly engineered eruption of long-standing differences, one that appears to be undermining the only functioning sub-regional organisation in the Middle East: the six-member Gulf Cooperation Council. The boycott of Qatar by neighbouring countries (along with Egypt) has imposed economic losses on Qatar and undercut its ability to manipulate regional conflicts by distributing financial largesse to radical political and military actors. The latter consequence has arguably been the most positive effect of the crisis so far. But Saudi Arabia and its allies, primarily the UAE, have not really succeeded in enforcing their will on their smaller neighbour. Rather than scaling down its relationship with Iran as demanded by Riyadh and Abu Dhabi, Doha has become dependent on Iranian airspace and imports, upgraded the countries' relationship and invited Turkey to enlarge its military presence in the emirate.

Saudi Arabia's increasingly assertive regional policy should not be seen in isolation from the ambitious and much-needed efforts of the Crown Prince to embark on a form of belated nation-building in a state that since its inception has defined itself more in religious than in national terms. The prince's Bismarckian 'Vision 2030' programme, which aims at preparing Saudi Arabia for a less carbon-dependent future, represents an attempt to reform the country's society and economy, and to mobilise the Kingdom's younger generations. The leadership wishes to make fuller use of Saudi Arabia's male and female workforce, to promote scientific and technical education, to downgrade the influence of the religious establishment and the appeal of radical Wahhabi Islam, and to foster a sense of nationalism.

History offers more than one example of similar endeavours that were accompanied by aggressive foreign policies.

It is an irony of sorts that both the Saudi Crown Prince and Iranian President Hassan Rouhani, who was re-elected with a convincing majority in 2017, have identified a need for domestic reform in their respective countries. Both would stand to gain from enhanced cooperation between their countries. Yet they could easily lose the opportunity to implement their reform programmes by engaging in costly external confrontations.

While his regional policies have so far brought mixed results at best, Mohammed bin Salman was doubtless able to boost his domestic and regional stance by securing the personal support of US President Donald Trump and US acknowledgement of Saudi Arabia's lead role in a loose coalition of Arab states. It was certainly easy for the Crown Prince to align himself with the Trump administration's two priorities in the region: the fight against terrorism (however defined) and a rollback of Iran.

Regional actors react to signals from the great powers

While the Middle East policies of the US and other extra-regional players are not the main focus of this article, it is clear that regional actors react to signals, or what they perceive as such, from the great powers. Thus, it is little wonder that the Saudi, Emirati and Israeli leaderships, among others, are eager to integrate the Trump administration's more hardline stance on Iran into their own political projects. Other US allies, meanwhile, are wary of an approach that seems to place military expediency above alliance considerations – this is certainly the case for Turkey – and to be marginalising the US in the political and diplomatic domains, not least by encouraging the perception that US policy favours the Saudi and Israeli governments in an overly partisan way. By de-emphasising diplomacy and taking decisions, such as his recognition of Jerusalem as the capital city of Israel, that alienate friends and foes alike, Trump has arguably been undermining the US role as the ultimate mediator in a region that is accustomed to relying on it, despite its long-standing support of Israel.

Russia, by contrast, seems to have learned something from previous US policy books for the Middle East, particularly that it should make itself a non-ignorable interlocutor for all the relevant parties, and to make no secret of its strategic interests. Thus, Russia is cooperating with Iran to stabilise the Assad government, but also receiving the Saudi monarch in Moscow, even before the King had visited Washington. Russia is Syria's most important military ally, but Moscow has also been demonstrating its excellent relationship with Israel, not least by means of a much-publicised visit of its defence minister to Tel Aviv. There have even been suggestions that Russia may be acceptable as a mediator on Jerusalem. And whereas the US has been ignoring, in Ankara's view at least, some of Turkey's main national-security priorities, Russia has been able to transform a relationship that was on the verge of war in 2015 into a form of co-ownership over a settlement process for Syria – never leaving any doubt, however, who arranges the seating order.

This is not to say that Russia is a benign actor. Among other things, the Russian defence ministry's proud announcement that its military had used the war in Syria to test new weaponry will certainly be seen as cynical by those members of Syria's opposition who are now supposed to accept Russia as a peace broker. Still, Moscow, unlike Washington, appears to have a plan, both to end the war in Syria and to enhance its own posture in the wider region.

The United States, meanwhile, seems to have become a diplomatic eyewitness to other powers' political initiatives in the region, despite its military leadership of the anti-Islamic State coalition and its strikes against Syria's chemical-weapons facilities. This is most visibly the case with regard to Syria. Consider that in 2015 and 2016, the US secretary of state and the Russian foreign minister co-chaired four ministerial meetings of the so-called International Syria Support Group, which helped to launch the UN-led intra-Syrian talks in Geneva, and to bring about a first (albeit short-lived) cessation of hostilities. By contrast, in 2017 the US was content with observer status in the Russian-led Astana talks. Even the new US Syria policy, as laid out by then-secretary of state Rex Tillerson in January 2018, has confirmed the military's lead on Syria. It calls for an open-ended US military presence in the country even after the defeat of the Islamic State, mainly to deny an expansion of Iranian influence, but displays no ambition to reassume a leading political role with regard to Syria's future.

One could be forgiven for seeing a certain parallel here with the position the European Union has been in for a long time, perhaps minus its preparedness to commit substantial sums of money to regional development schemes. It remains unclear whether the EU, most likely under French leadership, will be able to fill some of the diplomatic void that the US has left in the region. Given the habit of Middle Eastern leaders to balance their external relations, rather than allowing the political–diplomatic game to be dominated by a single great power, it is likely that there would be takers for such a European role.

Macron, l'américain?

Fabrice Pothier

US President Donald J. Trump and French President Emmanuel Macron are worlds apart: one is an impulsive populist, the other a cerebral centrist. Yet in this case, opposites appear to attract. Macron in particular has made a point of building a relationship with his US counterpart despite Trump's often disdainful attitude towards Europe. The question is whether Macron's calculated embrace of Trump can deliver positive results for French and European interests. Macron's state visit to the White House on 23–24 April revealed a rather mixed picture.

Macron's opportunity

There are some similarities between the two leaders' political stories. Both reached the highest offices in their respective countries in 2017 despite having never held elected office before, and both succeeded by challenging established party lines. But the similarities end there. While Macron triumphed by carving out new centre ground, Trump won by energising a disgruntled and putatively marginalised base, shifting the Republican Party farther to the right. While many saw his election as the beginning of the end of the liberal order, Macron has been celebrated as the unexpected saviour of liberal values against a threatening wave of populism. It would have been politically expedient for Macron to highlight these differences and distance himself from Trump, as German Chancellor Angela Merkel and others did.

Fabrice Pothier is IISS Consulting Senior Fellow for Defence Policy and Strategy.

Survival | vol. 60 no. 3 | June–July 2018 | pp. 105–111   DOI 10.1080/00396338.2018.1470761

But Macron opted for a more pragmatic approach that started with a now famous handshake on the sidelines of the NATO summit in July 2017. This was followed by Macron's surprising invitation to Trump to attend French National Day ceremonies in Paris on 14 July. Although granting Trump the international recognition he both craved and lacked was politically risky, Macron also put France and himself in the global spotlight, showcasing the grandeur of the French Republic.

Macron also had a geopolitical angle. Germany was heading for elections at the time, with German public opinion about Trump among the most negative in Europe. The United Kingdom, customarily the United States' strongest European ally, was engulfed in difficult and distracting Brexit negotiations, and buffeted by Trump's insulting and poorly informed comments on British domestic affairs. For the first time in decades, the field was clear for France to present itself as the United States' go-to partner in Europe. Having served under the previous government, Macron was well aware of the depth of the military and intelligence cooperation between the two countries. Senior French military officers like to boast that the true special relationship is now Franco-American, especially in the Sahel and in the fight against the Islamic State. With UK forces and capabilities diminishing, the Franco-American security relationship has rarely looked stronger.

Leveraging that relationship also fits into Macron's broader historic vision. Like some of his predecessors, starting with Charles de Gaulle, Macron wants to restore France's position as a pivotal power. His first bilateral meeting with Russian President Vladimir Putin at the Palace of Versailles signalled this intention. Although Macron delivered some warnings, especially about Moscow-sponsored media outlets, according to senior officials he also tried to find some points of cooperation with Putin, particularly on the Syrian conflict. Overall, in the space of a few months, Macron has succeeded in reinvigorating France's central role as a world power.

Divisive issues

Any Macron–Trump agenda would be loaded with fraught issues. Of these, global climate change is by far the most divisive. According to Macron, environmental policy is not a mere addendum to a government's programme:

in his pre-campaign essay 'Revolution', he stated that addressing the effects of climate change should be part of all government policies, including those on technological innovation and economic growth. The 2016 Paris climate agreement was the first instance since the 1997 Kyoto Protocol in which leading world carbon emitters, China and the United States in particular, could agree on emissions-curbing targets. The Paris accord closed a difficult decade of failed attempts to build a succeeding framework to the Kyoto accord, which the United States had never ratified. Key to the Paris agreement's success was a new US–China *entente* on climate change, which the Obama administration had patiently forged. Since the Paris agreement was one of the few major international policy successes of François Hollande's presidency, Macron was keen to build on it.

Beyond his substantive conviction that climate change is one of the greatest contemporary threats to human welfare, Macron also saw an opportunity to place France in a leading role on a global issue. Yet he also wanted to avoid a head-on collision with his US counterpart, who has repeatedly expressed deep scepticism about the scientific veracity of climate change, and has made a point of dismantling the Obama administration's domestic and international environmental policy. In particular, he has withdrawn the United States from the Paris agreement. Macron's approach has been to openly criticise that US decision – even sardonically, by echoing Trump's signature slogan 'Make American Great Again' in his own call to Congress to 'Make the Planet Great Again' – while also maintaining a dialogue with Trump on the need to fight climate change even if there is little chance this fight will succeed.

The same can be said for another difficult issue: the nuclear deal with Iran, known as the Joint Comprehensive Plan of Action (JCPOA). During his campaign, Trump repeatedly characterised the JCPOA as the worst deal in history, something he has continued to do in office. This opprobrium evidently has more to do with politically undermining his predecessor's legacy than with the actual effectiveness of the deal, as most experts, including many within the Trump administration's own Defense and State departments, believe that the deal is working. While the White House has not yet crossed the line of disavowing the deal, the president appears determined to do so, having just appointed two key officials – Mike Pompeo as secretary of state and John Bolton as national security advisor – who oppose the JCPOA. Trump has already declined to recertify the deal once, asking Congress to impose new sanctions on Iran. This prompted a strong adverse response from his European counterparts, including Macron. The Europeans' chief concern is that a US exit from the JCPOA would provide Iran's hardliners with leverage for marginalising the country's reformist president, Hassan Rouhani, who supports the deal; and with a pretext for stirring up national-ist sentiment in the midst of a crucial religious-leadership transition in Iran. They fear that such developments could trigger a nuclear arms race between Iran and Saudi Arabia, and put Iran and Israel on a collision course.

According to French officials, Paris is trying to convince the Trump administration not to withdraw from the agreement by finding ways to address the White House's concerns about Tehran's ballistic-missile pro-gramme and aggressive posture in the region – concerns which many senior French officials have long shared. As expected, Macron proposed to his US counterpart something along those lines, which was later touted as a 'new Iran deal'. Although the proposal was reportedly coordinated with the UK and Germany, it is less clear if the other signatories of the JCPOA, Russia and China, support this new approach. And, importantly, Iran's president rejected point blank any new plan. French Foreign Minister Jean-Yves Le Drian's visit to Tehran earlier in April reportedly failed to convince the Iranian leadership of the need for additional measures. Macron was presumably well aware of the low probability of success. But he may have concluded that introducing the idea, and showing European willingness to meet some of the administration's concerns, could in itself be a diplomatic victory of sorts, and help gain some allies in the adminis-tration and Congress.

Although Trump seems set on breaking away from the JCPOA, his administration has failed to define a coherent strategy for the wider Middle East. Despite its hawkish tone, especially on Iran, it has remained unwilling to commit the military and diplomatic resources necessary to change the balance of power in the region, maintaining only a minimum presence in conflicts, such as the war in Syria, in which Iran is playing a critical role. The looming summit between Trump and North Korean leader Kim Jong-un in May could strengthen Macron's hand in moderating Trump's position. Even the Iran hawks within the US administration may realise that repudiating a nuclear agreement on the eve of a 'denuclearisation' summit would damage Washington's credibility with Pyongyang.

Common ground

There are several issues on which Macron and Trump share some common ground. Chief among these is their focus on countering terrorism. American and French military and intelligence personnel have cultivated very close cooperation. In the Sahel region, where thousands of French forces have been stretched thin since the launch of *Operation Serval* in Mali in 2012, the US and, to a lesser extent, the UK are providing critical support to French forces, including intelligence and reconnaissance capabilities and strategic airlift, which the French army sorely lacks. In turn, French fighter jets and special-operations forces are deployed in support of the US-led coalition against ISIS in Syria and Iraq. From a homeland-security standpoint, France and other European countries are directly exposed to terrorist groups operating in the Middle East, while the United States enjoys geographical protection; yet European powers alone cannot lead a region-wide counter-terrorism campaign without US support.

As the counter-terrorism effort in Iraq and Syria is wound down, however, Paris is becoming concerned that the Trump administration might disengage more widely from the region, including Syria. This would be consistent with the US president's stated distaste for extensive foreign interventions, and his preference for insulating America from regional conflicts. It would also be in line with his decision to devote more resources to Afghanistan, and his assertion in a 29 March speech that the United States would withdraw from Syria 'very soon'. Broader opposition to an abrupt US pullback in the Middle East within the US government, and the Assad regime's apparent use of chemical weapons in Douma on 8 April, are, however, likely to impede any quick American withdrawal from the region.

Macron himself claimed on French television that Trump had reconsidered his decision to withdraw US troops from Syria thanks to France's stubborn diplomacy. Macron added that he had tempered American plans to strike Syria in retaliation for the attack on Douma by convincing Trump to focus on a few critical sites. Only time and continuous pressure will tell if the joint American–British–French strikes have restored deterrence and drawn a red line. But it is clear that Macron's France played a driving role in launching the strikes. While the UK government only explicitly joined the mini-coalition late in the planning process, Macron was apparently the one who made the call to Putin to warn him about the strikes. Again, by embracing Trump, Macron is not only trying to ensure that the United States stays involved in the Middle East, but is placing France in a pivotal role. While this is unlikely to be enough to spur the development of a coherent American strategy on conflicts such as Syria, Macron's efforts to channel some of the US administration's instincts has still been worthwhile.

The two presidents have some improbable points of convergence on international trade. Like other EU leaders, Macron was unequivocal in rejecting US 'blackmail' after Trump threatened to impose tariffs on steel and aluminium. But Washington and Paris are broadly in agreement about Chinese trade practices. Macron's repeated call for reciprocity and fairness during his visit to China was essentially a subtle concurrence with Trump's more accusatory rhetoric about Beijing's abuse of global trade. Like the US, France faces a large structural trade deficit – some €62 billion in 2017. While Macron understands that the deficit is largely due to an uncompetitive French industrial sector, he has also joined those in the EU calling for fairer trade arrangements. In fact, at his first European Council meeting as French president in June 2017, Macron proposed a new EU screening mechanism for foreign investment to better control Chinese investments in Europe's strategic sectors. This would emulate the United States' advanced screening procedure under the inter-agency Committee on Foreign Investment.

*　　*　　*

There are more issues that divide Trump and Macron than bring them together. Yet even on the most divisive subjects, such as climate change, Macron has already earned some political dividends by continuing a dialogue with the US president, all the while offering the wider world an alternative vision. At the very least, a French demonstration of resolve not to let the United States off the hook could encourage US states and cities to continue their efforts to curb emissions pending Trump's departure from office. On the issues that bring the two leaders together, Macron's goal is to secure the United States' ongoing counter-terrorism support in North Africa and the Sahel, and to harness Trump's preoccupation with reducing the US trade deficit to France's benefit in substantially curbing China's trade-distorting practices, which France and the EU probably cannot do without American help.

Overall, Macron's embrace of Trump is probably more about damage limitation than carving out an affirmative agenda. Although the French public is broadly critical of Trump and US policy, Macron's nurturing of a good relationship with the American president has yielded the symbolic benefit of positioning France at the centre of world affairs, and the substantive benefit of providing a potential check on US policies adverse to French and European interests. That said, the picture that emerges from Macron's much-celebrated state visit is more nuanced. Even if the French president purposefully asserts a different global vision – something he did eloquently in his address to Congress – his strategy exposes him to Trump's fundamental transactionalism and binary vision of politics. Other leaders, such as Canada's Justin Trudeau and Japan's Shinzo Abe, are still paying the price of their own embrace of Trump. As a student and assistant of the late French philosopher Paul Ricoeur, Macron appreciates the value of maintaining constructive tension between two opposites. It is less likely, however, that Trump fully appreciates such dialectical subtlety.

Noteworthy

2,202
Number of disaster-related deaths in Fukushima, Japan, attributed to evacuation stress, interruption to medical care and suicide

0
Number of cases of cancer attributed to the nuclear disaster at Fukushima[1]

Last to know

'You may get a tweet.'
White House Chief of Staff John Kelly warns secretary of state Rex Tillerson on 9 March 2018 that his job may be at risk.[2]

14
Number of Asian countries that increased their trade with China between 2011 and 2016

5
Number of Asian countries that increased their trade with the US[3]

Bad old days

'This is the first time since 1989 that Polish–Jewish relations have experienced such an earthquake … Like many other people, I sadly admit I keep asking myself: were we living in an illusion that things were going so well?'
Anna Chipczynska, president of the Jewish Community of Warsaw, comments on the effects of a new law in Poland that makes it an offence to attribute Nazi crimes to the Polish nation or state.[4]

'For years we were terribly proud that whereas in western Europe the best way to identify a synagogue was to look for the tank parked in front of it, here security was a fuddy-duddy who asks to look at your bag if he remembers. Now we've got slightly more serious about security.'
Konstanty Gebert, a columnist for the Gazeta Wyborcza newspaper.[5]

'Take off your yarmulke, sign the bill.'
Words on a banner held by far-right activists demonstrating in favour of the bill in February 2017.[6]

Read very closely

'The North Korean side clearly stated its willingness to denuclearise.'
South Korean officials comment on their talks with North Korean leader Kim Jong-un in Pyongyang on 5 March 2018.[7]

'He said that no nuclear test and intermediate-range and inter-continental ballistic rocket test-fire are necessary for the DPRK now, given that the work for mounting nuclear warheads on ballistic rockets was finished … He added that the mission of the northern nuclear test ground has thus come to an end … we will discontinue nuclear test and inter-continental ballistic rocket test-fire from April 21, Juche 107 (2018).'
North Korean news agency KCNA announces on 21 April 2018 the suspension of all missile tests and the closing of one nuclear-test site.[8]

Survival | vol. 60 no. 3 | June–July 2018 | pp. 112–114   DOI 10.1080/00396338.2018.1470762

From Russia with…

'There are therefore only two plausible explanations for what happened in Salisbury on 4 March. Either this was a direct act by the Russian state against our country, or the Russian government lost control of its potentially catastrophically damaging nerve agent and allowed it to get into the hands of others.'

UK Prime Minister Theresa May speaks to the House of Commons on 12 March 2018 about the poisoning of Russian national Sergei Skripal, who had been jailed in Russia for spying for Britain before moving to the UK in a spy swap, and his daughter.[9]

'Don't choose England as a place to live. Whatever the reasons, whether you're a professional traitor to the motherland or you just hate your country in your spare time, I repeat, no matter, don't move to England. Something is not right there. Maybe it's the climate. But in recent years there have been too many strange incidents with a grave outcome. People get hanged, poisoned, they die in helicopter crashes and fall out of windows in industrial quantities.'

Russian news presenter Kirill Kleymenov speaks on state television on 9 March 2018.[10]

'Turnout is higher than we expected, by about 8–10 per cent, for which we must say thanks to Great Britain. We were pressured exactly at the moment when we needed to mobilise. Whenever Russia is accused of something indiscriminately and without any evidence, the Russian people united around the centre of power. And the centre of power is certainly Putin today.'

Andrei Kondrashov, spokesman for Vladimir Putin's presidential campaign, speaks at Putin's victory party after he was re-elected president of Russia.[11]

Erdogan's Turkey

'They sit on a bench that is two meters high. They wear black robes with red collars. In a few hours they will decide my destiny. I look at them. They have loosened their ties out of boredom.'

Ahmet Altan, a novelist and former newspaper editor in Turkey, writes about being sentenced to life imprisonment without parole for sending 'subliminal messages' during a television broadcast said to have contributed to a coup attempt in July 2016.[12]

'I assure you that day will come when this Mafia sultanate comes to an end.'

Turkish reporter Ahmet Sik speaks to the press after being released on bail from Silivri prison after being held for more than a year on terror-related charges related to his work for the opposition newspaper Cumhuriyet.[13]

3.5 million
Estimated number of cases of Guinea worm infestation worldwide in 1986

30
Number of cases in 2017[14]

Zuckerberg's Monster

'Falsehood diffused significantly farther, faster, deeper, and more broadly than the truth in all categories of information … Whereas the truth rarely diffused to more than 1000 people, the top 1% of false-news cascades routinely diffused to between 1000 and 100,000 people.'

From a study published in Science investigating the 'Spread of True and False News Online.'[15]

'I'm afraid that Facebook has now turned into a beast.'

Yanghee Lee, special rapporteur on the situation of human rights in Myanmar at the UN, cites Facebook as having played a role in the outbreak of violence against the Rohingya.[16]

Sources

1 Robin Harding, 'Fukushima Nuclear Disaster: Did the Evacuation Raise the Death Toll?', *Financial Times*, 11 March 2018, https://www.ft.com/content/000f864e-22ba-11e8-add1-0e8958b189ea?emailId=5aa5dd6935f4a200043e2e50&segmentId=22011ee7-896a-8c4c-22a0-7603348b7f22.

2 Mark Landler, Maggie Haberman and Gardiner Harris, 'In Replacing Tillerson with Pompeo, Trump Turns to Loyalists Who Reflect "America First" Views', *New York Times*, 13 March 2018, https://www.nytimes.com/2018/03/13/us/politics/trump-tillerson-pompeo-america-first.html?hp&action=click&pgtype=Homepage&clickSource=story-heading&module=first-column-region&region=top-news&WT.nav=top-news.

3 Max Fisher and Audrey Carlsen, 'How China Is Challenging American Dominance in Asia', *New York Times*, 9 March 2018, https://www.nytimes.com/interactive/2018/03/09/world/asia/china-us-asia-rivalry.html?module=WatchingPortal&region=c-column-middle-span-region&pgType=Homepage&action=click&mediaId=wide&state=standard&contentPlacement=10&version=internal&contentCollection=www.nytimes.com&contentId=https%3A%2F%2Fwww.nytimes.com%2Finteractive%2F2018%2F03%2F09%2Fworld%2Fasia%2Fchina-us-asia-rivalry.html&eventName=Watching-article-click.

4 James Shotter, 'Poland: The Damage Done by Nazi Crimes Law', *Financial Times*, 12 March 2018, https://www.ft.com/content/16dd754c-21f8-11e8-9a70-08f715791301?emailId=5aa5dd6935f4a200043e2e50&segmentId=22011ee7-896a-8c4c-22a0-7603348b7f22.

5 *Ibid.*

6 *Ibid.*

7 Bryan Harris and Katrina Manson, 'North Korea Says It Is "Open to Ending Nuclear Programme"', *Financial Times*, 6 March 2018, https://www.ft.com/content/f5bb4c58-20fe-11e8-a895-1ba1f72c2c11?emailId=5a9f6a33cd19590004a3faf8&segmentId=22011ee7-896a-8c4c-22a0-7603348b7f22.

8 'Third Plenary Meeting of Seventh C.C., WPK Held in Presence of Kim Jong Un', KCNA Watch, 21 April 2018, https://kcnawatch.co/newstream/1524268891-973786350/third-plenary-meeting-of-seventh-c-c-wpk-held-in-presence-of-kim-jong-un/.

9 'PM Statement on Salisbury Incident: 12 March 2018', 12 March 2018, https://www.gov.uk/government/speeches/pm-commons-statement-on-salisbury-incident-12-march-2018.

10 Marc Bennetts, 'Russian State TV Warns "Traitors" Not to Settle in England', *Guardian*, 9 March 2018, https://www.theguardian.com/world/2018/mar/09/russian-state-tv-warns-traitors-not-to-settle-in-england.

11 Kathrin Hille, Henry Foy and Max Seddon, 'Moscow Thanks UK for Helping Putin Win Landslide Vote in Russia', *Financial Times*, 18 March 2018, https://www.ft.com/content/efab0a30-2ad4-11e8-a34a-7e7563b0b0f4?emailId=5aaf3a4f92ba4800049585ec.

12 Ahmet Altan, 'I Will Never See the World Again', *New York Times*, 28 February 2018, https://www.nytimes.com/2018/02/28/opinion/ahmet-altan-turkey-prison.html?utm_source=Canongate+newsletter&utm_campaign=633fd674cb-EMAIL_CAMPAIGN_2018_03_05&utm_medium=email&utm_term=0_337d0ea33a-633fd674cb-80457797.

13 'Turkey Releases Two More Journalists on Bail', *Guardian*, 10 March 2018, https://www.theguardian.com/world/2018/mar/10/turkey-releases-two-more-journalists-on-bail.

14 Donald G. McNeil Jr, 'South Sudan Halts Spread of Crippling Guinea Worms', *New York Times*, 22 March 2018, https://www.nytimes.com/2018/03/22/health/south-sudan-guinea-worms.html?module=WatchingPortal&region=c-column-middle-span-region&pgType=Homepage&action=click&mediaId=thumb_square&state=standard&contentPlacement=11&version=internal&contentCollection=www.nytimes.com&contentId=https%3A%2F%2Fwww.nytimes.com%2F2018%2F03%2F22%2Fhealth%2Fsouth-sudan-guinea-worms.html&eventName=Watching-article-click.

15 Soroush Vosoughi, Deb Roy and Sinan Aral, 'The Spread of True and False News Online', *Science*, March 2018, vol. 359, no. 6,380, http://science.sciencemag.org/content/359/6380/1146.full.

16 'UN: Facebook Has Turned into a Beast in Myanmar', BBC News, 13 March 2018, http://www.bbc.co.uk/news/technology-43385677.

Reaching an Understanding on Baltic Security

Nadezhda Arbatova

Since the beginning of the Ukrainian conflict, the littoral states of the Baltic Sea – despite not being directly affected by the war – have become preoccupied with matters of regional security. If the current crisis between Russia and the West were to escalate, it is the Baltic Sea region that would become the site of conflict, because it is where Russian and NATO forces come into direct contact. This is a region particularly sensitive to tensions between East and West.

The Russian threat has turned into a predominant theme in the three Baltic states – Latvia, Estonia and Lithuania – and in Poland. The foreign policy of the Baltic states, since they regained their independence in 1990–91, has grown out of their past: the painful history of being occupied and forcibly absorbed into the USSR.[1] Consequently, the countries form the avant-garde of opposition to the Russian challenge. Two neutral states in the region, Sweden and Finland, have pursued dialogue with Russia, although they also firmly reject Moscow's current foreign policy. Finding the right format for dialogue with Russia is not an easy endeavour, however, since Russia and the West look at the same facts and events through very different lenses. Their differences stem from profound disagreement, as well as misunderstanding, over the acceptable foundations of European security and interests across the post-Soviet space.

Nadezhda Arbatova (Nadia Alexandrova-Arbatova) is Head of Department of European Political Studies at the Primakov Institute for World Economy and International Relations (IMEMO), Russian Academy of Sciences.

Survival | vol. 60 no. 3 | June–July 2018 | pp. 115–132   DOI 10.1080/00396338.2018.1470766

Who was it that violated the post-Cold War order?

Russia is portrayed in the West as a revisionist state which ruptured the post-Cold War status quo first in the Caucasus crisis of 2008 and then in Ukraine in 2014. Conversely, as seen in Russia, it is the West – and above all NATO – that should be viewed as a violator of international order.

This inevitably raises the question of what that order really is. It could be argued that it began with the Paris Charter for a New Europe in 1990. But the charter was adopted when the USSR still existed: Mikhail Gorbachev never intended to revise the bipolar world order; he simply wanted to preserve the socialist system with a 'human face', and hoped for a new detente to end Cold War tensions. Perhaps the starting point for the current order was the end of bipolarity itself, which happened one year later in 1991, after the collapse of the USSR. But the most important changes that would then radically transform Europe's security landscape were not finalised in a new peace conference on the post-bipolar order.

Arguably, the real turning point was instead NATO's military campaign against Serbia in 1999, conducted without UN Security Council authorisation for the use of force. This military campaign became the first act of the newly enlarged NATO, fuelling concerns in Russia about the real intentions behind the Alliance's expansion. This event, together with the US military operation in Iraq in 2003, and recognition of Kosovo's independence, has become, in the eyes of Russia's political elite, the most vivid evidence that the world order and norms that emerged after the Second World War have ceased to exist. As seen in Moscow, a UN-led world order was replaced by a US-led order. Kosovo was presented by NATO and the EU member states as an exception. Russia saw it as a precedent, and carte blanche to behave accordingly. The question for our purposes is not so much who is right, but rather the implications of the disagreement. Recall Henry Kissinger's warning in 1999:

> The rejection of long-range strategy explains how it was possible to slide into the Kosovo conflict without adequate consideration of its implications … The transformation of the NATO alliance from a defensive military grouping to an institution prepared to impose its values by force

... undercut repeated American and allied assurances that Russia had nothing to fear from NATO expansion.[2]

Unlike Russia, the West proceeds from the deep conviction that the post-bipolar status quo was blatantly breached by Moscow in the war of 2008 against Georgia and then in Ukraine in 2014; Russia drew a red line around both states' Euro-Atlantic aspirations, and violated their territorial integrity. As one typical Western analysis put it, 'The consistent goal of each of these interventions has been to keep independent-minded or Western-oriented territories that Russia views as within its sphere of influence away from the West and within the Russian orbit'.[3] According to this interpretation, the Euromaidan should be viewed as the most striking evidence of the democratic choice of the Ukrainian people. As punishment, Russia annexed Crimea; it is supporting separatists in eastern Ukraine and continues to provide them with heavy weapons, other military equipment and financing; and it allows militants to enter Ukraine freely. While Russia says it seeks peace, its actions do not match its rhetoric.[4]

'The most fundamental problem of politics', wrote Kissinger, 'is not the control of wickedness but the limitation of righteousness'.[5] It is impossible to reach agreement over who is to blame for the breaking of the status-quo order, because both sides are sincerely convinced they are right. It is possible, however, to search for the 'original sin' of the current dispute in a more fundamental way. The diverging views of Russia and the West about acceptable principles of European security, and their rivalry over the countries in the Commonwealth of Independent States (CIS), can be explained by two interrelated phenomena: the uneven end of the era of bipolarity, and the uneven dissolution of the USSR.

Uneven end of bipolarity

European wars have tended to end in peace conferences – from the Peace of Westphalia to the Yalta Conference – establishing a new order and new rules of behaviour in international relations. The collapse of the USSR did not result in a new order to replace the 40-year-old system based on confrontation and the balance of terror. Moreover, the collapse of the Eastern bloc convinced the West of the rightness of its policies. Russia's economic and political weakness in the early 1990s was just another reason not to take its concerns seriously. Russia simply followed in America's wake; its interests were not considered, and its opinions were ignored. Prominent British strategic thinker Lawrence Freedman observed in 1999 that Russia's weakness meant that it could not 'expect the privileges, respect and extra sensitivity to its interests normally accorded a great power. Increasingly it lacks the clout to enforce its objections to developments it considers harmful or to take on the sort of responsibilities that can earn it international credit.'[6]

The end of bipolarity had a paradoxical impact on international relations. On the one hand, it removed the threat of a global conflict, but, on the other, it marginalised the distinctive attributes that had formed the core of detente in the Cold War era, such as the Helsinki principles and arms-control negotiations. The post-bipolar euphoria of the West created an impression that the old rules of behaviour that helped us survive the East–West confrontation had lost their importance once that confrontation ended, and that the old Westphalian system of sovereign states was becoming irrelevant, to be replaced with a preoccupation with democracy and human rights.[7] The contradiction between nations' right to sovereignty and other nations' right to humanitarian intervention was exacerbated by America's overall commitment to the spread of democracy, human rights and free markets by all means, including the use of force. The export of democracy through regime change became a source of worry to those authoritarian regimes that remained outside the orbit of American influence. During the Cold War, the principles of territorial integrity and the inviolability of borders had been defined in relation to external aggression. The rise of secessionist movements in the newly independent states changed that paradigm. International actors started to apply the Helsinki principles selectively, according to their ideological and political preferences.

The Russian leadership sees the current international order as being dominated by the United States and NATO, presenting an existential threat to Russia's security and interests. This system, found generally satisfactory by the West, has failed to satisfy Russia in its recovery from the crisis of the 1990s. Attempts to transform the existing Euro-Atlantic security system have not yielded any noticeable results. While other countries were able to join NATO (and the EU) en masse, Moscow had to make do with a range of palliatives, such as the Partnership for Peace, the Permanent Joint Council and the Russia–NATO Council. As a result, the post-bipolar system of European security became a jumble of Cold War institutions and hasty innovations. These institutions and bodies were able to resolve none of Europe's post-Cold War conflicts.

Russian President Vladimir Putin's speech in Munich on 10 February 2007 was simply a reflection of contradictions that had been building for some time.[8] Seven years later, in his speech at the Valdai International Discussion Club's annual meeting in 2014, Putin urged the development of a world order more friendly to Russian interests:

> Instead of establishing a new balance of power, essential for maintaining order and stability, [the Americans] took steps that threw the system into sharp and deep imbalance. The Cold War ended, but it did not end with the signing of a peace treaty with clear and transparent agreements on respecting existing rules or creating new rules and standards.[9]

The appeal to the international community to come back to the unfinished business of the past and create a genuine post-bipolar order, or at least agree on commonly agreed rules of behaviour, appears justified. The ultimate irony, however, is that this goal cannot be achieved without peace in Ukraine, which is the main precondition for any security arrangements in Europe. Aside from this, a great deal will depend on the Kremlin's own perception of post-bipolar order and norms, defined by Russia's post-imperial complexes, security concerns and vulnerabilities.

It is possible to identify several fundamentals of the Russian posture. Firstly, it finds a unipolar world unacceptable. As seen from Moscow, we live in a multilateral world, the crux of which is the US–Russia–China triangle. Secondly, the international order is led by the UN Security Council – where Russia has a permanent seat – and not by the United States. Thirdly, Russia supports the idea of multilateralism, which in the eyes of the Russian political elite is not so much about multilateral cooperation but rather about

Russia's equality with other great powers in international affairs. Russia wants to be recognised as a great power, and wants this recognition not just in words but in deeds. Moscow demands respect for its legitimate interests and consideration for its views on the most important issues, even if they differ from those of the United States and its allies. Fourthly, the Kremlin wants a peace conference that could establish legally binding rules of behaviour for all participants. Past experience offers different models of such conferences: Yalta, which has become a symbol of bipolarity, and Paris, which proclaimed that 'the era of confrontation and division of Europe has ended'.[10] Moscow's idea of a peace conference is interpreted in the West as a new Yalta, in which partners will have clearly defined spheres of influence. The idea for such a conference appeared alongside president Dmitry Medvedev's proposal for a treaty on European security in 2009, although the Kremlin has not described it as a 'new Yalta'; that phrase has so far been put forward by individuals from the State Duma or the expert community.[11] But what is clear is that the Kremlin wants Georgia, Ukraine, Azerbaijan and Moldova (the so-called GUAM countries) to remain neutral in terms of security arrangements. Lastly, Moscow argues that the principle of sovereignty and non-interference in domestic affairs should be an absolute value in international relations.

The Kremlin fully understands that the West will not 'trade' Ukraine – a symbol of the Russia–West divide – for Syria or any other hotspot. The settlement of the Ukrainian conflict is a key condition for a new summit, whether 'Helsinki-plus' or 'Paris 2.0', which should address the main contradictions of the post-bipolar order. President Putin's idea of deploying a UN contingent along the line of contact in Donbas, similar to the situation in Cyprus, has the potential to become the first step toward ending the crisis and, hopefully, toward building a new world order. Unfortunately, however, this idea is failing to gain traction.

Uneven dissolution of the USSR
The way the USSR was dissolved – at the stroke of a pen by the leaders of Russia, Ukraine and Belarus in December 1991, without serious negotiations on what the newly independent states would inherit from the USSR

– largely predetermined the fate of the CIS, and relations between Russia and its post-Soviet neighbours. This later became clear when Russia plunged into never-ending tensions with its neighbours over issues of territory, economics, defence and minorities. The CIS was created not only to manage a 'velvet divorce' of former Soviet Union republics, but as an integrationist body for the states that emerged on the territory of the former USSR, with the exception of the three Baltic republics. Latvia, Lithuania and Estonia unambiguously moved toward the Western institutions: NATO and the European Union.

With Russian troops off the Baltic states' territory, the political incentive for good relations with Russia disappeared, despite the fact that the Russian government, at the time of the Soviet Union's dissolution, had decisively supported Baltic independence. Generally speaking, relations between Russia and Estonia, Latvia and Lithuania in the 1990s were defined by low-intensity crisis. This was the product of several factors; most importantly, a post-colonial syndrome in the Baltic states resulted in a negative attitude to Russia as the heiress of the USSR, and the depiction of large Russian-speaking communities (except in Lithuania) as a fifth column. The latter have become a bargaining chip in the heated rhetoric of both Russian and Baltic nationalists.

Looking back, it is clear that the new Russian leadership failed to formulate a well-thought-out strategy vis-à-vis its neighbours.[12] Russia's post-Soviet euphoria was replaced with a sense of defeat, the loss of a large empire – not at distant approaches, like other colonial powers before it, but in its immediate neighbourhood – and the end of great-power status. Moscow's major dilemma regarding policy in its so-called 'near abroad' was to strike a balance between treating the other former Soviet Union republics as independent while establishing close links with them. The reassembling of the CIS under Russian auspices, and Russia's involvement in local conflicts, pushed the Kremlin, after all, to cultivate 'special relations' with its neighbours. The latter half-heartedly accepted this model, which turned out to be a bad bargain: economic benefits for political loyalty. This ultimately led to the split of the CIS into the anti-Russian GUAM and the pro-Russian Collective Security Treaty Organisation (CSTO, comprising Russia, Belarus, Armenia, Kazakhstan, Uzbekistan, Tajikistan and Kyrgyzstan). In liberal Russian circles it is widely recognised that, as Alexei Arbatov puts it,

> Russia made its fair share of policy mistakes in the post-Soviet area during the 1990s by trying to establish its dominance in the region through openly encouraging separatism in neighboring countries, supporting loyal but repressive regimes, making use of the military presence that remained from the Soviet years and brazenly using energy supplies as a means of blackmail.[13]

It is also recognised that, in the 1990s, although it was suspicious about the CIS project, the West did not let this overshadow relations with Russia, because the rest of Moscow's foreign and domestic policy suited it perfectly well. In any event, the West was focused on the task of integrating the Central and Eastern European countries into the EU and NATO.

The Western dichotomy in relation to Russia's post-Soviet policy – suspicion of Russian neo-imperialism, combined with reluctance to assume a greater burden in cooperating with Russia to resolve post-Soviet problems – had a negative impact on both Russia's attitude to its near abroad and its perceptions of the West's role and intentions there. The EU and NATO regional strategies – the Eastern Partnership and the Individual Membership Action Plan – which aimed at encompassing some of Russia's closest neighbours, became for the Kremlin a clear confirmation of Western plans to elbow Russia out of its natural habitat.

The divergence in views between the West and Russia simply reflects a new contradiction between nations' right to freely choose security alliances, on the one hand, and other nations' right to oppose the expansion of alliances and to organise national security accordingly. From the very beginning of NATO's enlargement strategy, Russia was fearful that it would be an open-ended process, which is why it drew a red line around Georgia and Ukraine. Russia's policy in the post-Soviet space has been, and remains, the main factor shaping the development of its relations with the West. Conversely, Western policy towards the CIS countries is a kind of litmus test for the Russian political elite in understanding the true aims of EU and NATO post-communist strategy.

The Ukraine crisis in a Baltic context

Security and stability in the Baltic region depend on the state of Russia–West relations; at the same time, growing rivalry in the Baltic area, including unintended incidents, could provoke a sharp conflict at the global level. Taking a closer look at the regional security landscape after the Ukraine conflict, there emerge several tensions in the regional postures of four NATO members – Latvia, Estonia, Lithuania and Poland – and two neutral states: Finland and Sweden.

Latvia, Estonia and Lithuania fear that Russia could invade them in a version of the Crimea scenario, either under the pretext of protecting Russian-speaking minorities or, in the case of a new Russia–West crisis, to break a blockade of the Kaliningrad exclave. As a European Parliament think-tank study put it:

> Russia appealed to the fate of Russian-speaking communities to justify its annexation of Crimea and its posture regarding the subsequent armed conflict in eastern Ukraine. Unsurprisingly, this has reinforced concerns in the Baltics and those who perceive the Russian-speaking minorities as a potential Trojan horse in the heart of their societies.[14]

It follows that the Baltic countries should be vitally interested in full integration of Russian speakers into their societies, since unequal treatment of the Russophone population only exacerbates a feeling of alienation.[15] A well-executed strategy of integration could help solve the 'loyalty' issue and ease domestic tensions. Authorities in the Baltic states, however, prefer to use the possibility of Russian intervention as a means of getting more military support from NATO.

Not wishing to remain a buffer zone between Russia and the West, Latvia, Estonia, Lithuania and Poland sought security within NATO. They are subject to the collective-security pact under Article V of the North Atlantic Treaty. Yet, were a Russia–West conflict to escalate, these countries would find themselves on the front line, with unpredictable consequences. The Baltic members of NATO are deeply concerned about what they call a destabilising Russian military build-up near their borders, in the form of Russia's increasing military activity in the Western Military District. In their view, as one analysis puts it, Russia 'has been conducting a far more aggressive, anti-Western foreign policy, significantly ratcheting up provocative military maneuvers near NATO members' borders with Russia, intimating nuclear threats, and deploying nuclear-capable missiles in the Russian exclave of Kaliningrad'.[16]

Yet, it was not Russia which came to NATO's border – rather the opposite. Moscow proceeds from the understanding that it has a right to organise security on its own territory according to the perceived threat, which is NATO's conventional superiority over Russia. As Russian Defence Minister Sergei Shoigu pointed out at the annual meeting of the Defence Ministry Board,

> Since 2012, the number of military contingents deployed by NATO near Russia's western frontiers has increased threefold. Four battalion tactical groups have been deployed in the Baltics and Poland as well as a U.S. Army armored brigade and command staffs of NATO's multinational divisions in Poland and Romania. The number of engagement-ready forces of the alliance has grown from 10,000 to 40,000 troops, while their notice period has been reduced from 45 to 30 days.[17]

Unsurprisingly, Moscow is very sensitive to debates in Finland and Sweden about their potential membership of NATO. Finland shares a border with Russia; joining the Alliance would mean extending the NATO–Russia border. From the perspective of the US military, Sweden might play an important role in basing aircraft in the event of a military crisis in the Baltic region, during which the United States would need basing outside Russia's anti-access/area-denial (A2/AD) bubble, which extends from Kaliningrad and western Russia over the eastern Baltic Sea. Sea lanes of communication via the Danish straits might also be important for certain types of operations deeper into the Baltic Sea.[18]

The security postures of Finland and Sweden are linked by virtue of geography and strategy. If Sweden decided to join NATO, Finland would likely follow for fear of being isolated. Polls conducted after Crimea showed only a marginal effect on support for membership in both countries, however, which remains low.[19] At the same time, according to René Nyberg, former ambassador of Finland to the Russian Federation, the relationships of Sweden and Finland with NATO have changed fundamentally. Joining NATO's Partnership for Peace and making full use of the tool kits it has offered to develop interoperability and participating in operations both in Kosovo and Afghanistan have *peu à peu* resulted in the full compatibility of Finnish and Swedish armed forces with NATO.[20]

Moreover, both states have embarked on new forms of bilateral and Nordic cooperation, and they have welcomed the Alliance's decision to deploy troops in Poland and the Baltic states (under the programme of Enhanced Forward Presence). The Kremlin has already reacted negatively to these debates over NATO membership, warning both countries that it would have consequences for their relations.

Given their mutual concerns, it seems natural that a dialogue on regional security between Russia and the four littoral-state members of NATO and the EU would significantly improve the situation in the Baltic Sea region. One topic should be the risk of incidents in the air. Renewed tensions with Russia after the Ukraine conflict have resulted in a growing number of narrowly avoided mid-air collisions, in which Russian pilots have behaved more riskily than necessary. In 2016, President Putin supported a proposal by Finnish President Sauli Niinistö for planes to fly with transponders activated in the Baltic Sea region; this was rejected by NATO, however, on the grounds that it would do little to improve air safety. Russia has also proposed to hold a meeting of military experts in the field of air safety. This idea, too, was rejected because, according to diplomats from NATO countries, such a meeting would violate the Alliance's decision to suspend practical cooperation with Russia.[21] Needless to say, NATO's unwillingness to establish a working relationship with Russia on such practical issues does not improve regional security. The prevention of unintended incidents, and arms-control treaties in general, should be an exception to NATO's matters of principle, because they serve the interests of all parties.

While Sweden and Finland, countries stuck in between Russia and NATO, would welcome any initiative aimed at strengthening regional security,[22] the Baltic countries seem presently uninterested in a security dialogue with Russia, since it could curtail NATO's military deployments on their territories. Lithuania, Latvia and Estonia were in the group of states calling for the 1997 Founding Act and the 2002 Rome Declaration to be deemed no longer binding in view of Russia's violations of their provisions.[23] In political terms, this would mean Russia would officially cease to be treated as NATO's partner. From the Baltic states' point of view, in military terms such a decision would pave the way for the permanent deployment of significant NATO forces on the eastern flank, constituting a clear confirmation of the collective-defence guarantee and sending a deterrent signal.[24]

Appeasement or deterrence?

From the very beginning of Russia's emergence as an independent state, the West was split on the question of how to deal with it in foreign-policy terms. Unlike the EU and NATO countries in southern and western Europe which were more prone to engagement with Russia, the Baltic and Nordic states have always been suspicious about authoritarian trends in Russia's domestic evolution that could lead, in their view, to the revival of the Russian empire. The alternative to deterrence is held to be 'appeasement', a strategy of identifying and addressing the grievances that gave rise to Russia's dissatisfaction with the West. In a 2017 essay for the Latvian Institute of International Affairs, British analyst James Sherr identified the steps which such a strategy would demand of the West:

- 'withdrawing its infrastructure, missile defence units and forward-based forces from Poland, Romania and the Baltic states;
- agreeing to statutory limitations on the development of prompt global strike and other "destabilizing" systems;
- strictly observing the non-alignment of Sweden and Finland (irrespective of the wishes of these two states), reversing recent trends toward NATO–EU security cooperation and the integrated defence of the Nordic–Baltic region;
- respecting the "rights" of Russia's citizens abroad and, *vide* Medvedev, Russia's "unquestioned priority … to defend the rights and dignity of our citizens wherever they live";
- binding, "non-bloc" status for Ukraine and the withdrawal of

NATO's "presence" (training and advisory teams, liaison, and information offices); annulling the EU–Ukraine Association Agreement and formalizing Ukraine's "federalization" (autonomy for the Donetsk and Luhansk Republics and their right of veto on Ukraine's foreign and defence policies);

• transforming the NATO–Russia Council into an effective working organ, operating on the basis of "equality" (i.e., a de facto right of veto on issues of importance to Russia).'[25]

These terms, as seen from the Nordic–Baltic Sea strategic community, are incompatible with the security of the Baltic states, and in any case could not be implemented over their heads. By this logic, the only response to Russia's resurgence is therefore deterrence, both by denial and by punishment. (The linkage between the two forms of deterrence will be reinforced if Russia perceives that Finland and Sweden would not stand aside in the event of an attack against the Baltic states.) The goal of this strategy is to persuade Moscow that even a short war will have harrowing costs and inexorably lead to the long war that Russia fears and is likely to lose.[26] This argument, however, only reinforces the Kremlin's thinking: if Russia is to lose a long war, the only option is a short war.

Russia's short-war concept, potentially including the selective use of nuclear weapons for 'de-escalation' of a conflict, has not appeared out of nowhere. For ten years, Russia has repeatedly expressed its concerns about high-precision, long-range conventional weapons whose destructive potential was most vividly demonstrated in the former Yugoslavia in 1999, Iraq in 2003 and Libya in 2011. These concerns were ignored by the West. Aside from this, US defence policy has always implied the possibility of using nuclear weapons first, from plans for limited first use during the Cold War through to the Nuclear Posture Review released in 2018. That review calls for low-yield nuclear weapons as a 'flexible' nuclear option, and explicitly states that the United States could employ nuclear weapons in response to 'significant non-nuclear strategic attacks'. This includes, but is not limited to, 'attacks on U.S., allied, or partner civilian population or infrastructure'.[27] The US did not have to wait long for the Kremlin's response. In Putin's annual address to the

Federal Assembly of the Russian Federation, he delivered a message to the world that Russia has restored its military might, and has developed a new line of nuclear-capable or dual-purpose weapons that can evade US defences.

Additional sub-strategic US nuclear options might indeed deter a pre-meditated Russian attack in the case of a crisis in the Baltic states or Poland; on the other hand, in the more probable scenario of uncontrolled crisis escalation, it could provoke the early use of nuclear weapons. Poland and the Baltic states have previously been supporters of strengthened US extended nuclear deterrence to NATO, with some speculation that they might even welcome the deployment of tactical nuclear weapons on their own soil.[28] Neither Sweden nor Finland, for their part, have publicly supported the idea of deploying tactical nuclear weapons in the Baltics. However, the fact that Finland did not support the UN resolution to negotiate a treaty outlawing nuclear weapons is being interpreted by some experts as a departure from Finland's previously straightforward position on multilateral non-proliferation and disarmament treaties.[29]

Art of the possible

American and Russian bragging about new destructive capabilities is a dangerous major-power game. Deterrence is not a panacea, and if nuclear deterrence worked in the bipolar world there is no guarantee that it will continue to work in the future. Russia and the West need to find a new balance between deterrence and dialogue to safeguard security in Europe. Dialogue plays an essential role in managing what has become an adversarial relationship.[30] It therefore makes sense to look more closely at the 'appeasement' option, and to identify which aspects represent a genuine effort to tackle problems of mutual concern.

The bullet-point list of putative Russian demands provided above can be classified as realistic or unrealistic, and the realistic items should become the subject of negotiations. Withdrawing missile-defence units from Romania and Poland looks unrealistic, and 48 interceptors per se do not present a threat to Russia.[31] With regard to ballistic-missile defence (BMD), Russia has two major concerns. Firstly, it fears that US BMD is an open-ended programme pursued in all environments (at sea, ashore, air-based and space-based). Secondly, Mk-41 launchers, which the United States has deployed in Romania and Poland, can technically be converted to launch intermediate-range cruise missiles; doing so would be a direct violation of the Intermediate-Range Nuclear Forces Treaty. Russia's general concern about BMD can be overcome only in a different political environment, which would require a new dialogue between Russia and the United States. But its second claim can be resolved by agreed verification inspections in Romania and Poland to exclude the deployment of a ground-launched version of US submarine-launched cruise missiles on Mk-41 launchers. As for NATO forward-based troops, and Russian forces near the borders of the Baltic states, Russia and NATO could agree to freeze military deployments at the present level and then to gradually reduce them.

Russia's concern over prompt global strike is justified: high-precision, long-range conventional weapons are destabilising systems. The Russian strategic community has repeatedly expressed concern that US long-range, high-precision conventional weapons could be used to hold Russian nuclear forces at risk. Joint management of this problem could be achieved either in discrete negotiations or in the context of negotiations over strategic nuclear forces.

Strictly enforcing the non-aligned status of Sweden and Finland is unrealistic. Finland and Sweden are sovereign states, and Russia, so obsessed with its own sovereignty, should accept this reality. The future direction of the two states' foreign policy will depend in large part on Russian actions, both in the region and at the international level.

Respecting the rights of Russian citizens is a worthy goal, a fact recognised not only by Russians but by Western experts as well. A RAND report, for example, argues that 'better integration of Russian speakers may help to build more-cohesive societies in the Baltics'.[32]

The non-bloc status of Ukraine and Georgia cannot be achieved as a deal between Russia and the US or NATO. It could be discussed at a 'Helsinki-plus' peace conference when the conflict in Ukraine is resolved. Peace in Ukraine itself is the necessary precondition for such a forum. Only after that is achieved should the OSCE and the UN promote serious new arrangements for the post-Soviet space. Neutrality for Ukraine, Moldova,

Georgia and Azerbaijan should guarantee them security, sovereignty and the integrity of existing de facto borders. These are general principles, and as always, the devil lies in the detail. But there is reason for hope. After the Cuban Missile Crisis of 1962, nobody could have foreseen that the USSR and the West would be able to agree on the Helsinki Decalogue in 1975.

Transforming the NATO–Russia Council into an effective working organ also does not contradict the interests of NATO member states. Indeed, since the creation of the council there have been fears that it would turn into a purely decorative body, and these have unfortunately been realised by its inability to resolve either the Caucasian crisis or the conflict in Ukraine.

The present situation presents a circular dilemma. On the one hand, Russia is presented in the West as an aggressor whose concerns and vulnerabilities should not be taken into account. On the other hand, the current Russia–West conflict would not have erupted if Russia's concerns had been taken seriously. The main danger of armed conflict stems not from Moscow's grand expansionist designs, but rather from its sense of vulnerability and isolation, and its determination to take risks in order to stand its ground and avoid ever being seen as weak.[33] History should teach Russian and Western politicians that they must choose from among realistic options, and deal with the partners they have.

Notes

1   Dovile Jakniunaite, 'Changes in Security Policy and Perceptions of the Baltic States 2014–2016', *Journal on Baltic Security*, vol. 2, no. 2, 2016, p. 7, http://www.baltdefcol.org/files/files/JOBS/JOBS.02.2.pdf.

2   Henry Kissinger, 'New World Disorder', *Newsweek*, 30 May 1999, http://www.newsweek.com/new-world-disorder-166550, quoted in Matthew Dal Santo, 'The Shortsightedness of NATO's War with Serbia Over Kosovo Haunts Ukraine', *National Interest*, 2 September 2014, http://nationalinterest.org/blog/the-buzz/the-shortsightedness-natos-war-serbia-over-kosovo-haunts-11180.

3   Stratfor, 'Putting Russia's Crimean Intervention into Context', 12 April 2014, https://worldview.stratfor.com/article/putting-russias-crimean-intervention-context.

4   Nadia Alexandrova-Arbatova [Nadezhda Arbatova], 'The Ukraine Crisis Is Exposing Some Uncomfortable Truths', *Europe's World*, 29 October 2014, http://www.friendsofeurope.org/views/

the-ukraine-crisis-is-exposing-some-uncomfortable-truths.

5   Henry Kissinger, *A World Restored: Metternich, Castlereagh and the Problems of Peace, 1812–22* (Boston, MA: Mariner Books, 1973), p. 206.

6   Lawrence Freedman, 'The New Great Power Politics', in Alexei Arbatov, Karl Kaiser and Robert Legvold (eds), *Russia and the West: The Twenty First Century Security Environment* (Armonk, NY: Sharpe, 1999), p. 26.

7   Javier Solana, 'Securing Peace in Europe', speech in Mnster, 12 November 1998, https://www.nato.int/docu/speech/1998/s981112a.htm.

8   Alexei Arbatov, 'Moscow and Munich: A New Framework for Russian Domestic and Foreign Policies', Carnegie Moscow Center, 2007, p. 13.

9   Vladimir Putin, speech to the Valdai International Discussion Club, Sochi, 24 October 2014.

10 'Charter of Paris for a New Europe', Paris, 19–21 November 1990, p. 3, https://www.osce.org/mc/39516?download=true.

11 See, for example, Mikhail Khazin, 'New Yalta Is Inevitable: World Forecast for 2017 from a Well-Known Economist', business-gazeta.ru, 23 January 2017, https://www.business-gazeta.ru/article/335125.

12 Alexei Arbatovet et al. (eds), *Managing Conflict in the Former Soviet Union: Russian and American Perspectives* (Cambridge, MA: MIT Press, 1997), p. 24.

13 Arbatov, 'Moscow and Munich', p. 17.

14 Nicolás de Pedro et al., 'Facing Russia's Strategic Challenge: Security Developments from the Baltic to the Black Sea', European Parliament, 17 November 2017, p. 12, http://www.europarl.europa.eu/RegData/etudes/STUD/2017/603853/EXPO_STU(2017)603853_EN.pdf.

15 The three Baltic republics are states parties to the Framework for the Protection of National Minorities (FCNM), which came into force in 1998 and underscores minority protection as a core value of the Council of Europe. But none of them has yet ratified the European Charter on Regional or Minority Languages (ECRML), which aims to protect and promote traditional regional and minority languages in Europe.

16 Richard Sokolsky, 'The New NATO–Russia Military Balance: Implications for European Security', Carnegie Endowment for International Peace, 13 March 2017, http://carnegieendowment.org/2017/03/13/new-nato-russia-military-balance-implications-for-european-security-pub-68222.

17 Kremlin, 22 December 2017, http://kremlin.ru/events/president/news/56472.

18 Christopher S. Chivvis, 'Sweden, Finland and NATO', German Marshall Fund, 30 June 2017, http://www.gmfus.org/publications/sweden-finland-and-nato.

19 Suvi Turtiainen, 'Despite Crimea, Finland and Sweden Stay Wary of NATO', 22 April 2014, European Council on Foreign Relations, https://www.ecfr.eu/article/commentary_despite_crimea_finland_and_sweden_stay_wary_of_nato250.

20 René Nyberg, 'Finland and Sweden and Security in the Baltic Sea Region', Polish Institute of International

Affairs, Warsaw, 12 June 2017, http://www.anselm.fi/finland-sweden-security-baltic-sea-region/.

21 Julian E. Barnes, 'NATO Rejects Russian Air-Safety Proposal for Planes in Baltic Region', *Wall Street Journal*, 20 September 2016, https://www.wsj.com/articles/nato-rejects-russian-air-safety-proposal-for-planes-in-baltic-region-1474391644.

22 'Sipilä: Finland Has Sweden's Support for Continuing Dialogue with Russia', *Helsinki Times*, 12 July 2016, http://www.helsinkitimes.fi/finland/finland-news/politics/14093-sipilae-finland-has-sweden-s-support-for-continuing-dialogue-with-russia.html.

23 Justyna Gotkowska, 'NATO's Presence in the Baltic States – Reassurance of Allies or Deterrence for Russia?', Centre for Eastern Studies (OSW), https://www.osw.waw.pl/en/publikacje/osw-commentary/2015-04-29/natos-presence-baltic-states-reassurance-allies-or-deterrence.

24 *Ibid*.

25 James Sherr, 'The Baltic States in Russian Military Strategy', in Andris Spruds and Maris Andzans (eds), 'Security in the Baltic Sea Region: Realities and Prospects', *Riga Conference Papers*, 2017, p. 163, http://liia.lv/en/publications/security-in-the-baltic-sea-region-realities-and-prospects-the-riga-conference-papers-2017-643.

26 *Ibid*., p. 166.

27 US Department of Defense, '2018 Nuclear Posture Review', https://www.defense.gov/News/SpecialReports/2018NuclearPostureReview.aspx.

28 See, for example, Steve Cimbala and Adam B. Lowther, 'Ukraine and the American Nuclear Arsenal', 2014, p. 3, https://www.atlcom.nl/ap_archive/pdf/AP%202014%20nr.%203/Lowther.pdf.

29 See Katarina Simonen, 'Treaty on the Prohibition of Nuclear Weapons: Why Finland Is Not Supporting It', 28 August 2017, http://www.6d.fi/index.php/102-starters/1058-treaty-on-the-prohibition-of-nuclear-weapons-why-finland-is-not-supporting-it.

30 Claudia Major and Jeffrey Rathke, 'NATO Needs Deterrence and Dialogue: Defining the New Balance in View of the Warsaw Summit', *SWP Comments*, 18 April 2016, p. 4, https://www.swp-berlin.org/fileadmin/contents/products/comments/2016C18_mjr_Rathke.pdf.

31 Alexei Arbatov, 'Ugrozy strategicheskoi stabilnisti – mnimye i realnye' [Threats to Strategic Stability – Imaginary and Real], *Polis*, 2018, no. 3, p. 12.

32 Andrew Radin, 'Hybrid Warfare in the Baltics: Threats and Potential Responses', RAND Corporation, 2017, p. 31, https://www.rand.org/content/dam/rand/pubs/research_reports/RR1500/RR1577/RAND_RR1577.pdf.

33 Alexei Arbatov, 'Understanding the US–Russia Nuclear Schism', *Survival*, vol. 59, no. 2, April–May 2017.

After Nuclear First Use, What?

Vince A. Manzo and John K. Warden

At some point in our lifetime, we may awaken to the horrifying news that, for the first time since 1945, a country has carried out an attack with nuclear weapons. This dark possibility is something we must vigorously attempt to prevent. But it is also a plausible event for which the United States and its allies must prepare. If a conflict breaks out in Asia or Europe, an adversary of the United States and its allies may believe it can conduct limited nuclear strikes and, rather than precipitate its own destruction, win the war – not in the sense of defeating the United States militarily, but by convincing Washington to refrain from bringing its full strategic–military power to bear on the conflict. However dangerous this logic may sound, there is reason to believe that it resonates in Russia and North Korea.[1] Whether either country would ever act on such a dangerous strategy in a war is impossible to predict, but evidence suggests that their governments have the guiding strategic concepts, military capabilities, plans and, thus, the means to conduct nuclear attacks should they decide that doing so is their best, or perhaps least bad, option.

If an adversary were to cross the nuclear threshold, whatever happened next would have profound near- and long-term consequences. In most circumstances, a nuclear strike would cause substantial, immediate loss of life and potentially long-term humanitarian and economic consequences.

Vince A. Manzo (@VAManzo15) is a defence and nuclear policy analyst based in Arlington, VA. **John K. Warden** (jkwarden@gmail.com) is a defence policy and strategy analyst based in Washington DC. The views expressed here are their own.

Survival | vol. 60 no. 3 | June–July 2018 | pp. 133–160   DOI 10.1080/00396338.2018.1470770

In any scenario, it would shatter the more than 70-year-old tradition of nuclear weapons not being used in conflict.[2] The potential for further nuclear escalation would place countless lives at risk, and the outcome of the conflict would influence other countries' perceptions of the utility of nuclear weapons, and of the reliability of the United States as an ally and steward of the international system. These epochal stakes demand a serious analysis of how the United States might lead an international effort to minimise the loss of life, secure a just peace and reinforce the tradition of non-use of nuclear weapons.

US interests after an adversary's first nuclear use

Following an adversary's nuclear strike, the underlying interests that compelled the United States to become involved in the war would endure. US strategic interests might include protecting US allies, opposing territorial conquest or preserving freedom of navigation. Military operational objectives might include seizing key cities or choke points; maintaining control of critical terrain, waters or airspace; or halting an enemy's military advance.

A separate but related US interest would be ending the war in a manner that minimised the loss of life and treasure both for itself and its allies.[3] Following nuclear use, it would seek to avoid, or at the very least limit, additional nuclear strikes by the enemy, either by re-establishing deterrence or limiting the adversary's ability to carry out additional nuclear strikes by conducting counterforce operations against its nuclear forces.[4] At the same time, the United States would attempt to avoid a protracted conflict that could result in more death and destruction.

A third US interest would be preserving the US alliance system. The United States extends deterrence to allies by committing to come to their aid if attacked. If the US not only failed to deter a country from initiating a conventional conflict with an American ally, but also failed to deter said country from using nuclear weapons, this would shake allied confidence in the reliability of US security guarantees, potentially leading allies to build alternative regional security architectures or acquire nuclear weapons.[5] Therefore, the US would have a strong interest in restoring the credibility both of its security guarantee to the affected ally and, by proxy, of its global alliance network more generally. To do so, the United States would need to demonstrate, firstly, that a nuclear strike would not cause it to abandon its ally and, secondly, that it would not enable the adversary to successfully trample on the ally's vital interests. It would need to send a message to the world that the adversary's attempt to terminate a conventional conflict using nuclear weapons had failed, and that other states would be foolish to challenge US extended nuclear deterrence in the future.

A fourth US interest would be to shape the perceptions and norms of nuclear use.[6] Indeed, all of humanity has an interest in preserving a world in which nuclear weapons – still the most destructive weapons on earth – remain in the background. Following an adversary's use of nuclear weapons, the United States would seek to re-establish the consensus supporting the non-use of nuclear weapons.[7] At a minimum, it would attempt to demonstrate that its adversary had failed to achieve its goals via nuclear attack and faced significant costs for attempting nuclear coercion, thus dissuading other potential adversaries from travelling a similar path.[8] The United States also would need to consider how its own use of nuclear weapons in response to a nuclear attack could shape global perceptions and norms.

A final US interest would be to convince the world that its response was legitimate and moral. At first glance, framing the international narrative would seem to be a trivial concern compared to terminating the conflict and avoiding further nuclear attacks. Yet, the United States would have a compelling interest in establishing a post-war environment that is conducive to a lasting peace and a durable, rules-based international system. The United States might choose to retaliate with nuclear weapons, an action that, however necessary, could have tragic human consequences. Acting in a way that is consistent with just-war principles and explaining US decision-making would help the United States to continue as a leader in the post-war world order.[9]

Variables shaping the US response to a nuclear attack

Following an adversary's use of nuclear weapons, a number of variables would influence how the United States pursued its interests and prioritised among them:

The adversary's nuclear arsenal. The adversary's remaining nuclear forces following an attack would directly affect the risk of subsequent nuclear attacks. Several attributes of these forces would be particularly important: the number of nuclear weapons at the adversary's disposal; the number, availability, range and effectiveness of its delivery vehicles; its command and control system; its forces' overall survivability against a counterforce attack; and its ability to overcome US and allied defences. If Russia were to use several nuclear weapons in an attack against US or allied targets, it would have thousands remaining, giving it the ability to conduct nuclear attacks on a global scale. A country such as North Korea, by contrast, may only have a handful of remaining weapons, a more rudimentary command and control system, and a less reliable ability to carry out nuclear strikes with intercontinental-range missiles. The make-up of the adversary's nuclear forces would affect the attractiveness of US damage-limitation options, as well as the cost and risks of further nuclear escalation.

US objectives in the conventional conflict. As noted, the interests that had drawn Washington into the conflict in the first place would remain intact following an adversary's nuclear attack. The United States might be fighting to regain an ally's territory, defend an ally from a sustained invasion, topple an adversary's regime or degrade an adversary's military forces. At the time of the nuclear attack, the United States might have already achieved these goals, or be in the midst of a successful but incomplete campaign. Alternatively, the United States might be mobilising its forces in the target region and preparing the battlefield to begin a campaign. The degree of progress toward achieving US and allied objectives would affect both the US military posture in the region and the measures deemed necessary to demonstrate that using nuclear weapons against the United States is not a winning strategy.

US deterrence messaging. The messages the United States had delivered prior to a nuclear attack would influence American perceptions of the country's interests once nuclear deterrence had failed. US officials might relay deterrence messages to the adversary before and during the conflict. These messages could take the form of explicit threats or vague warnings, delivered publicly or via private backchannels. If an adversary's use of nuclear weapons contravened a public, explicit threat, it would be a direct affront to

US extended-deterrence credibility. The United States would be worried that this loss of credibility would invite further escalation by the adversary and send a signal to other potential adversaries that US threats against nuclear use were hollow.[10] US credibility might be less directly affected, however, if it had issued only vague, backchannel warnings. The 2018 Nuclear Posture Review (NPR) illustrates the importance of this variable. While US standing declaratory policy toward Russia and China states that nuclear attack against the United States will fail to achieve its objectives and is incalculably dangerous, the United States has issued a more precise deterrence message to North Korea: 'any North Korean nuclear attack against the United States or its allies and partners is unacceptable and will result in the end of that regime. There is no scenario in which the Kim regime could employ nuclear weapons and survive.'[11] Assuming the United States does not modify this policy in a crisis, it could face severe credibility challenges if it chose to refrain from regime change following a North Korean nuclear attack.

The adversary's motivation. Understanding the adversary's motivation for crossing the nuclear threshold would be important for assessing whether US response options stood a fair chance of restoring deterrence rather than provoking further nuclear attacks.[12] An adversary could be motivated to use nuclear weapons to avoid losing something it values, such as territory or military capabilities, or it might conclude that using nuclear weapons is its only viable means of ensuring regime survival, either because it fears US-led regime change or judges that losing a limited war would endanger the regime internally. Alternatively, an adversary could use nuclear weapons to consolidate gains. It might already have achieved its wartime objective (such as seizing territory), deciding to use nuclear weapons to stymie or deter attempts by the United States to restore the status quo ante. In addition, the degree of certainty over the adversary's motivation would be an important factor for US decision-makers. In some plausible scenarios, the adversary's motivation could be unclear. The Soviet Union, for example, sent conflicting messages in two different letters during the Cuban Missile Crisis, which caused considerable debate and confusion among president John F. Kennedy's advisers.[13] In other scenarios, US officials might not believe the explanation the adversary provided.

The purpose of the attack. The primary purpose of an adversary's nuclear attack could be to suggest further escalation or to achieve instrumental effects.[14] Coercive attacks are primarily intended to send a signal about the risk of nuclear escalation. Such strikes could range from a demonstration shot over the ocean to a terror-inducing attack on a military target, and would be intended to shape the perceptions of national decision-makers or vulnerable populations, with the goal of deterring US intervention or compelling the United States and its allies to moderate their war aims. Instrumental attacks, meanwhile, are primarily intended to achieve concrete battlefield effects that provide the attacker with a military advantage. In cases where it faced a difficult target set or possessed only limited conventional firepower, an adversary might calculate that using nuclear weapons would help it achieve its objectives in a conflict. Targets of such an attack could include facilities required to transport US forces to the conflict region or capabilities that were critical to the US campaign. While analytically distinct from a primarily coercive nuclear strike, a limited instrumental nuclear attack would nonetheless also be coercive. If an adversary were to withhold certain nuclear forces, it would raise the spectre of further escalation. Moreover, degrading US conventional military operations might alter US perceptions about the military costs of continuing to prosecute its military campaign.

The consequences of the nuclear attack. The physical effects of a nuclear attack would vary widely depending on the number and type of weapons used, the yields of the weapons, the way the weapons were detonated and the targets attacked.[15] US assessments of the scope of the attack, in particular the estimated casualties and fatalities, would influence how Washington evaluated the appropriateness and proportionality of various response options. A militarily significant nuclear strike might constrain what the United States and its allies could accomplish with conventional forces in the days, weeks or months following the attack. An attack that killed a large number of people or had catastrophic economic and environmental effects might increase pressure for the United States and its allies to expand their war aims.

The opinions of allies, US constituencies and other countries. The reactions of various constituencies to the adversary's nuclear attack, and their opinions about various potential US response options, would be important factors in

US decision-making. The preferences of allies that were involved in the conflict, and that may have suffered a nuclear attack or loss of territory, would weigh heavily on American decision-makers. The views of the public, media and members of Congress would also shape perceptions in Washington, as would public opinion around the world. The United States would also seek to shape these perceptions.

US objectives and response options

Given the many potential operational objectives, types of weapons and choices of targets open to the US, there is a near infinite number of responses the country could make to an adversary's use of nuclear weapons. Conceptually speaking, however, there are only a few broad categories of US response options. To start with, the United States would need to determine whether to maintain, narrow or expand its conflict objectives. In certain circumstances, the United States might choose to narrow its conflict objectives by, for example, making it clear that the United States was not seeking to change the adversary's regime. In other circumstances, the United States might make the opposite decision and expand its objectives, seeking to either conquer more territory, impose more punishment or even topple the adversarial regime. In a third scenario, the United States might continue to pursue its pre-nuclear-use objectives without making any adjustments.

Next, the United States would have to match appropriate military operations to its objectives. If it decided to narrow its objectives, it might simultaneously choose to restrict its military operations – by, for example, withholding certain weapons or targets – in order to signal restraint to the adversary. If Washington assessed that it could achieve its objectives without nuclear weapons, it might keep its operations constant and choose to continue fighting with conventional forces. If it were to decide that previously restricted military operations were required to achieve its objectives, it could choose to incorporate nuclear weapons into its response.

To better understand the relationship between the circumstances of an adversary's nuclear use and US response options, we have devised two vignettes involving North Korea and two vignettes involving Russia. These are meant to be plausible and illustrative. In each, the adversary uses nuclear weapons in an attempt to achieve its objectives in a conventional conflict with the United States and its allies.

A North Korean nuclear demonstration

The first vignette posits an aggressive, revisionist North Korea that has a nuclear-weapons force capable of striking targets in South Korea, Japan and the continental United States.

In this scenario, North Korea goes beyond its previous provocations around the disputed maritime border in the Yellow Sea in an attempt to conquer an island near the North Korean coast, but south of the disputed maritime Northern Limit Line.[16] South Korea, caught by surprise, is only able to mount a moderate local defence. North Korea takes the island in less than 24 hours, capturing many South Korean soldiers and civilians. In the days that follow, the United States and South Korea deem North Korea's invasion an unacceptable act of war and begin massing troops to retake the island. In addition, the United States reaffirms that 'any North Korean nuclear attack will mean the end of the Kim regime'.

Before the United States and South Korea launch their counter-attack, North Korea explodes a nuclear weapon delivered by a medium-range ballistic missile over the Sea of Japan. The explosion is followed by a public message from North Korea that its 'peaceful nuclear test' will be followed by 'decisive nuclear blows' against any country that tries to take back what is 'rightfully North Korean territory'. Following the demonstration, the international community universally condemns North Korea for its aggressive and escalatory behaviour. Yet there are calls from Europe and China for the United States to avoid launching a nuclear response or pursing regime change. Seoul and Tokyo, by contrast, conclude that a US nuclear counter-demonstration is necessary to deter follow-on nuclear strikes. Some voices within the United States, South Korea and Japan argue that North Korea's demonstration constitutes a nuclear attack and therefore merits regime change under US policy.

In this vignette, North Korea attempts to present South Korea and the United States with a fait accompli.[17] Pyongyang succeeds in using military force to acquire territory, and uses nuclear weapons to try to deter South

Korea, the United States and Japan from attempting to restore South Korea's control over its territory. By conducting a nuclear demonstration early in the conflict – indeed, before the United States and South Korea have committed significant military forces – North Korea is attempting to generate fear of intervention by highlighting the risk of nuclear escalation. At the same time, Pyongyang has avoided a direct strike on South Korea, Japan and the United States, stopping short of testing the US threat to pursue regime change if North Korea conducts a 'nuclear attack'.

North Korea's clear attempt to use nuclear coercion to consolidate its territorial gains would significantly raise the stakes for the United States. If North Korea succeeded in achieving its objectives at an acceptable cost, it would signal to Pyongyang and other US adversaries that nuclear weapons not only deter regime change, but also create cover for revisionist military aggression. The key question for American decision-makers would be whether to keep US wartime ambitions limited to restoring the previous territorial arrangement, or to expand its aims and pursue regime change.

If it selected the limited option, the United States would need an overarching political strategy for bringing the conflict to an end, including some type of off-ramp for Pyongyang and a mechanism for communication and negotiation. The United States and South Korea could move forward with military operations to retake the conquered island, while making it clear to North Korea that they were willing to accept the pre-conflict status quo. At the same time, the United States would need to threaten escalation to deter North Korea from carrying out additional nuclear strikes. But this option would only succeed if Pyongyang clearly understood US intentions and resolve. The ability of US officials to communicate with key interlocutors in Pyongyang would take on strategic significance.

Alternatively, the United States could expand its wartime objectives and move to topple the regime. If it chose that path, the United States would undoubtedly conduct counterforce strikes to disable as much of North Korea's nuclear force as possible and to reduce the cost of the war to South Korea and Japan, as well as to itself. Because North Korea's nuclear arsenal in this vignette is limited and only somewhat survivable, damage limitation would likely be a realistic option. But pursuing regime change would all

Table 1: **North Korean nuclear demonstration – key variables**

Adversary's nuclear arsenal	• Limited but growing • Somewhat survivable • Capable of threatening regional targets and the continental United States, but of uncertain reliability
US objectives in conventional conflict	• Restore sovereignty of South Korean island • Military operations not yet under way
US deterrence messages before nuclear attack	• Explicit warning that nuclear attack would result in regime change
Motivation for nuclear attack	• Fait accompli
Instrumental or coercive	• Coercive
Consequence of nuclear attack	• No casualties or destruction
Opinions of allies, US and other countries	• United States and allies are unified in their objectives • Some countries oppose a nuclear response

but guarantee retribution in the form of an artillery barrage against Seoul, and possibly incite a nuclear strike on a major US or allied city. Therefore, pursuing regime change and conducting a counterforce strike would only be the most attractive option if 1) Seoul and Tokyo were in agreement; 2) the United States were confident that it could significantly limit the potential for nuclear reprisal; and 3) the United States concluded that attempting to achieve limited objectives while managing escalation was the more dangerous option, either because US officials doubted that any strategy would succeed in convincing North Korea not to use nuclear weapons again, or because leaving the Kim regime in power carried a prohibitive risk of another war in the future.

An additional question for US decision-makers would be the role that nuclear weapons should play in the US response. If the United States were conducting counterforce strikes, it would have to balance the military benefit of using nuclear weapons against the humanitarian cost. It might determine that it needed to use nuclear weapons to increase its chances of destroying mobile launchers and deeply buried facilities associated with North Korea's nuclear programme.[18] Alternatively, it might forgo nuclear weapons after calculating that the collateral damage involved in a nuclear strike would be too high, or that using nuclear weapons would bring only marginal improvement in prospects for military success compared with sticking to conventional weapons.

If the United States were instead to decide to pursue limited objectives, the decision about whether, and if so how, to use nuclear weapons would be more complicated. In a strict military sense, nuclear weapons likely would not significantly enhance the ability of the United States and South Korea to retake the lost island, their key strategic and operational objective. Moreover, if the United States were able to achieve its objectives while avoiding a nuclear response, it might be able to garner more international support for economic sanctions and other means of punishing North Korea. This would also, as George Quester puts it, reinforce 'the world's current intuition that nuclear weapons are not some kind of "ultimate weapon"', potentially discouraging future nuclear proliferation and use.[19] On the other hand, the need to deter a subsequent North Korean nuclear strike might prompt Washington to include nuclear weapons in its response. US nuclear use could contribute to deterrence by demonstrating US resolve and signalling the risks and costs of further nuclear escalation by the adversary. In addition, a nuclear reprisal might enhance the credibility of US deterrence in the eyes of its allies by demonstrating its willingness to run nuclear risks to uphold its security commitments.

North Korean counter-intervention against military targets
The second vignette features a more significant North Korean nuclear strike under more ambiguous circumstances.

What starts as a clash between North and South Korean patrol vessels near the Northern Limit Line becomes an escalating conventional conflict.[20] After a North Korean patrol boat is sunk by a South Korean corvette, North Korea retaliates by firing artillery against South Korean military targets on the Northwest Islands. South Korea returns fire on the source of the attack and conducts a missile strike against a Korean People's Army headquarters element near Pyongyang. North Korea accuses South Korea of trying to assassinate leader Kim Jong-un and retaliates by firing artillery at military targets in and around Seoul, resulting in thousands of casualties.

High-readiness US and South Korean military units launch a military offensive against North Korean military units near the Demilitarised Zone (DMZ), with some allied forces moving into North Korean territory. The United States reiterates that any nuclear attack on the United States or its allies will result in regime change. Simultaneously, South Korea, the United

States and Japan begin mobilising for war; they are privately deliberating about whether to overthrow the Kim regime, but have not arrived at a policy. During the US–South Korean offensive, North Korea strikes the Port of Busan and US military bases in Japan with nuclear weapons delivered by medium-range ballistic missiles, killing thousands and leaving the facilities badly damaged.[21] North Korea proclaims that the United States and South Korea are preparing to invade North Korea and warns that a subsequent attack on its territory would result in nuclear strikes against Tokyo, Guam and Honolulu. Some significant international voices blame South Korea and the United States for forcing North Korea to escalate the conflict. Public opinion in the United States, South Korea and Japan is divided between those calling for retribution and those calling for de-escalation.

In this scenario, North Korea's nuclear strikes are designed to be both militarily advantageous and coercive. Having become involved in a conflict that it fears could result in regime change, North Korea uses nuclear weapons to prevent the United States and South Korea from fully mobilising and positioning forces for an invasion. By conducting a nuclear strike early in the conflict, Pyongyang appears to be attempting to delay US reinforcements from arriving, while sending a clear coercive message that any invasion of North Korea would risk significant nuclear escalation. Unlike in the previous vignette, North Korea has opted for a large initial nuclear strike to shock the United States and its allies into accommodation.

Again, the key decision for Washington would be whether to keep its objectives limited or pursue regime change accompanied by counterforce strikes against North Korea's nuclear forces. In this case, however, a number of variables have shifted. Firstly, North Korea appears to be attempting to forestall regime change rather than trying to consolidate a territorial conquest, which makes its threat to further escalate the conflict highly credible. If the United States chooses to de-escalate the situation and deter additional nuclear use, it will need to do so in a way that assures Pyongyang that it is not pursuing regime change. Secondly, US strategic and military objectives are less clear. The pre-nuclear-strike American objective was to limit the military threat to Seoul. Regime change was under consideration, but was not an outward US goal. Thirdly, North Korea's strikes had a signifi-

Table 2: **North Korean nuclear counter-intervention – key variables**

Adversary's nuclear arsenal	• Limited but growing • Somewhat survivable • Capable of threatening regional targets and the continental United States, but of uncertain reliability
US objectives in conventional conflict	• Reduce the military threat to Seoul • Regime change under consideration prior to nuclear strike
US deterrence messages before nuclear attack	• Explicit warning that nuclear attack would result in regime change
Motivation for nuclear attack	• Stated fear of regime change
Instrumental or coercive	• Instrumental *and* coercive
Consequence of nuclear attack	• Significant casualties and destruction • Degraded US and allied military operations
Opinions of allies, US and other countries	• International community divided • Public opinion in US and allied countries split

cant impact on the ability of the United States to quickly supply additional forces to the Korean Peninsula. With fewer conventional military capabilities available, the United States may require nuclear weapons to achieve certain short-term military objectives.

In this scenario, the three most salient US objectives following North Korea's nuclear strike are limiting the impact of the war, shaping how Pyongyang and other US adversaries perceive the effectiveness of nuclear coercion, and convincing the international community that the US response to the attack is legitimate despite the perception that Seoul and Washington provoked the conflict. There are two ways in which the US could try to achieve its objectives.

One option would be to publicly state that the United States and its allies were not pursuing regime change, return US and South Korean troops to positions south of the DMZ and carry out limited military operations to set the stage for potential negotiations. Implicitly, the United States would acknowledge that the risks and costs of trying to convince North Korea to refrain from using additional nuclear weapons were less than those of trying to disarm North Korea's nuclear forces. Nonetheless, the United States might choose to incorporate nuclear weapons into its response. Nuclear weapons could improve US chances of efficiently destroying certain massed, fleeting, mobile or hardened targets, or compensate for the reduced effectiveness of US conventional forces. Given the scope of North Korea's strikes on US and allied bases and ports, US nuclear strikes could be required to stave off a North Korean attack on US and South Korean forces operating near the DMZ. Moreover, there is evidence that the US public would likely support US nuclear use if it were convinced that nuclear weapons would provide a military advantage over conventional options.[22]

The biggest downside of keeping constant or narrowing US conflict objectives would be the risk that the United States would be viewed as capitulating to nuclear coercion after issuing an explicit deterrent threat. If North Korea were able to conduct a serious nuclear strike and live to fight another day, other countries might conclude that nuclear weapons can terminate conventional conflicts on terms favourable to those who first use them. As a result, the United States would have a strong interest in countering this message. It might insist that it was never interested in pursuing regime change, and highlight that North Korea had made no political or territorial gains. Beyond that, the United States might opt to add punitive strikes to its response to signal to North Korea and other US adversaries that using nuclear weapons to try to terminate a conventional conflict is an extremely costly endeavour. Such strikes would carry a risk, however, that the Kim regime would conclude that the US was seeking regime change and launch another nuclear attack.

Even if the United States succeeded in de-escalating the conflict while imposing significant costs on North Korea, it would face serious credibility challenges. By drawing an explicit red line – 'any nuclear attack will mean the end of the Kim regime' – Washington put its reputation on the line. In this scenario the warning fails, leaving the United States to either follow through on its threat or suffer a blow to its reputation. Of course, the US president could decide, as did Barack Obama following the 2013 chemical attack in Ghouta, Syria, to forgo following through on his or her military threat. But as the Syria case demonstrates, choosing not to act would result in concerns about US credibility, both at home and around the world, and potentially weaken Washington's ability to issue credible deterrent threats in future conflicts.[23] Given the catastrophic potential for nuclear escalation in this vignette, successfully ending the conflict without further nuclear attacks would put the United States in a strong position to argue that its restrained response ultimately saved more lives than moving forward with regime change. Due to the prevailing view that South Korea and the United States bore responsibility for triggering the nuclear attack, other countries might respond favourably to the US argument, provided its strategy succeeded. How this argument would be received in Japan and South Korea is an open question, however.

A second option would be to disarm as much of North Korea's nuclear forces as possible and pursue regime change. This course of action would send the strongest possible signal to US allies and adversaries alike that nuclear coercion would not deter the United States from achieving its war objectives. But successfully limiting the war's impact on the United States and its allies would hinge on the effectiveness of US and allied intelligence, surveillance, reconnaissance, strike and missile-defence capabilities. The US decision to use nuclear weapons would depend on the extent to which nuclear strikes would increase the probability of limiting damage. Moreover, considering the scope of the initial North Korean nuclear strike, the United States might be less concerned than in the previous vignette about nuclear counterforce strikes being perceived as disproportionate either domestically or internationally, though the perception of US responsibility for North Korea's escalation would factor in US calculations. The main downside of this option would be the risk of damage limitation coming up short, leaving the United States and its allies vulnerable to significant nuclear retaliation.

A Russian coercive nuclear strike on a single military target
A third vignette involves Russia using nuclear coercion to try to terminate an escalating conventional conflict in Lithuania.[24]

Following assaults on ethnic Russians during a riot in Vilnius, Russian troops enter Lithuania. Lithuania invokes Article V of the North Atlantic Treaty as Russia rapidly entrenches its position on Lithuanian soil and warns NATO not to contest its occupation, stating that protecting ethnic Russians abroad is a core Russian interest.[25] The United States and NATO publicly declare their intent to restore Lithuanian sovereignty. Washington considers privately assuring Moscow that the United States has no intention of invading Russia or threatening the Putin regime, but decides against it. The United States sticks to its standard declaratory policy of calculated ambiguity and refrains from issuing any specific messages to deter Russian nuclear use.

As the United States begins transporting additional forces into Europe in preparation for a NATO operation to retake Lithuania, Russia launches a salvo of conventional ballistic and cruise missiles against military-infrastructure targets throughout Europe. In response, the United States reiterates its determination to restore Lithuanian sovereignty, continues mobilising forces, and employs sea- and air-launched conventional cruise missiles against Russian integrated air defences and logistics units supporting Russia's conventional-strike operations. Russia then launches an SS-26 *Iskander*-M ballistic missile from Kaliningrad that detonates a low-yield nuclear warhead over a sparsely populated rail station in Poland that NATO has been using to transit forces.[26] Russia releases a video recording of President Vladimir Putin declaring that 'Russia will not allow the Western aggressors to mass an existential threat on its border. This missile was but the tip of our nuclear sword that we will use to protect the Russian state. We call on the United States to come to the table in dialogue to avert a tragic war.' The international community condemns Russia's use of nuclear weapons, but several influential countries urge NATO to negotiate rather than escalate the conflict. Several NATO countries also privately call for de-escalation, though they remain committed to defending Lithuania.

In this vignette, the nuclear demonstration magnifies the shared interest of the US and NATO in removing Russian forces from Lithuania. Any outcome in which they accepted the new status quo would signal that NATO members were vulnerable to nuclear blackmail. At the same time, however, the United States would need to try to manage escalation and prevent a large-scale US–Russia nuclear war. In contrast to North Korea, the size of Russia's arsenal precludes targeting the regime.

Russia's nuclear use is intended in this case to be limited and coercive. The strike has a moderate military impact by delaying the movement of NATO forces through Poland, but additional transit routes are available for NATO operations – a fact of which Russian officials are almost certainly aware. In addition, Russia is attempting to signal that its actions are defen-

Table 3: **Russian coercive nuclear strike – key variables**

Adversary's nuclear arsenal	• Sophisticated, large and survivable • Holds targets at risk in Europe, Asia and North America
US objectives in conventional conflict	• Restore sovereignty of Lithuania • Has carried out conventional strikes but not yet initiated a military campaign
US deterrence messages before nuclear attack	• Continuation of calculated ambiguity regarding US responses to nuclear use coupled with statement of limited NATO goals
Motivation for nuclear attack	• Unclear; plausibly to consolidate gains or avoid losses
Instrumental or coercive	• Coercive
Consequence of nuclear attack	• Limited casualties • Some destruction
Opinions of allies, US and other countries	• Unity within NATO, with some members calling for de-escalation • Mixed opinions within the international community

sive, motivated by an imperative to prevent the United States from invading Russia and destroying the Putin regime.

Russia's decision to go nuclear so early in the conflict raises a key question for the United States: is Moscow trying to avert losses or consolidate gains? Russia has signalled that it fears regime change despite the fact that NATO clearly conveyed limited war aims. One plausible interpretation is that Russia based its decision to enter Lithuania on the assumption that NATO would fracture. Russia's nuclear demonstration, therefore, is an attempt to avert losses, an act of desperation to avoid a war that Moscow did not expect to fight and fears might result in regime change.[27] An alternative interpretation is that Russia's goal is to consolidate its position in Lithuania. From this perspective, Russia's purported fears of regime change are a ruse intended to scare the United States into accepting Russian revanchism and to sow disagreement within NATO.

If Washington judged that Russia was acting to avert losses and looking for a palatable off-ramp, the United States might look for an opportunity to restore Lithuania's sovereignty while avoiding a costly war and further nuclear escalation. For this type of response, the United States could focus on encouraging Russia to withdraw its military forces from Lithuania peacefully, including through diplomatic efforts to rally other nations to reinforce this message, while offering clear assurances that NATO had no interest in invading Russia. But NATO also would have to signal its resolve to fight a war if need be lest Russia calculate that it could hold on to Lithuania at an acceptable cost. Therefore, the United States might continue with its mobilisation to signal to Moscow that a refusal to withdraw would bring about the war that Russia fears. In addition, Washington would have an interest in restoring nuclear deterrence. One obvious way of doing so would be to put America's reputation on the line by issuing a more specific and direct deterrence message to Russia about the consequences of subsequent nuclear use.

The potential downside of showing restraint is that it might send the wrong signal about the cost of nuclear use. If the international community came to believe that Russia had faced little or no cost for its nuclear adventurism, this would further contribute to the erosion of the tradition of non-use of nuclear weapons. Nonetheless, if a restrained response resulted in Russian forces leaving Lithuania, NATO countries could argue that they had honoured their security commitments. Because the Alliance had already stated that its war aims were limited to restoring the status quo ante, the United States and its allies could argue that Russia's nuclear attack was reckless and ineffective. By claiming the moral high ground, the United States could lead an international effort to impose sanctions and other punitive measures on Russia after the crisis abated and thus reinforce the view that nuclear use is an unattractive option for US adversaries.

Alternatively, if Washington determined that Russia was in fact trying to consolidate gains, a different type of response would be warranted. In this case, the United States and its allies would need to convince Moscow that it had misjudged their stakes in the conflict by clearly demonstrating their resolve to use military force to restore Lithuania's sovereignty.

Because Russia's nuclear strike does not have a significant military impact in this scenario, one option for NATO would be to forgo a nuclear response and continue with its previous plan for pushing Russia's military out of Lithuania. As discussed above, this course of action might give the United States the moral high ground and allow it to garner support for punitive measures. But it also might encourage Russia to escalate further. If Russia interpreted the absence of a nuclear response as evidence that its stakes in the conflict were significantly higher than NATO's, it might calculate that it need only press harder with a more expansive nuclear strike.

Another option for the United States and NATO would be to incorporate a limited nuclear strike into their operation to restore Lithuania's sovereignty. The primary purpose of the nuclear component of the NATO response would be coercive: to convince Russia that it cannot bully the Alliance, and to deter a second Russian nuclear attack while the conventional campaign was unfolding.[28] Certain options, such as a US nuclear demonstration over the open ocean, would be solely intended to send a signal. With other nuclear-strike options, however, the United States could achieve an additional instrumental benefit by using nuclear weapons to degrade military targets that were critical to Russia's ability to defend Lithuania. In choosing the character and scope of its nuclear response, Washington would have to balance the coercive and instrumental benefits of nuclear strikes against the risk of triggering further Russian escalation.[29] As a result, Washington might, for example, avoid a nuclear strike against targets in Russian territory if it judged that such a strike would likely provoke Moscow to escalate further.

An additional consideration for US decision-makers would be the need to sustain solidarity with allies and, just as important, to signal NATO unity to Moscow. If the Alliance appeared strong and united, Moscow would be less confident in its ability to achieve its objectives at an acceptable cost. In certain circumstances, maintaining broad NATO support might push the United States to opt for a more restrained nuclear response than it would otherwise prefer. Alternatively, the US might work with its nuclear-armed allies to send a signal of collective resolve to Moscow. For example, the United States could employ a demonstration shot, coupled with a trilateral statement from the United States, the United Kingdom and France in support of the action and pledging that Russia would face three united nuclear powers if it used nuclear weapons again.

A significant Russian nuclear attack on military targets

This final vignette departs from the previous scenario to explore a more severe Russian nuclear attack on military targets further along in a conventional conflict.

Following Russia's conventional-missile strike, the United States continues to mobilise, and initiates a suppression campaign against Russia's integrated air defences and select elements of the country's conventional-strike operations. A conventional campaign against Russian forces in Lithuania is launched, and the United States significantly degrades Russia's anti-access/area-denial (A2/AD) posture and its position in Lithuania. Without warning, Russia employs several nuclear-tipped sea-launched cruise missiles and intermediate-range ground-launched cruise missiles against military–logistic targets in the Baltic states (except Lithuania) and Poland, and against US *Aegis Ashore* ballistic-missile defence sites in Poland and Romania. Russia then releases a message offering to begin negotiations on a political agreement to secure the safety of the Russian state. The nuclear attack galvanises NATO, but protests break out throughout Europe and in the United States calling for an end to the war. The international community condemns Russia as global financial markets enter a free fall.

The key differences between this and the previous vignette are that, in this case, the conventional war is further along, US–NATO operations are succeeding and Russia's nuclear attack is larger, resulting in tens of thousands of casualties. The attack also significantly disrupts NATO's ability to operate from the Baltic states and Poland, creating a window of vulnerability during which Russia could resolidify its military position in Lithuania. It is uncertain whether Russia's primary motivation in using nuclear weapons was to maintain its presence in Lithuania or to end the war, thus forestalling an invasion of Russia. Russia's fear of invasion and regime change is, however, potentially more credible than in the previous vignette because of the significant degradation of the country's A2/AD capabilities. Even though NATO operations were only seeking to remove Russian forces from Lithuania, Russian leaders may have believed that the United States was setting the military conditions for an invasion.[30] It may be that from Moscow's perspective, nuclear weapons were its best means of resisting US coercion and preventing a US-supported colour revolution.

This scenario of Russian nuclear use would pose familiar dilemmas for US decision-makers as they contemplated the appropriate response. The critical factor for sustaining the credibility of NATO and US global security commitments, and re-establishing the tradition against nuclear-weapons use, would be whether the Alliance succeeded in restoring Lithuanian

Table 4: **Significant Russian nuclear attack – key variables**

Adversary's nuclear arsenal	• Sophisticated, large and survivable • Holds targets at risk in Europe, Asia and North America
US objectives in conventional conflict	• Restore sovereignty of Lithuania • In the midst of a conventional conflict
US deterrence messages before nuclear attack	• Continuation of calculated ambiguity regarding US responses to nuclear use coupled with statement of limited NATO goals
Motivation for nuclear attack	• Unclear; plausibly to consolidate gains or avoid losses
Instrumental or coercive	• Instrumental *and* coercive
Consequence of nuclear attack	• Significant casualties and destruction • Militarily significant effect on US/NATO military operations
Opinions of allies, US and other countries	• Unity within NATO, with protests cropping up in Europe and the United States • Panic spreading throughout the international community, with widespread criticism of Russia

sovereignty. But the United States would need to find a way to achieve its conventional military objectives while convincing Moscow to forgo further nuclear attacks. While some variables in this scenario would push the United States toward a more forceful response, others would encourage caution and restraint.

The scale of Russia's nuclear strike, and its military effect, would increase the attractiveness of a more forceful US response. A decisive US response might be necessary to show Russia and other US adversaries that future nuclear use would be counterproductive. Some NATO members and US allies in Asia would likely question the reliability of extended deterrence if they viewed the US response to a nuclear attack resulting in thousands of casualties as tepid.[31] Furthermore, if the United States did choose to conduct nuclear strikes to degrade Russia's ability to restore its position in Lithuania, this choice would have an important military impact. Such strikes would prevent Russia from exploiting US and NATO conventional vulnerabilities following the attack, providing NATO with time to reconstitute its forces near Lithuania and to develop operational workarounds to account for lost bases.

On the other hand, clear indications that Moscow genuinely feared regime change would advise a more restrained response. The United States and NATO had already specified that their war aims were limited, but it appears Russia was nonetheless afraid of being left defenceless against an invasion. At the very least, it would be in the US interest to provide a public, political assurance to Moscow that it had no interest in invading Russia. But if US military action did not match its words, the message might ring hollow. If, for example, the United States conducted a nuclear attack on critical conventional military capabilities in Russia's Western Military District, this might exacerbate Russia's fears of invasion and incite Moscow to conduct additional nuclear strikes.

As a result, the United States would have an interest in balancing the competing risks of sending a weak message and stoking Russian fears. A potential middle-ground option would be to pair a coercive nuclear strike with a diplomatic off-ramp for Moscow. Rather than using nuclear weapons to degrade Russia's ability to conduct military operations in Lithuania, the United States could target something that Russia values away from the battlefield (such as a port, airfield or military production facility not directly relevant to the defence of Moscow and St Petersburg). Such a strike would be punitive and coercive, demonstrating US resolve to run nuclear risks to recover Lithuania, while avoiding a military effect that might contribute to Russian fears that the US was considering an invasion. Moreover, given the size and survivability of Russia's arsenal, a limited US nuclear response would be unlikely to create use-or-lose pressure in Moscow, provided the target selected was not tied to Russia's strategic nuclear posture (and assuming Russia did not perceive it as the leading edge of a decapitation strike).

*   *   *

As these scenarios demonstrate, there will be no easy answers after a nuclear attack. A range of context-specific variables will determine the pros and cons of different options, and in many instances the evidence regarding the attacker's motivations will be open to multiple interpretations. The final decision will ultimately require a judgement call by the American president and his or her advisers based on myriad factors. Some of these will be quantitative assessments that rest upon a mixture of intelligence and uncertain assumptions, such as estimates of the US ability to destroy the adversary's remaining nuclear forces. Other considerations will be more political, such as the preferences of US allies and other nations.

As long as the potential for conflict between nuclear-weapons states endures, the United States and its allies have a responsibility to their publics and the wider world to prepare for the aftermath of an adversary's first use. Mapping out every likely contingency ahead of time would be impossible, but US officials can prepare to navigate an adversary's nuclear use through further study of the various interests, objectives and variables that would inform US response options, and simulate conflict decision-making in table-top exercises and war games. Preparing to answer questions from senior decision-makers, to articulate the assumptions and uncertainties of their underlying assessments, and to adjust military options to meet the president's strategic intent are important capacities that American policymakers can improve in peacetime.[32] Making these intellectual preparations for the failure of nuclear deterrence would better position the United States to choose political strategies and military operations that ultimately safeguard American and global interests while minimising the risk of escalation, and to convincingly explain its actions to the world.

In some instances, the United States would best accomplish its objectives through a combination of diplomatic, economic and military actions short of nuclear retaliation. In other scenarios, a nuclear response would improve US prospects for achieving its objectives and safeguarding its interests. Regardless, possession of effective nuclear-response options would be essential for securing US, allied and global interests. Nuclear weapons have an obvious utility in cases where the United States judges that incorporating nuclear weapons into its response offers the best chance of either re-establishing deterrence or limiting damage. If nuclear attack severely limits the United States' ability to protect its allies with conventional forces, US nuclear weapons would be the primary means to achieve operational and coercive effects in support of US strategy while it regenerates its conventional posture.

The role of nuclear weapons in cases where the United States would opt for a purely non-nuclear response is subtle but important. The ability to respond effectively in the event that the non-nuclear response fails provides an important backstop. In North Korea scenarios, Washington's ability to limit the damage if the Kim regime used more nuclear weapons underwrites any strategy that seeks to elicit North Korean restraint. In Russia scenarios, effective limited nuclear-response options to hold high-value targets at risk or to stymie Russian military operations hedges against Russian efforts to double down on its coercive strategy or exploit post-attack vulnerabilities in US and allied conventional forces.

There is no doubt that the primary purpose of US nuclear weapons is deterrence. After an adversary's nuclear first use, however, US nuclear weapons would have important additional missions. Analysis of the forces needed for achieving US objectives after deterrence fails should continue to inform the ongoing debate about US nuclear modernisation.

Acknowledgements

The authors wish to thank Dr Brad Roberts for his valuable comments on an earlier draft.

Notes

1   See Barry D. Watts, *Nuclear–Conventional Firebreaks and the Nuclear Taboo* (Washington DC: Center for Strategic and Budgetary Assessments, 2013); Brad Roberts, *The Case for Nuclear Weapons in the 21st Century* (Palo Alto, CA: Stanford University Press, December 2015); Dave Johnson, *Nuclear Weapons in Russia's Approach to Conflict*, Recherches & Documents No. 6, Foundation pour la Recherche Stratégique, November 2016; Dave Johnson, *Russia's Conventional Precision Strike Capabilities, Regional Crises, and Nuclear Thresholds*, Livermore Papers on Global Security No. 3, Lawrence Livermore National Laboratory, Center for Global Security Research, February 2018; and John K. Warden, 'North Korea's Nuclear Posture: An Evolving Challenge for US Deterrence', *Proliferation Papers*, Institut Français des Relations Internationales (Ifri), March 2017.

2   T.V. Paul, 'Taboo or Tradition? The Non-use of Nuclear Weapons in World Politics', *Review of International Studies*, vol. 36, no. 4, October 2010, pp. 853–63.

3   Leon Wieseltier, 'When Deterrence Fails', *Foreign Affairs*, vol. 63, no. 4, Spring 1985, pp. 827–47; and Robert Scher, 'Nuclear Modernization: Is It Needed and Can We Afford It?', speech at the Center for Strategic and International Studies Conference on US Nuclear Policy Post-2016, Washington DC, 5 May 2016, https://csis-prod.s3.amazonaws.com/s3fs-public/event/ASD%20Scher%20Modernization%20Remarks_0.pdf.

4   US Department of Defense, *The Nuclear Posture Review Report* (Washington DC: Department of Defense, 2018), p. 23.

5   See Jennifer Lind, 'Keep, Toss, or Fix?

Assessing US Alliance in East Asia', in Jeremi Suri and Benjamin Valentino (eds), *Sustainable Security: Rethinking American National Security Strategy* (New York: Oxford University Press, 2016), pp. 297–31; Philipp C. Bleek and Eric B. Lorber, 'Security Guarantees and Allied Nuclear Proliferation', *Journal of Conflict Resolution*, vol. 58, no. 3, 2014, pp. 429–54; and M. Elaine Bunn, Waheguru Pal Singh Sidhu, Sugio Takahashi and Christopher Twomey, 'How Might Nuclear Deterrence Fail in a Limited Way and What Should We Do About It If It Does?', panel discussion, US Strategic Command Deterrence Symposium, LaVista, NE, 14 August 2014, available on YouTube at https://www.youtube.com/watch?v=16gD4So6Mlk&index=13&list=PLzO_KvP4phUYPNAqhWK_cDE73i7FteVQ5.

6   Paul, 'Taboo or Tradition?', pp. 852–63; and Nina Tannenwald, 'Stigmatizing the Bomb: Origins of the Nuclear Taboo', *International Security*, vol. 29, no. 4, Spring 2005, pp. 5–49.

7   Mark Fitzpatrick, 'The World After: Proliferation, Deterrence and Disarmament if the Nuclear Taboo Is Broken', *Proliferation Papers*, Ifri, Spring 2009.

8   George H. Quester, *Nuclear First Strike: Consequences of a Broken Taboo* (Baltimore, MD: Johns Hopkins University Press, December 2005), p. 116.

9   Brad Roberts, 'Rethinking How Wars Must End: NBC War Termination Issues in the Post-Cold War Era', in Victor Utgoff (ed.), *The Coming Crisis: Nuclear Proliferation, US Interests, and World Older* (Cambridge, MA: MIT

Press, 2000), pp. 266–72.

10 On the importance of the United States' credibility and reputation for action, see Alex Weisiger and Keren Yarhi-Milo, 'Revisiting Reputation: How Past Actions Matter in International Politics', *International Organization*, no. 69, Spring 2015, pp. 473–95.

11 US Department of Defense, *The Nuclear Posture Review Report*, p. 33.

12 On the importance of understanding an adversary's motivations and tailoring deterrence accordingly, see M. Elaine Bunn, *Can Deterrence Be Tailored?*, Strategic Forum No. 225 (Washington DC: National Defense University Press, January 2007); and Kevin Chilton and Greg Weaver, 'Waging Deterrence in the 21st Century', *Strategic Studies Quarterly*, vol. 3, no. 1, Spring 2009, pp. 31–42.

13 See David Welch and James Blight, 'An Introduction to the ExComm Transcripts', *International Security*, vol. 12, no. 3, Winter 1987–88, pp. 5–20; McGeorge Bundy and James Blight, 'October 27, 1962: Transcripts of the Meetings of the ExComm', *International Security*, vol. 12, no. 3, Winter 1987–88), pp. 30–92; and Michael Dobbs, *One Minute to Midnight: Kennedy, Khrushchev, and Castro on the Brink of Nuclear War* (New York: Vintage Books, 2008).

14 See Forrest E. Morgan et al., *Dangerous Thresholds: Managing Escalation in the 21st Century* (Santa Monica, CA: RAND Corporation, 2008); and Kerry M. Kartchner and Michael S. Gerson, 'Escalation to Limited Nuclear War in the 21st Century', in Jeffrey A. Larsen and Kerry M. Kartchner (eds), *On*

Limited Nuclear War in the 21st Century (Stanford, CA: Stanford University Press, 2014), pp. 144–71.

15 See Michael Frankel, James Scouras and George Ullrich, *The Uncertain Consequences of Nuclear Weapons Use* (Laurel, MD: Johns Hopkins University Applied Physics Lab, 2015); and Samuel Glasstone and Philip J. Dolan, *The Effects of Nuclear Weapons* (Washington DC: US Government Printing Office, 1977).

16 A similar scenario is envisioned in Brad Glosserman, 'Struggling with the Gray Zone: Trilateral Cooperation to Strengthen Deterrence in Northeast Asia', *Issues & Insights*, vol. 15, no. 13, October 2015, pp. C-1–C-2; and Warden, 'North Korea's Nuclear Posture', pp. 27–8.

17 Dan Altman, 'By Fait Accompli, Not Coercion: How States Wrest Territory from Their Adversaries', *International Studies Quarterly*, vol. 61, no. 4, December 2017, pp. 881–91; and Ahmer Tarar, 'A Strategic Logic of the Military Fait Accompli', *International Studies Quarterly*, vol. 60, no. 4, December 2016, pp. 742–52.

18 See Austin Long, 'US Strategic Nuclear Targeting Policy: Necessity and Damage Limitation', H-Diplo/ ISSF Policy Roundtable 1–4 (2016) on US Nuclear Policy, 22 December 2016, https://issforum.org/round-tables/policy/1-4-nuclear; and Keir A. Lieber and Daryl G. Press, 'The Nukes We Need: Preserving the American Deterrent', *Foreign Affairs*, vol. 88, no. 6, November/December 2009, pp. 39–51.

19 Quester, *Nuclear First Strike*, p. 123. See also Adam Mount, 'The Logic of Nuclear Restraint', *Survival*, vol. 57,

no. 4, August–September 2015, pp. 53–76.

20 The risk of a low-level provocation escalating to a conflict is described in Warden, 'North Korea's Nuclear Posture', pp. 28–9.

21 There is evidence that North Korea would consider such a nuclear strike in a conventional conflict with the United States. See Warden, 'North Korea's Nuclear Posture', pp. 29–33; and Jeffrey Lewis, 'North Korea Is Practicing for Nuclear War', *Foreign Policy*, 9 March 2017, http://foreignpolicy.com/2017/03/09/north-korea-is-practicing-for-nuclear-war/.

22 Daryl G. Press, Scott D. Sagan and Benjamin A. Valentino, 'Atomic Aversion: Experimental Evidence on Taboos, Traditions, and the Non-Use of Nuclear Weapons', *American Political Science Review*, vol. 107, no. 1, February 2013, pp. 188–206.

23 For an account of the Obama administration's deliberations on Syria, its military strikes and the potential impact on US credibility of not enforcing US 'red lines', see Jeffrey Goldberg, 'The Obama Doctrine', *Atlantic*, April 2016, https://www.theatlantic.com/magazine/archive/2016/04/the-obama-doctrine/471525/. See also Alex Weisiger and Keren Yarhi-Milo, 'What American Credibility Myth? How and Why Reputation Matters', *War on the Rocks*, 4 October 2016, https://warontherocks.com/2016/10/what-american-credibility-myth-how-and-why-reputation-matters/.

24 For analyses of the role of non-nuclear and nuclear escalation in Russian strategy, see Johnson,

Nuclear Weapons in Russia's Approach to Conflict and *Russia's Conventional Precision Strike Capabilities, Regional Crises, and Nuclear Thresholds*; Roberts, *The Case for Nuclear Weapons in the 21st Century*, pp. 128–38; Kristin Ven Bruusgaard, 'Russian Strategic Deterrence', *Survival*, vol. 58, no. 4, August–September 2016, pp. 7–26, and 'The Myth of Russia's Lowered Nuclear Threshold', *War on the Rocks*, 22 September 2017, https://warontherocks.com/2017/09/the-myth-of-russias-lowered-nuclear-threshold/; and Anya Loukianova Fink, 'The Evolving Russian Concept of Strategic Deterrence: Risks and Responses', *Arms Control Today*, vol. 47, no. 6, July–August 2017, pp. 14–20.

25 This scenario is drawn from Thomas G. Mahnken, 'Future Scenarios of Limited Nuclear Conflict', in Larsen and Kartchner (eds), *On Limited Nuclear War in the 21st Century*, p. 137. However, we posit a different Russian nuclear attack than the one in Mahnken's scenario.

26 For a summary of Russia's nuclear forces, see Hans Kristensen and Robert Norris, 'Russian Nuclear Forces, 2017', *Bulletin of Atomic Scientists*, vol. 73, no. 2, March 2017, pp. 115–26. For an interactive tool showing the threat radius of *Iskander* systems in Kaliningrad, see Ian Williams, 'The Russia–NATO A2AD Environment', Center for Strategic and International Studies, 3 January 2017, https://missilethreat.csis.org/russia-nato-a2ad-environment. For an example of a Russian statement regarding the deployment of nuclear-capable systems in Kaliningrad,

see 'Russia Moves Nuclear-capable Missile into Kaliningrad', Reuters, 8 October 2016, http://in.reuters.com/article/russia-usa-missiles-confirm/russia-moves-nuclear-capable-missiles-into-kaliningrad-idINKC-N1280JB.

27 It is possible that deterrence could fail because an adversary's calculus changed during a conflict. See Chilton and Weaver, 'Waging Deterrence in the 21st Century', p. 35. In this scenario, Russia may have come to regard its regime as jeopardised.

28 Scher, 'Nuclear Modernization'.

29 For a discussion of the historic rationale for US limited nuclear options, see James R. Schlesinger, *Annual Defense Department Report, FY 1975* (Washington DC: Government Printing Office, 1974); and Elbridge A. Colby, 'The United States and Discriminate Nuclear Options During the Cold War', in Larsen and Kartchner (eds), *On Limited Nuclear War in the 21st Century*, pp. 49–79.

30 In this hypothetical case, Russian leaders might have concluded that 'the very existence of the state is under threat', which is a rationale for nuclear-weapons use in Russia's 2014 military doctrine. See Ven Bruusgaard, 'The Myth of Russia's Lowered Nuclear Threshold'. For a description of Russia's naval non-strategic nuclear weapons, see Kristensen and Norris, 'Russian Nuclear Forces, 2017', pp. 122–4.

31 Bunn, Sidhu, Takahashi and Twomey, 'How Might Nuclear Deterrence Fail in a Limited Way and What Should We Do About It If It Does?'.

32 Roberts, 'Rethinking How Wars Must

End', p. 273. Moreover, the *Nuclear Posture Review* calls for improving the analyses and technology to support presidential decision-making and consultations in nuclear crises (see *The Nuclear Posture Review Report,* p. 58). These efforts should focus on the type of scenarios presented in this article.

European Defence: Give PESCO a Chance

Sven Biscop

> It is easier to deal with an open objection than with a profession of agreement in principle which covers an underlying reluctance to translate it into practice. While clear opposition presents an obstacle that can be surmounted, hesitant acquiescence acts as a constant break on progress.

> *Basil H. Liddell Hart*[1]

Sir Basil Liddell Hart's remarks about his attempts to promote the reform of the British Army between the two world wars unwittingly capture the current state of European defence. At their 1998 Saint-Malo Summit, the UK and France initiated the creation of a military arm for the European Union, now known as the Common Security and Defence Policy (CSDP). Ever since, EU member states have consistently claimed that more cooperation between their armed forces is the only way to significantly increase military capability. Successive projects have been proposed, yet none has ever really been implemented.

Sceptics can therefore be forgiven for eyeing the EU's latest initiative, known as Permanent Structured Cooperation (PESCO), with some suspicion – not least because the EU has already tried and failed to activate PESCO, in 2010 after the entry into force of the Lisbon Treaty.[2] Yet the latest attempt,

Sven Biscop, an Honorary Fellow of the European Security and Defence College (ESDC), is the director of the Europe in the World programme at the Egmont – Royal Institute for International Relations in Brussels, and a professor at Ghent University.

Survival | vol. 60 no. 3 | June–July 2018 | pp. 161–180   DOI 10.1080/00396338.2018.1470771

formally launched in December 2017, feels different. Success is obviously not guaranteed, but seems more likely in this case than in the past.

Why PESCO is different

The EU's Council of Ministers decided to establish PESCO on 8 December 2017, with the involvement of 25 member states – all but the UK (for obvious reasons), Denmark (which has a standing opt-out from the CSDP) and Malta.[3] The remaining 25 members have signed up to 20 commitments.

The most tangible of these is the obligation to take part in at least one of a list of capability projects that the participating states agree to be 'strategically relevant'. This obligation is linked to a general commitment to help address, through collaborative projects, the common capability shortfalls that the EU identifies, and to look for collaborative options first even when filling a national shortfall. Furthermore, all projects should help make the European defence industry more competitive and avoid unnecessary overlap, thus supporting the European Defence Technological and Industrial Base. Member states have also committed to make available strategically deployable formations, in addition to the battalion-strength EU Battlegroups, in order to achieve the EU's military level of ambition, and to provide substantial support every time the EU launches an actual operation.

All of this comes at a price, hence states have further committed to 'regularly increas[e] defence budgets in real terms, in order to reach agreed objectives', as well as to allocate 20% of their defence spending to investment, and 2% to research and technology (R&T). The 'agreed objectives' in question are not spelled out, because many states will likely never reach the objective that they signed up to as NATO members to spend 2% of GDP on defence. The fact that the NATO allies had already committed to the 2% threshold made it impossible, however, for the EU to specify a lower number. A commitment under PESCO to spend 20% on investment and 2% on R&T means that states that now spend two-thirds or more of their defence budget on salaries will be forced to increase their budgets.

What makes PESCO different from previous initiatives? Firstly, because Council decisions are legally binding, PESCO, unlike other initiatives, will not go away. Previous schemes typically fizzled out after a year or two once it became clear that states were not actually going to do anything. Not so PESCO: because it has been written into EU law, the Council of Ministers will annually assess whether the member states are fulfilling their commitments, on the basis of a report by the High Representative. The states themselves are required to produce an annual National Implementation Plan. As with the NATO Defence Planning Process (NDPP), this does not guarantee that states will meet all of their targets, but does mean that they will have to explain any failure to do so to their fellow member states, as well as to their publics and parliaments. Moreover, the commitment to enter into collaborative capability projects will mean collective engagements, which are more difficult to renege on: once a state commits to a specific multinational project, it cannot withdraw without incurring the wrath of the other states taking part. In this area at least, the participating states will serve to keep each other in line, potentially making PESCO more forceful than the NDPP.

PESCO may come with a stick, but for the first time there is also a carrot. The European Commission has proposed a European Defence Fund that, as of the next budgetary cycle (2021–27), will include a 'development window' of up to €5 billion per year, from which up to 20% can be funded from the EU budget, for multinational projects that address a commonly identified shortfall.[4] For projects falling within the PESCO framework, an additional bonus of 10% is foreseen. Compared to the €35bn or so that the PESCO states annually spend on investment today, that is not a negligible sum. Of course, the EU budget also comes from the member states, but the European Defence Fund represents a new pot of common funding. If it is used to launch a limited number of key projects, it may help to orient member states' decisions.

Whereas defence was traditionally seen to fall outside its remit, the EU Commission has now become a key driver of the defence debate within the EU. That is good news, given that things usually advance once the Commission puts its shoulder to the wheel. Even more importantly, the initiative to launch PESCO came not from Brussels, but from member states, who took it upon themselves to enhance their defence effort without being exhorted to by the US, NATO or the EU. France and Germany took the initiative at a bilateral summit on 13 July 2017, tabling a detailed proposal that was underwritten by Italy and Spain. Belgium, Estonia, Finland and the Netherlands were also invited to co-sign the proposal and its successive updates.[5] Strong Franco-German leadership led to the countries' proposals being adopted in record time: less than half a year elapsed between the Franco-German summit and the Council decision.

Making PESCO work

Continued leadership will be necessary to ensure that PESCO fulfils its potential and does not fall victim to its own success. In its current form, it embodies a compromise between France and Germany as to the number of states that have joined it. The French expectation was that a core group of around a dozen members would pull the others along, and therefore Paris emphasised ambitious criteria, conceiving of PESCO as a platform to generate forces for operations. Germany, on the other hand, had a more inclusive vision. Both views were to shape the ultimate outcome, but it is clear that PESCO was not designed to have so many members. All decision-making, except when it comes to the admission of new members, is unanimous, a set-up that has had consequences from the start, notably for the first list of 17 PESCO projects.[6]

'Medical HQ to Spearhead EU Military Push' read one implicitly sceptical headline when the list was announced.[7] In fact, deployable medical assets constitute a real strategic shortfall, and no government will deploy its troops if medical support is not available. But most of the other projects, while useful for the states that proposed them, do not meet any of the collectively identified European shortfalls. In many cases, the states concerned were going to undertake them anyway, PESCO or no PESCO. A prior assessment by the EU Military Staff told member states as much, but the suggestion that it should formally validate project proposals was discarded. France and Germany had initially aimed at five to ten projects, but when it became clear that member states were joining en masse, it became politically impossible not to accept at least some of their project proposals (nearly 50 in total). Nor could Paris and Berlin simply impose their views on the others; indeed, they dropped some of their own projects to keep the list to a manageable number. On the bright side, some of the projects are expected to produce results in the near term, which will serve to demonstrate the value of PESCO to political leaders and publics alike, and help to keep the momentum going.

Nevertheless, this lack of focus should be rectified in the next round of project proposals, scheduled to take place before the end of 2018. For PESCO to add real value, it must focus on projects that, because they require a large critical mass of participating states and address a common rather than a national shortfall, would not otherwise happen – projects that really are 'strategically relevant', such as long-range air and sea transport; intelligence, surveillance, target acquisition and reconnaissance (from drones to satellites); air-to-air refuelling; and deployable networks. These are the strategic enablers that Europeans need to project military force beyond the borders of Europe. Some EU members may acquire a limited national capacity in some of these areas, but certainly not enough to allow them to conduct significant operations without relying on US assets. Most simply cannot afford any capacity at all in these areas, except at the expense of their basic war-fighting capabilities.

The first list of PESCO projects does not distinguish between 'strategically relevant' projects and others. It would be advisable if the next one did. All projects could count towards PESCO states' general obligation to engage in collaborative projects, but states should be obliged to participate in at least one 'strategically relevant' project. By limiting the number of these to three to five per annual round of projects, PESCO could generate the critical mass that each of them needs. (Of course, this would present the political difficulty of telling some states that their projects are less relevant than others.) Ideally, PESCO would only use Commission co-funding for the strategic projects, given that scattering the means of the European Defence Fund across a plethora of projects will greatly reduce its effectiveness.

A system to assess member states' performance in terms of their PESCO commitments is already in place, and the Council is scheduled, before summer 2018, to specify more precise objectives and to sequence their fulfilment in two phases (2018–20 and 2021–25). But developing a culture of compliance will be crucial. The only sanction provided for non-compliance, once a state has been given a time frame for consultation and rectifying the situation, is suspension from PESCO, a nuclear option that is unlikely to be used. Yet member states must be made to understand that they cannot join PESCO just to make up the numbers. This will require clear and firm language (something the EU is not necessarily known for) in the annual report on every state's performance, as well as complete transparency so as to generate pressure both from peers and the public. Most importantly, the original authors of the PESCO proposal, namely France, Germany, Italy and Spain, must lead by example.[8] They must demonstrate not only that they are implementing the commitments in full, but also that they truly respect the spirit of PESCO, and put the collective European interest first. It is incumbent upon them to propose genuinely strategic projects that smaller states do not have the scale to initiate.

France and Germany set the course at their July 2017 bilateral summit, at which they announced joint initiatives to develop major land-combat, artillery and maritime-patrol systems, as well as a combat aircraft (among other projects), while confirming their support for the Eurodrone programme with Italy and Spain. These initiatives represent a departure from the status quo, under which European states seek to satisfy their own national requirements for any new equipment. A host of companies will usually compete for national contracts, which typically represent only a very small share of the market as each state requests its own national variant of the equipment on offer. If, however, Paris and Berlin, along with Rome and Madrid (the 'big four'), were to systematically join hands and harmonise requirements in all major capability areas under the auspices of PESCO, Europeans could finally be in a position to design, build and procure a single system in each domain. Like in the US, there could still be competition between two or three big industrial consortia, but in the end Europeans too would opt for a single project, which would then be significantly more competitive, including vis-à-vis the American alternatives on the market.

If the big four were thus to gradually integrate requirements and procurement, the other EU members would have no choice but to join in. Lacking the necessary scale to launch alternative projects, their national defence industries (comprising mostly small and medium-sized enterprises) would not survive outside the large consortia competing for big-four projects. Indeed, not even the big four are capable of reaching the critical mass of investors and customers needed to make a project economically viable without the participation of other members. This implies that the defence firms of smaller states will have a fair chance of joining the main consortia.

A cultural shift is clearly needed that only France, Germany, Italy and Spain can initiate. If they are serious about PESCO, they must abandon all protectionism, including offsets (the practice of returning money spent on procurement in another country to a purchasing state in the form of sub-contracts to its own defence industry, or even investments in other economic sectors), in defence procurement. This may seem a distant prospect, but the alternative – national defence industries engaging in ruinous competition that ultimately leaves Europe with no defence industry at all – is already on the horizon. For its part, the European Commission has sent a strong signal by taking legal action, for the first time, against EU member states accused of violating EU defence-market legislation. Italy, Poland and Portugal have been cited for awarding contracts to national industries without public tender, and Denmark and the Netherlands for demanding undue offsets.

Towards integration

The implementation of PESCO is understandably focused on capability pro-jects, its most tangible dimension. But the fact that states participating in any given project will acquire the same equipment could serve as the founda-tion for more integrated forces, in which any additional capabilities can be operated in the most cost-effective way. Once a project has been completed, it only makes sense for the resulting capability to be co-owned, as part of a unified force, by all the states that helped to develop it, rather than being divided between them. This would apply in particular to strategic enablers, such as transport aircraft and ships, drones, and satellites, the development of which requires a large critical mass of participating states to take off. Individual drones, ships and aircraft could still be owned by individual states and even operated by national personnel, but they could be incor-porated into a single structure with multinational personnel for command, logistics, maintenance and training, and subject to a standardised upgrade programme. Not only would this reduce duplication between states, but it would also enhance the availability of capabilities for operations, as compared with small, national capabilities, some portion of which is always in maintenance. The experience of the European Air Transport Command in Eindhoven, which operates the transport fleets of France, Germany, Italy, Spain and the Benelux countries, shows how important efficiency gains can be achieved, even without merging logistics and maintenance, which could be the next step.

Combat units could be operated more cost-effectively as well. Even Europe's smaller states could maintain a significant combat capacity if, rather than having to field all support units themselves, combat support and combat service support were provided through a combination of pooling and a division of labour among several states. Belgian–Dutch naval cooperation is an example of this model. Manoeuvre units remain nationally staffed: ships sail either under the Belgian flag with a Belgian crew, or the Dutch flag with a Dutch crew. But there is only one, pooled, naval command and one naval-operations school; and there is a division of labour with regard to logistics, maintenance and training, with the Dutch providing these services for all frigates and the Belgians for all minehunters.

This dimension of PESCO has received far less attention since 2017 than it did in 2010, though one of its (less stringently worded) commitments states that members 'could commit' to an active role in existing and future multinational structures, such as the Eurocorps, meaning that states would go beyond interoperability (making sure that their forces can be deployed alongside each other) toward integration (creating permanent multinational capabilities to support their national forces). Such a move would arguably maximise the impact of PESCO. Furthermore, although the Council decision states that this commitment does not 'cover a readiness force, a standing force [or] a stand by force', it is difficult to see how states can meet operations-related commitments or make strategically deployable formations available without to some degree creating more permanently integrated force packages with collective enablers. Without readiness, a force does not constitute a capability. If this commitment refers only to the existing EU practice of declaring the theoretical availability of non-identified national forces, it is meaningless. Instead, integration ought to be wired into PESCO from the start.

One of the first 17 PESCO projects to be announced is a Crisis Response Operation Core (CROC) that should facilitate force generation for expeditionary operations.[9] To achieve this goal, which was first proposed in a Franco-German 'food-for-thought' paper, a generic contingency plan for a crisis-response operation would be developed and a force package derived from it that would consist of one land division or three brigades, plus the required strategic enablers. Participating states would then assign capabilities to this package, which would be logged in a database to be maintained by the EU Military Staff. The list of projects annexed to the Council decision states that CROC 'will decisively contribute to the creation of a coherent full spectrum force package'. The original Franco-German paper, however, had stated that 'no concrete names and figures of assigned capabilities/forces are foreseen',[10] leading one senior military officer to describe CROC as 'no more than an Excel sheet'. If, by contrast, participating states assign pre-identified forces and anchor them permanently in a CROC with pre-assigned enablers, this could be the beginning of a move from interoperability to integration.

PESCO vs other initiatives

Many of the states that have joined PESCO are simultaneously engaged in another scheme, NATO's Framework Nations Concept (FNC), which also seeks to promote cooperation and possibly integration. The way in which the FNC involves a larger nation offering a framework, such as a corps or headquarters, to which smaller nations make specific contributions in the collective pursuit of the states' capability targets, invites a direct comparison with PESCO.[11] The fact that the FNC was originally a German idea raises questions about why it was tabled in NATO rather than the EU. Bringing together 19 allies, the German-led FNC group started out with a focus on capability development, with sub-groups of various sizes addressing specific capability areas. It now also functions as a framework for generating deployments, notably on Europe's eastern borders, in the context of NATO's Enhanced Forward Presence there. The extent to which participating states are willing to integrate with German forces remains to be seen, although bilateral German–Dutch cooperation between land forces has already progressed very far indeed. Dutch armoured and air-mobile units have been anchored within larger German formations, and effectively rely on specific German-only support elements, which seems to prove that integration can work.

While Germany takes the lead in the development of the FNC, France has launched yet another scheme. The European Intervention Initiative (EII), which focuses on territorial defence, was announced by French President Emmanuel Macron in a speech at Sorbonne University in September 2017. In view of the timing of the speech, which was delivered just as work on PESCO was accelerating, many assumed that Macron was referring to CROC, but it has since become clear that EII is meant to be a separate scheme falling outside the framework of PESCO and even of the EU. Macron apparently envisages that, by the beginning of the next decade, participating states will have achieved a common intervention force, a common defence budget and a common doctrine for action.[12] France has initially invited nine countries in total to join the scheme (Belgium, Denmark, Estonia, Germany, Italy, the Netherlands, Portugal, Spain and the UK), but the precise form the initiative will take remains unclear. The emphasis seems to be on doctrine, planning, intelligence and strategic culture rather than on force packages. The participation of the UK would not prevent the launching of the EII as a PESCO project, since third-country participation in individual PESCO projects will be provided for, and indeed will help the larger projects to achieve critical mass.

The emergence of CROC, the FNC and EII suggests that at least some European states are convinced of the need to build more integrated force packages. But too many parallel initiatives risk undermining each other. Many states are involved in all three projects. If all were to be pursued at the same pace, overlap and competition would be bound to occur. It is possible to make a state's forces interoperable with many others in the context of different frameworks. But as soon as a state moves toward integration, choices must be made: a capability that has been integrated into one framework cannot simultaneously be merged with another. Given the importance of French and German leadership to the success of PESCO, will they be able to take the lead on EII and the FNC at the same time? Who will take the lead on CROC? Is PESCO's top priority territorial defence, or power projection, or both? Neither France nor Germany has clarified its ultimate plans. While the German foreign ministry and the political leadership of the defence ministry appear to be backing PESCO, many in the Bundeswehr still prioritise NATO and the FNC.[13] Meanwhile, many within the French defence establishment seem disillusioned with the EU, believing that only the UK and the US can be relied upon in combat. EII could be the result of French disappointment with PESCO, which turned out differently than Paris expected.

In order to ensure that all initiatives fit together with PESCO, states need to be more clear about its purpose, which remains surprisingly vague. The established EU practice of pushing on with concrete measures that member states can agree on, while leaving the more contentious end goal undefined, risks failure in this case, because the ongoing non-EU schemes could hollow out PESCO. Without a long-term view, it will be difficult to maintain any sort of coherence between successive annual rounds of project proposals, let alone to decide what the priority projects should be. Participating states need to think carefully about what PESCO might allow them to do that they cannot do today.

PESCO and European security

The Council decision states only that PESCO members have made commitments to each other 'with a view to [preparing for] the most demanding missions, and contributing to the fulfilment of the Union level of ambition'. The EU's military level of ambition has not been updated since 1999, however, when the EU adopted the (land-centric) Headline Goal of achieving the capacity to deploy, and to sustain for at least one year, 60,000 troops, with concomitant air and naval support, for expeditionary operations.

In 2016, the EU Global Strategy (which guides all EU external policies) added the qualitative objective of strategic autonomy. In operational terms, strategic autonomy means the capacity to undertake certain military tasks at all times and therefore, if necessary, alone. The precise nature of the operations the EU should be capable of was defined by the Council of Ministers, which on 14 November 2016 adopted the Implementation Plan on Security and Defence, intended to operationalise the Global Strategy. The plan lists an ambitious range of operations, from 'joint crisis management operations in situations of high security risk in the regions surrounding the EU' and 'joint stabilisation operations, including air and special operations', through air-security and maritime-security operations, to capacity-building. However, it specifies neither how many operations the EU should be able to conduct simultaneously, nor the envisaged scale of these operations. Member states were not willing to enter into detail, most likely because doing so would have revealed that the existing Headline Goal, which has not been attained, is actually insufficient to achieve a significant degree of concurrency. Moreover, member states have hitherto been reluctant to undertake high-intensity operations under the EU flag. As a result, the Implementation Plan's list of operations seems already to have been forgotten; military staffers in Brussels refer to it as 'the annex of the annex'. The CROC food-for-thought paper, however, is more explicit, translating the existing Headline Goal into a need for a corps headquarters, three divisions and nine to 12 brigades, with the three brigades that it calls for in the short term constituting only a first step.

The CSDP was created for expeditionary purposes only, but the Global Strategy, besides introducing the need for strategic autonomy, also added a new task: the protection of Europe. The idea is not for the EU to take charge of collective territorial defence, even though there is a legal basis for this in the Lisbon Treaty;[14] that will remain the prerogative of NATO. There is a range of contingencies, however, that fall below the threshold of NATO's Article V, in which the armed forces have a mostly supporting role to play, and which the EU is arguably better placed to address, such as homeland security, cyber security and border security. Of course, such contingencies exist on a continuum: homeland security may require defeating an enemy abroad, such as the Islamic State, in addition to patrolling the streets at home; border security may be conditional upon creating a safe and secure environment in Europe's neighbouring countries; and cyber security may be the theatre of confrontation that replaces, or precedes, warfare between regular forces. Capability requirements sit along a continuum as well: the shortfalls in European arsenals identified by NATO and the EU are nearly identical. The key to defining PESCO's place in Europe's security architecture would be to acknowledge this continuum, and to break through the organisational divide between the EU and NATO that hinders any serious strategising by Europeans.

At present, Europe's capability shortfalls are such that it can neither meet its NATO obligations for territorial defence, nor achieve strategic autonomy with regard to the protection of Europe and expeditionary operations as demanded by the EU Global Strategy. Defence spending is going up in nearly all European states, but spending more is not in itself the answer, given that the nature and scale of many key shortfalls (notably strategic enablers) is such that no single European state is capable of acquiring sufficient capabilities to make a difference. Even if all European states were to spend 2% of GDP on defence, they would still be dependent on US strategic lift, intelligence and more to actually employ their forces. Thus, cooperation and integration is needed. By pooling their defence efforts, Europeans can make the best use of the available resources to address their forces' shortfalls. By working together to achieve synergies and effects of scale, and by minimising duplication, they might even do so by spending less than 2% of GDP. After all, this spending target should not be seen as an objective in its own right: the real aim is to achieve all capability targets. If that can be done for less money, so much the better. Of course, spending less than 2% is not an objective in its own right either.

PESCO, NATO and the EU

PESCO could be the single umbrella under which European states engage in cooperation and integration to meet all of their capability targets, for both NATO and the EU. This is what the 25 PESCO members actually stated in the 13 November 2017 notification document in which they announced their intention to launch the initiative. According to the document, 'A long term vision of PESCO could be to arrive at a coherent full spectrum force package – in complementarity with NATO, which will continue to be the cornerstone of collective defence for its members'.[15] The Council decision did not repeat this wording, but this is precisely what PESCO should (and not just could) be.

Achieving this will require that a number of taboos be broken, and some artificial limitations be superseded. The EU, for example, would have to accept that developing capabilities within an EU framework does not mean that they will necessarily be put to use under the EU flag. The type of capabilities that PESCO focuses on should therefore not be limited by the kinds of operations that states have hitherto undertaken through the EU (which have mostly been of a smaller scale and at the lower end of the spectrum), nor even by the military tasks of the EU. Instead, PESCO should envisage the full spectrum of expeditionary operations, which Europeans can choose to conduct through either the EU, the UN or NATO, or as part of an ad hoc coalition, depending on the circumstances of each contingency, and the full spectrum of capabilities needed for territorial defence. Likewise, NATO would have to accept that setting capability targets for each ally does not mean that capabilities will necessarily be developed within a NATO framework or by each ally separately. In addition to working with individual allies, NATO should work with European allies and partners as a group[16] that will meet a series of targets collectively. The fact that the EU as such is not a member of NATO should not be allowed to hinder this work, since the most suitable framework for such collective action is the EU's PESCO mechanism.

PESCO in practice serves both the EU and NATO

PESCO's first list of projects shows that, in practice, it already serves both the EU and NATO, even though this has not been stated explicitly. Its military-mobility project is a prime example. The aim is to facilitate the movement of armed forces across the EU, by tackling both procedural obstacles and infrastructure problems (such as roads and bridges that are unsuitable for heavy military vehicles). NATO itself used to take charge of this, but after the end of the Cold War the existing mechanisms were neither updated nor extended to new allies in Central and Eastern Europe. Today, the EU is much better placed to assume this responsibility, even though the primary objective is to enhance the capacity for rapid reaction in the context of collective defence. The project has therefore been explicitly welcomed by NATO and the US. The EuroArtillery project is another example. Aiming to develop a new mobile precision artillery platform, this capability is clearly suited to the type of high-intensity operations that, at least until now, European states have conducted through NATO or ad hoc coalitions rather than the EU.

Since PESCO already serves both expeditionary operations and territorial defence, there is no need to choose between them (or indeed homeland security), nor to create additional schemes outside PESCO. States that today are mostly concerned with the defence of their territory, such as Finland and Poland, as well as states that are focusing more on operations abroad, such as Belgium, could pursue their defence policies within the PESCO framework. This is not to say that PESCO's participating states will need to do everything together, in every capability area. It would be perfectly possible, in the field of land capabilities, to create two cores within PESCO. France could bring EII under the PESCO umbrella, merge it with the CROC project, and take the lead in building an integrated multinational force package geared towards expeditionary operations, from which forces could be generated quickly in times of crisis. Germany could likewise bring the FNC group under the PESCO umbrella and continue with the integration of a force package geared toward territorial defence. The idea would not be a strict division of labour: France and Germany should obviously engage in both cores (as they do in operational terms, with German troops deployed in Mali and French troops in Lithuania). This would rather be a division of leadership, with each country taking the lead in the project that fits best with its strategic culture. France and Germany together, with Italy and Spain, should propose projects to acquire the strategic enablers required to support all operations. In this way, contrasting dynamics would strengthen rather than undermine each other.

By using PESCO as the sole umbrella for multinational capability development, complete consistency between the EU and NATO could be assured. Although the NDPP and the EU's Capability Development Plan logically identify the same shortfalls, they do not necessarily produce the same order of priorities. More importantly, ensuring the strategic autonomy of Europe is not an objective of the NDPP, which currently sets targets only for individual allies and for NATO as a whole, without guaranteeing that the European allies (and partners) will be able to conduct certain operations autonomously. Putting the EU and NATO targets together would allow the PESCO states to create a capability mixture that enables them, on the one hand, to assume their share of the burden of collective defence and to contribute to expeditionary operations together with other allies; and, on the other hand, to ensure European security and to launch by themselves the expeditionary operations identified by the EU level of ambition.

In this context, the European states that belong both to NATO and PESCO should consider merging the two National Implementation Plans they currently have – one detailing how they will achieve NATO's 'Wales pledge' of spending 2% of GDP on defence, and the other detailing how they will meet the PESCO commitments – to produce a single plan. This plan would be systematically assessed by NATO, via the established NDPP, and by the EU, which has launched a Coordinated Annual Review on Defence that will focus on the extent to which states have harmonised requirements and engaged in collaborative projects.

NATO targets are of course well established. As for the EU targets, the November 2016 Implementation Plan already identifies the types of operations that Europeans should be able to run on their own. Quantitatively, the existing Headline Goal could continue to be used, since the fact it will now have to be achieved without the UK means that it actually represents an increased level of ambition for the 25 PESCO states. If the EU were to achieve a degree of strategic autonomy thanks to PESCO, it would be able to assume first-line responsibility for crises in its neighbourhood (that remain below the threshold of Article V), without having to rely on US assets. It could then also take the lead politically and address crises according to its own values and interests. The US, in turn, could focus its strategy and capabilities on its own priorities. In other words, PESCO would help the European allies and partners to achieve the more equitable burden-sharing within NATO that the US has been demanding for so long.

PESCO and the US

It therefore came as a surprise to many European officials and observers when, on the eve of the NATO Defence Ministers Meeting in Brussels on 14–15 February 2018, first the US and then NATO Secretary-General Jens Stoltenberg suddenly voiced concerns about PESCO.[17] Kay Bailey Hutchison, US ambassador to NATO, stated that the EU's defence plans should not lead to a duplication of NATO, nor create transatlantic economic barriers. This view of European defence harks back to Madeleine Albright's initial negative reaction to the idea in the late 1990s, at which time she called for no duplication, no discrimination and no decoupling.[18] Yet at least since 2008 (the final year of George W. Bush's second term as president), the US has had a much more pragmatic view, seeming to be saying to Europeans that 'if you want to continue merely talking about European defence, don't waste our time; but if you want to really do something about it, by all means, go ahead – we welcome any scheme that produces more capability, regardless of its logo'.

If the current US administration has reverted to the more critical view, perhaps that is because of its strong focus on trade and a fear that PESCO will negatively affect American defence exports to Europe. It is one of PESCO's avowed objectives to strengthen the European defence industry, but even as it urges its members to 'buy European', this does not mean 'buy only European', especially as the European and American defence industries are closely intertwined. Still, strategic autonomy does also imply industrial autonomy. Surely nobody in the US sincerely expects the European allies to use increases in their defence budgets only on the purchase of more American equipment?

A strong plea by European leaders in favour of European defence, notably at the Munich Security Conference immediately after the NATO Defence Ministerial in 2018, shows that Washington has misjudged the mood in Brussels. It would be in the interests of the US, the EU and NATO alike if Washington adopted a more constructive attitude. In autumn 2017, when PESCO was still in the making, it was apparently suggested by members of US Defense Secretary James Mattis's inner circle that NATO might be granted observer status within PESCO. Such a suggestion is certain to raise hackles among those who prefer to maintain strict barriers between the EU and NATO, but it is just the kind of cross-cutting idea that is needed to maximise the performance of the stove-piped European security architecture. The NATO–EU relationship is already more transparent than it used to be: for example, NATO has been invited to the first set of bilateral meetings under the Coordinated Annual Review on Defence between the European Defence Agency and the individual PESCO states, in order to discuss their first National Implementation Plans. Offering NATO permanent-observer status within PESCO's central governance bodies would serve to solidify PESCO's role as the sole platform for multinational European capability development for both the EU and NATO. At the same time, the EU could be given a permanent-observer seat at the North Atlantic Council, thus creating full mutual transparency.

It could be argued that US concern can be taken as a good sign, demonstrating that PESCO has real potential – if it didn't, the US wouldn't be worrying about it. As with any complex scheme, it is possible to think of many reasons why it might not work, but it is too early to predict its failure. PESCO is qualitatively different from other schemes and could succeed where others have failed, but only if its member states (especially France, Germany, Italy and Spain) sustain an active leadership role and refrain from diluting it through uncoordinated parallel schemes. The role of the European Commission will also be crucial. One thing is certain: if European states want to significantly increase their military capacity, or even attain some degree of strategic autonomy, a collaborative scheme is the only option. They need to give PESCO a chance.

Acknowledgements

This article is based on a series of informal exchanges with diplomats, officials and military officers from various EU institutions and member states. The author warmly thanks all of them, for without them this article could not have been written.

Notes

1 Basil H. Liddell Hart, *The Memoirs of Captain Liddell Hart: Volume II* (London: Cassel, 1965), p. 73.

2 Sven Biscop and Jo Coelmont, 'CSDP and the "Ghent Framework": The Indirect Approach to Permanent Structured Cooperation?', *European Foreign Affairs Review*, vol. 16, no. 2, 2011, pp. 149–67.

3 Council of the European Union, 'Council Decision Establishing Permanent Structured Cooperation (PESCO) and Determining the List of Participating Member States', Brussels, 8 December 2017.

4 There will also be an 'R&T window' of €500 million per year.

5 The involvement of Belgium, Estonia, Finland and the Netherlands has not always been as substantial as

they might have wished: they have sometimes received drafts already approved by Paris, Berlin, Rome and Madrid with a request for comments by noon.

6 The full list of 17 projects encompasses the European Medical Command; the European Secure Software-defined Radio (ESSOR); the Network of Logistic Hubs in Europe and Support to Operations; Military Mobility; the European Union Training Mission Competence Centre (EU TMCC); the European Training Certification Centre for European Armies; Energy Operational Function (EOF); the Deployable Military Disaster Relief Capability Package; Maritime (semi-) Autonomous Systems for Mine Countermeasures (MAS MCM); Harbour & Maritime Surveillance and Protection (HARMSPRO); Upgrade of Maritime Surveillance; the Cyber Threats and Incident Response Information Sharing Platform; Cyber Rapid Response Teams and Mutual Assistance in Cyber Security; the Strategic Command and Control (C2) System for CSDP Missions and Operations; the Armoured Infantry Fighting Vehicle / Amphibious Assault Vehicle / Light Armoured Vehicle; Indirect Fire Support (EuroArtillery); and the EUFOR Crisis Response Operation Core (EUFOR CROC).

7 Andrew Rettman and Nikolaj Nielsen, 'Medical HQ to Spearhead EU Military Push', EU Observer, 13 December 2017.

8 France and Germany invited Italy and Spain to co-sign their proposals. Ideally, Poland would have been included in this group, as the most important eastern EU member state, but under the current Polish government, this was not possible. Indeed, Poland only joined PESCO at the last minute, after everybody else did (and after having tried in vain to have the texts modified).

9 In a highly competitive field, CROC must surely win the prize for 'worst acronym ever'.

10 'Food for Thought Paper on the CROC', prepared by France and Germany, September 2017.

11 Diego A. Ruiz Palmer, The Framework Nations Concept and NATO: Game-Changer for a New Strategic Era or Missed Opportunity? (Rome: NATO Defence College, July 2016).

12 Emmanuel Macron, 'Initiative pour l'Europe – Discours pour une Europe souveraine, unie, démocratique', Paris, 26 September 2017.

13 Rainer L. Glatz and Martin Zapfe, Ambitious Framework Nation: Germany in NATO (Berlin: Stiftung Wissenschaft und Politik, September 2017).

14 Article 42.7 of the Treaty on European Union, the so-called Mutual Assistance Clause, states that 'if a Member State is the victim of armed aggression on its territory, the other Member States shall have towards it an obligation of aid and assistance by all the means in their power'. The clause has been activated once, at the request of France following the 13 November 2015 terrorist attacks in Paris, but this was mostly a symbolic move. See Sven Biscop, 'The European Union and Mutual Assistance: More than Defence', International Spectator, vol. 51, no. 2, 2016, pp. 119–25.

15 Participating States, 'Notification on

Permanent Structured Cooperation (PESCO) to the Council and to the High Representative of the Union for Foreign Affairs and Security Policy', Brussels, 13 November 2017.

16 *Pace* Cyprus, the only EU member state that is neither a member nor a partner of NATO.

17 Michael Peel, Katrina Manson and Mehreen Khan, 'Pentagon Fires Warning Shot to EU over NATO Unity', *Financial Times*, 15 February 2018.

18 Madeleine Albright, 'Remarks to the North Atlantic Council Ministerial Meeting', Brussels, 8 December 1998.

India, the Indo-Pacific and the Quad

Rahul Roy-Chaudhury and Kate Sullivan de Estrada

The term 'Indo-Pacific', recently in fashion, describes a supposedly vital and contiguous strategic arena encompassing the eastern Indian and Western Pacific oceans. Accompanying the concept is the notion of a revived partnership: the Quadrilateral Security Dialogue between the United States, Australia, India and Japan (or 'Quad').

One of these countries is not like the others. India's maritime interests and strategy sit uneasily with those of the other Quad powers. India's is an Indian Ocean vision, rather than an Indo-Pacific vision. Bound by the strategic primacy of the Indian Ocean and by the constraints on its sea-power projection, in the short term, India's engagement with the Indo-Pacific framework will remain largely diplomatic, economic and rhetorical. India's core strategic focus lies west of the Strait of Malacca.

The return of the Quad

The Quad, previously initiated in 2007 by Japanese Prime Minister Shinzo Abe and discontinued after the withdrawal of Australia under then-prime minister Kevin Rudd, was revived at a meeting of senior diplomats from the four nations on the sidelines of the ASEAN summit in Manila in November 2017, resulting in parallel commitments to maintain a free and open order

Rahul Roy-Chaudhury is Senior Fellow for South Asia at the IISS and the author of two books on India's maritime security. **Kate Sullivan de Estrada** is Associate Professor in the International Relations of South Asia at the University of Oxford, a Fellow of St Antony's College and a Consulting Member of the IISS.

Survival | vol. 60 no. 3 | June–July 2018 | pp. 181–194   DOI 10.1080/00396338.2018.1470773

in the Indo-Pacific.[1] The Indo-Pacific construct is partly material, reflecting a vast increase in activity along the sea lines of communication that link the two oceanic regions in trade and energy – and in turn, it is partly strategic, as this greater interdependence brings greater vulnerability and risk.

Yet the currency of the Indo-Pacific idea lies also in its framing as a space of shared values. Prime Minister Abe's now widely cited 'Confluence of the Two Seas' speech, delivered before the Indian parliament in 2007, spoke not only of the 'dynamic coupling' of the Indian and Pacific oceans, but also of their identity as 'seas of freedom and of prosperity'.[2] Australia's 2017 foreign-policy White Paper referred to a vision of an 'open, inclusive and prosperous Indo-Pacific region, in which the rights of all states are respected'.[3] US President Donald Trump's five-nation tour of Asia late last year was punctuated by his frequent invocation of the phrase 'free and open Indo-Pacific region'.[4] And India's press release in response to the November quadrilateral meeting declared that 'a free, open, prosperous and inclusive Indo-Pacific region serves the long-term interests of all countries in the region and of the world at large'.[5]

Two ideas are implicit in this values-based framing: one about China, the other about India. Firstly, despite claims from the White House that the term is 'certainly not'[6] an effort to contain China's influence, it is clear that the Indo-Pacific construct is a response to perceptions that China is deploying infrastructure development and investments in the region for geopolitical gain, and that Beijing is, at best, weakly committed to a rules-based international order, particularly in the maritime domain. Secondly, in a way that the term 'Asia-Pacific' did not, 'Indo-Pacific' explicitly includes a rising India, whose significance to the future balance of power in Asia is obvious, and whose democratic credentials and rhetorical embrace of a rules-based order offer reassurance to Washington, Tokyo and Canberra. As a senior Trump-administration official put it, 'We talk about an Indo-Pacific in part because that phrase captures the importance of India's rise'.[7]

External recognition of India's growing influence and hopes for its co-operation in upholding freedom of navigation and overflight at sea resonate, in theory, with Indian ambitions. In recent years, a key part of India's rise has been a turn to the sea; its 2015 Maritime Security Strategy, for example, notes 'the incontrovertible link between secure seas and India's resurgence in the 21st century'. The language of Indo-Pacific summitry also chimes with India's rhetorical commitment to an open maritime order.[8]

Nevertheless, there are clear limits to India's enthusiasm for the Quad. For India, Japan and Australia alike, the fear of provoking China at a moment when US commitment to the security of the region is uncertain is a reason for caution. Beyond that shared caution, New Delhi has its own historical aversion to multilateral arrangements that can be construed as alliances, and has been ambivalent towards democratic collectives. The current Indian government, perhaps even more than its predecessors, also places great value on India's relationships with ASEAN member states through a revamped 'Act East' policy. This explains why the Indian government's press release following the Manila meeting in November avoided any explicit mention of a 'quadrilateral', unlike the US and Australian statements. (For that matter, it is noteworthy that four separate statements were issued by the four governments after the Manila meeting, rather than a single, joint statement.)[9] Nor did it mention freedom of navigation and overflight, respect for international law or maritime security, although New Delhi has in the past regularly voiced support for these principles.[10] The press release also clarified that Act East remains 'the cornerstone of [the Indian government's] engagement in the Indo-Pacific region'.[11]

Beyond this diplomatic inhibition, however, is something more fundamental: India's own idea of its maritime interests and strategy may not match the expectations of other Quad members.

Mapping the Indo-Pacific

The four Quad capitals define the Indo-Pacific differently. The US National Security Strategy, released in December 2017, states that the Indo-Pacific region 'stretches from the west coast of India to the western shores of the United States' and thereby neatly slices off the western Indian Ocean.[12] The regional map on the cover of the 2017 Australian foreign-policy White Paper highlights an area that extends just far enough to include the westernmost point in India and then arches southwards to exclude much of the western Indian Ocean.[13]

By contrast, the 2017 edition of Japan's Diplomatic Blue Book maps an Indo-Pacific that stretches from Japan, in the east, to the east coast of the African continent, in the west, including both the eastern and the western Indian Ocean. Japan and India do share a preference for cross-regional trade and infrastructural connections, as expressed in a May 2017 vision document for an Asia–Africa Growth Corridor, which some view as a bilateral response to China's Belt and Road Initiative (BRI).[14] But partnering on economic cooperation is about as far as India is willing to go. The 2015 Maritime Security Strategy specifically lists India's 'primary areas of maritime interests' as extending from, at the most westerly points, the Persian Gulf and the Gulf of Oman; the Gulf of Aden and the Red Sea; the east coast of Africa littoral and the southwest Indian Ocean region island nations to, at the most easterly reach, the Andaman Sea to India's east, whose littoral states include Myanmar, Thailand and Indonesia.[15] India's strategy document also lists around ten choke points that sit at the entry and exit points to, and the thoroughfares across, the Indian Ocean. The southeast Indian Ocean (stretching as far as Australia), South and East China seas, western Pacific Ocean, and southern Indian Ocean region (including Antarctica), are relegated to the status of 'secondary areas of maritime interest'.

The primacy of the Indian Ocean

The Indian Ocean's importance for India has a great deal to do with the nature of the country's rise. India's primarily economics-driven emergence has seen a marked increase in trade flows and a growing dependence on the transport of energy and raw materials, both of which depend primarily on sea lines of communication.[16] Pakistan's growing partnership with China has also helped ensure that New Delhi's rising ambitions have not been focused on land-based pre-eminence. The result is a new appreciation of the link between India's maritime development and its national power, illustrated by the burgeoning interest among contemporary Indian strategists in the writings of the nineteenth-century American naval theorist Rear-Admiral Alfred Thayer Mahan.[17]

More recently, a major driver of India's seaward turn has been China's expanding influence in the Indian Ocean through the launch of the BRI.

The initiative's flagship project, the $62 billion China–Pakistan Economic Corridor (CPEC), seeks to link China to the Indian Ocean through Pakistan's Gwadar port. In parallel, the BRI's Maritime Silk Road traverses key strategic nodes across the Indian Ocean. China's BRI is an affront to India, which believes that by virtue of simple geography it has a right to maritime pre-eminence in the Indian Ocean.

Although from the 1980s onwards India's leaders began to recognise the Indian navy's potential as an instrument of state power, it was not until the beginning of the twenty-first century that India's ocean geography began to receive the attention of its leadership. That decade saw, as David Scott puts it, 'a shift of maritime vision from a small coastal-hugging passive brown-water fleet to a larger ocean-going active blue-water fleet capable of power projection throughout the Indian Ocean'.[18] Under the current leadership of Prime Minister Narendra Modi, India for the first time aspires to become a 'leading' power in the Indian Ocean, seeking to take on greater roles and responsibilities in the region. In March 2015, Modi engaged in a purposeful spree of island hopping, visiting the Seychelles (the first ministerial visit in 34 years), Sri Lanka (the first in 28) and Mauritius, where Modi became the first Indian prime minister in decades to unveil an Indian Ocean vision.

That vision, declared Modi, 'is rooted in advancing cooperation in our region; and, to use our capabilities for the benefit of all in our common maritime home'.[19] His plan centres on shared maritime-security capabilities and mutual economic development, joint action in response to emergencies, and adherence to international maritime rules and norms.

Buried in this rhetoric is a pitch for regional connectivity distinct from that offered by China. India refused to participate formally in China's May 2017 BRI forum, citing objections to CPEC as a project that 'ignores [India's] core concerns on sovereignty and territorial integrity' (since it incorporates a highway that traverses territory claimed by India) as well as objections to BRI more broadly, for what India believes is absent: 'universally recognized international norms, good governance, rule of law, openness, transparency and equality'.[20] At a conference in Colombo in September of that same year, Indian officials pressed for a collective definition of Indian Ocean 'identity'.[21] India's Foreign Secretary S. Jaishankar declared, pointedly, that the Indian Ocean 'must be treated as a partner, not as an arena';[22] that it was 'naturally supportive of international norms and rule of law', and 'the world's only English-speaking ocean region'.[23] The implication of the language, albeit phrased diplomatically, is clear: China is not a natural part of the Indian Ocean.

For Modi, apart from the insistence that the region not be Chinese, the scope of the claim that the Indian Ocean is India's ocean has two further dimensions: economics and counter-terrorism. Modi has launched significant initiatives to develop India's port infrastructure, seeking to use the civilian maritime sector as a driver of employment and economic growth.[24] He has also placed an emphasis on coastal and maritime security in counter-terrorism. (Both India's deadliest terror attack, in March 1993 in Bombay, and the November 2008 attack on Mumbai, were seaborne.) The Modi government has overhauled coastal security, and maritime-domain awareness is a central theme in the 2015 Maritime Security Strategy.

This twin emphasis on development and security at home, however, points to a pervasive theme in India's rise and power projection under Modi's leadership: a recognition of limited capabilities and certain kinds of vulnerabilities, and an eagerness to consolidate and build up strength – but not to overstretch. Similarly, the desire to operate away from Chinese influence underscores the importance of the Indian Ocean, but diminishes the logic of projecting Indian power further eastwards, within or close to China's territorial waters. The Indian navy's activities have followed this logic. The navy has clear incentives for a strong operational role in the Indian Ocean and little such incentive for a role that extends to the South China Sea or the broader Pacific Ocean. Meanwhile, it has been pushing back on Chinese presence closer to home.

China: pushback and challenges

In 2017, China established for the first time a permanent naval presence in the Indian Ocean through its first overseas military base in Djibouti, on the Horn of Africa. New Delhi's concerns centre on both Beijing's increasingly assertive policies and China's growing influence in the Indian Ocean, which appears to India as a strategy of encirclement. China's initiatives include port-development projects at Hambantota and Colombo in Sri Lanka, Gwadar in Pakistan, Chittagong in Bangladesh, Kyaukpyu in Myanmar, and reports of the leasing of islets for this purpose in the Maldives, as well as a significant increase in naval deployments in the Indian Ocean, including submarine visits to the ports of Colombo and Karachi. China is also emerging as a supplier of critical naval hardware in the region: it sold two refurbished diesel-electric submarines to Bangladesh in November 2016 and is constructing eight submarines for Pakistan.[25]

India is responding in a number of ways – but each comes with its own challenges. Firstly, it aims to selectively challenge China's infrastructure projects in South Asia with Indian alternatives, including economic support, and port and energy development. In April 2017, for example, India agreed to provide its third line of credit to Bangladesh for $4.5bn, including for port upgrades, having provided $1bn in 2010 and $2bn in 2016. The two countries settled their maritime-border dispute in July 2014 and their land-border dispute in June 2015. India is also pursuing a $2bn investment in Sri Lanka for the development of the port, oil terminals and refinery at Trincomalee; it is also in talks to invest in an airport near Hambantota.

Secondly, India has made a point of appearing as one of the first contributors to humanitarian and disaster-relief operations in its neighbourhood. A key unspoken message of these missions is of India's proximity and preparedness to step in vis-à-vis China.

Thirdly, New Delhi has sought to expand bilateral maritime-security and -defence cooperation with island and littoral states, building on the work of the previous Congress-led government, which provided naval vessels and aircraft to select states while carrying out joint surveillance, patrols and hydrographic surveys of the exclusive economic zones (EEZs) of Mauritius, the Seychelles and the Maldives. The Modi government has provided defence-related lines of credit, and overseen the launch of a coastal-surveillance radar project in the Seychelles; it plans construction and upgrading of an airstrip and jetty on the Mauritian island of Agaléga and Assumption Island in the Seychelles for surveillance purposes.[26] That said, India faces difficulties in these bilateral partnerships. The Indian government's complicated relationship with the Maldives' authoritarian president,

Abdulla Yameen, has been exacerbated by Yameen's outreach towards China. The result is that India's three existing radar stations in the Maldives, connected to India's coastal radar network, are unlikely to be operational, and plans for the construction of seven additional Indian radars in the Maldives are on hold. Indian territory, in the form of Minicoy Island, begins just 90 nautical miles from the northernmost island of the Maldives, and even a medium-range Chinese surveillance radar in the northern Maldives (should the Maldives government allow one to be stationed there) could monitor air activity over India's entire southern peninsula. In the case of Sri Lanka, Indian anxieties centre on the political and security impact of Colombo's indebtedness to China and the December 2017 debt-for-equity swap that has resulted in a Chinese company's control of the Hambantota port. Meanwhile, there is concern in the Seychelles over the Indian construction of a Seychelles coastguard facility on Assumption Island, with a leak in March 2018 of the secret revised India–Seychelles agreement stalling its ratification by the Seychelles parliament.

Fourthly, as China has stepped up assertive patrolling in the South China Sea and increased naval deployments in the Indian Ocean, concerns in New Delhi about active patrols by nuclear-powered Chinese submarines have resulted in a greater emphasis on nuclear deterrence at sea.[27] This has led to a larger role for Indian surveillance and an acceleration of India's drive to put nuclear weapons to sea. The 2015 Maritime Security Strategy underscores that India's nuclear-powered ballistic-missile submarines (SSBNs) aim to give the country's nuclear deterrent 'credibility, effectiveness and survivability'.[28] The *Arihant*, commissioned in 2016 and expected to be the first of five such vessels, carries ballistic missiles with a range of 700 kilometres, with longer-range ballistic missiles of 3,000–5,000km currently under development.[29]

The *Arihant*, however, has been in dock for over a year undergoing repairs following an accident. More broadly, its operational deployment brings specific challenges. In order to prevent accidents and targeted attacks, India's non-sea-based nuclear weapons have traditionally been de-mated, with warheads physically separated from the delivery platforms of aircraft and ballistic missiles. Even if this is still the case for the *Arihant*, de-alerting at sea is unlikely to continue indefinitely, as the rationale for India's sea-based nuclear deterrent is to ensure a 'second-strike' capability. This will require its nuclear weapons and missiles to be pre-mated with the delivery vehicle (or 'canisterised') to form a ready arsenal. Such an arrangement, however, increases vulnerability both to accidents and to targeted attacks at dedicated naval facilities.

Ensuring a high degree of reliability in communication with the submarine at sea is another challenge. The importance of communication at a time of crisis is key. In the event that – unlike nuclear weapons on land or in the air – the submarine's communication from land suddenly ends and alternative means of communication are not successful, it is not clear what action the submarine commander should take. In such circumstances, if political control over nuclear weapons is essential, as required by India's nuclear doctrine, deterrence is likely to fail; but, if deterrence is not to fail, then political control needs to be 'weakened' or transferred to the submarine itself. Neither of these options currently appears acceptable.

Beyond the Indian Ocean: ambition and constraint

In terms of declaratory policy and defence diplomacy, India is certainly looking beyond the Indian Ocean, which helps explain why it is amenable to participating in the Quad, even if it remains reluctant to call it that. India has sought to significantly upgrade its bilateral strategic partnerships with the United States, Japan, Australia and Vietnam. In August 2016, India signed a memorandum of understanding with the United States to provide mutual military access to each country's support facilities, and in December 2016, the US accorded India the status of a 'major defence partner'. India and Japan upgraded their relationship to a 'special strategic and global partnership' in September 2014, institutionalising engagement through various ministerial dialogues. Relations with Australia were upgraded to the level of 'strategic partnership' in 2009, and defence cooperation was expanded in November 2014 to include research, development and industry engagement, with regular defence-ministerial meetings. India provided nine ships to the 2017 iteration of the trilateral *Malabar* exercise with the US and Japanese navies in the Bay of Bengal, its largest-ever contribution. India has also provided Vietnam with patrol boats, a $500 million line of credit for defence spending, access to satellite data for monitoring its own waters, and submarine and combat-aircraft training. A 2018 bilateral joint statement called for strengthening of cooperation in anti-piracy, security of sea lanes and exchange of white-shipping information (data on merchant or cargo ships).[30]

The Modi government has also stepped up its engagement with ASEAN. A joint statement at the January 2018 ASEAN–India Summit in Delhi sought to strengthen maritime cooperation,[31] and the biannual *Milan* exercise took place off the coast of the Andaman and Nicobar Islands, involving the participation of Indonesia, Singapore, Malaysia and Thailand. However, India's embrace of ASEAN, and the importance that the organisation holds in India's 'Act East' strategy, in itself poses an obstacle to India's embrace of the Quad, as India has traditionally supported ASEAN's centrality in matters of regional security.[32]

A similar pattern of rhetorical ambition and practical constraint is visible in India's attitude towards the South China Sea. Indian statements and strategy documents are replete with references to freedom of navigation and overflight, focusing on unimpeded lawful maritime commerce in the South China Sea in accordance with international law, as well as seeking the peaceful resolution of maritime disputes in the region. It is highly unlikely, however, that an Indian government would order the navy to operationally deploy in the South China Sea to protect India's commercial interests. India is also unlikely to carry out freedom-of-navigation operations (FONOPS) in the South China Sea, especially as India itself remains a target of US FONOPS over the issue of prior consent required for military exercises or manoeuvres in India's EEZ or operations at sea. India will almost certainly continue to reject formal invitations to join the United States in joint patrols in the South China Sea. Apart from significant volumes of maritime trade, the only asset India holds in the region is in Vietnam, with Indian oil firm ONGC Videsh conducting oil and gas exploration and exploitation activities on land, on its continental shelf and within its EEZ.

Moreover, even India's strategy in the Indian Ocean can only operate as far as the constraints set by India's naval-expansion programme. The ambitious warship-building programme reportedly seeks to develop a 212-ship navy within the next ten years, up from 138 ships at present (14 submarines, 27 principal surface combatants and nearly 100 patrol and coastal combatants). Virtually all of this is to be based on domestic warship construction, with some 40 ships currently being built in India.[33] India's warship-construction projects, however, continue to suffer from innumerable delays and cost increases. Moreover, only a quarter of the warships currently being built are principal combatants (including aircraft carriers, nuclear-armed ballistic-missile and conventional submarines, and destroyers and frigates).

Meanwhile, the navy is overstretched, compromising its operational effectiveness. A prominent example is the conventional submarine force, where India's total number of submarines is in decline with no follow-on acquisition programme in place. This situation is compounded by the lack of an adequate number of multi-role helicopters and minesweepers. India's defence budget for 2018–19 indicates a nominal increase of 9.5% for the capital side of the armed forces, just about covering 5% inflation and rupee depreciation, resulting in a real increase of less than 5%, with much of it to be spent to cover payments for ongoing acquisitions.[34] India has also, so far, made only partial use of the Andaman and Nicobar Islands in the Bay of Bengal, strategically located close to the Strait of Malacca and Singapore. Although a joint services command exists on the islands, local naval and air deployments remain limited. In short, beyond the Indian Ocean, the 'Pacific' part of Indian naval engagement in the Indo-Pacific will look stronger on paper than it does in practice.

*   *   *

The Indian Ocean is the focus of India's strategic ambition for several reasons. It occupies an influential place in both India's geography and its elite imaginations; it is the locus of India's most pressing strategic interests; and, potentially, it is also the place where India can build and lead a counter-order to China's BRI. Unlike Japan, India's strategic priorities and the intended reach of its sea power extend, to its east, only as far as the Andaman Sea.

Whether the newest iteration of the Quad will thrive where the 2007 edition failed will depend, in part, on understanding the primacy of the Indian Ocean to India and the constraints on its sea-power projection. Having raised expectations, however, the onus is now on the Indian bureaucratic and security establishments to fulfil the commitments it has already made in the Indian Ocean. India's track record in multilateral cooperation in the region is poor, and it is unclear whether existing forums – such as the Indian Ocean Rim Association, whose performance is weak, or the Indian Ocean Naval Symposium, whose achievements are more impressive – will be enough. India will also have to work on its bilateral relations with the Indian Ocean's island and littoral states. In military terms, it is imperative that India effectively build up its capabilities at sea in the Indian Ocean. This is the area where it still has tremendous relative advantage over the Chinese navy, even though Chinese naval expansion may well be narrowing this gap.

For powers outside the region seeking to engage India on maritime-security issues, a sense of Indian priorities combined with a spirit of equal (or preferably, from New Delhi's point of view, junior) partnership will work better than grandiose strategic or infrastructural plans that push India beyond its ambitions and its capabilities. French President Emmanuel Macron's recent visit showed how this can be done.[35]

Acknowledgements

The authors would like to thank Viraj Solanki, IISS Research Analyst for South Asia, for contributing valuable research assistance to this article.

Notes

1 Indian Ministry of External Affairs, 'India–Australia–Japan–U.S. Consultations on Indo-Pacific', 12 November 2017, http://mea.gov.in/press-releases.htm?dtl/29110/IndiaAustraliaJapanUS_Consultations_on_IndoPacific_November_12_2017.

2 Shinzo Abe, speech to the Indian Parliament, New Delhi, 22 August 2007, http://www.mofa.go.jp/region/asia-paci/pmv0708/speech-2.html.

3 Australian Department of Foreign Affairs and Trade, '2017 Foreign Policy White Paper', November 2017, https://www.fpwhitepaper.gov.au/.

4   Demetri Sevastopulo, 'Trump Gives Glimpse of "Indo-Pacific" Strategy to Counter China', 10 November 2017, https://www.ft.com/content/e6d17fd6-c623-11e7-a1d2-6786f39ef675.

5   Indian Ministry of External Affairs, 'India–Australia–Japan–U.S. Consultations on Indo-Pacific'.

6   Louis Nelson, 'In Asia, Trump Keeps Talking About Indo-Pacific', *Politico*, 7 November 2017, https://www.politico.com/story/2017/11/07/trump-asia-indo-pacific-244657.

7   *Ibid*.

8   Indian Ministry of Defence, 'Ensuring Secure Seas: Indian Maritime Security Strategy', October 2015, p. 32, https://www.indiannavy.nic.in/sites/default/files/Indian_Maritime_Security_Strategy_Document_25Jan16.pdf.

9   Premesha Saha, 'The Quad in the Indo-Pacific: Why ASEAN Remains Cautious', ORF Issue Brief, no. 229, 2018, http://www.orfonline.org/research/asean-quad/.

10 Ankit Panda, 'US, Japan, India, and Australia Hold Working-Level Quadrilateral Meeting on Regional Cooperation', *Diplomat*, 13 November 2017, https://thediplomat.com/2017/11/us-japan-india-and-australia-hold-working-level-quadrilateral-meeting-on-regional-cooperation/13 November 2017.

11 Indian Ministry of External Affairs, 'India–Australia–Japan–U.S. Consultations on Indo-Pacific'.

12 White House, 'National Security Strategy of the United States of America', 2017, pp. 45–6, https://www.whitehouse.gov/wp-content/uploads/2017/12/NSS-Final-12-18-2017-0905.pdf.

13 Australian Department of Foreign Affairs and Trade, '2017 Foreign Policy White Paper'.

14 Japanese Ministry of Foreign Affairs, 'Diplomatic Bluebook 2017', p. 27, http://www.mofa.go.jp/files/000290287.pdf.

15 Indian Ministry of Defence, 'Ensuring Secure Seas', p. 32.

16 David Scott, 'The Indian Ocean as India's Ocean', in David M. Malone et al. (eds), *The Oxford Handbook of Indian Foreign Policy* (Oxford: Oxford University Press, 2015), p. 469.

17 Michael Pugh, 'Is Mahan Still Alive? State Naval Power in the International System', *Journal of Conflict Studies*, vol. 16, no. 2, 1996. See also C. Raja Mohan, *Samudra Manthan: Sino-Indian Rivalry in the Indo-Pacific* (Washington DC: Brookings Institution Press, 2012).

18 Scott, 'The Indian Ocean as India's Ocean', p. 468.

19 Narendra Modi, 'Text of the PM's Remarks on the Commissioning of Coast Ship Barracuda', Port Louis, Mauritius, 12 March 2015, https://www.narendramodi.in/text-of-the-pms-remarks-on-the-commissioning-of-coast-ship-barracuda-2954.

20 Government of India, 'Official Spokesperson's Response to a Query on Participation of India in OBOR/BRI Forum', New Delhi, 13 May 2017, http://mea.gov.in/media-briefings.htm?dtl/28463/Official+Spokespersons+response+to+a+query+on+participation+of+India+in+OBORBRI+Forum.

21 P.K. Balachandran, 'India Presses for Consensus on "Indian Ocean Identity"', *South Asian Monitor*, 4 September 2017, https://southasianmonitor.com/2017/09/04/

india-presses-consensus-indian-ocean-identity/.

22 S. Jaishankar, address to the Indian Ocean Conference, Colombo, 1 September 2017, http://mea.gov.in/ Speeches-Statements.htm?dtl/28909/ Foreign+Secretarys+Address+to+the+ Indian+Ocean+Conference+Colombo.

23 Balachandran, 'India Presses for Consensus'.

24 Narendra Modi, 'PM Modi's address at the inauguration of Maritime India Summit 2016', Mumbai, 14 April 2016, https://www.narendramodi. in/pm-modi-at-the-inauguration-of-maritime-india-summit-2016-in-mumbai-440341.

25 Rahul Roy-Chaudhury, 'India Counters China in the Indian Ocean', IISS Voices, 25 August 2017, http:// www.iiss.org/en/iiss%20voices/ blogsections/iiss-voices-2017-adeb/ august-2b48/indian-ocean-ecba.

26 Rahul Roy-Chaudhury, 'India's Perspective Towards China in Their Shared South Asian Neighbourhood: Cooperation Versus Competition', Contemporary Politics, vol. 24, no. 1, p. 107.

27 Sylvia Mishra, 'Nuclear Weapons and Capabilities in the Indian Ocean: An Indian Perspective', ORF Commentaries, 26 April 2017, http:// www.orfonline.org/research/nuclear-weapons-and-capabilities-in-the-indian-ocean-an-indian-perspective/.

28 Indian Ministry of Defence, 'Ensuring Secure Seas', p. 48.

29 Vice Admiral (Retd) Vijay Shankar, 'Deterrence at Sea: India's Evolving Options', IISS, London, 31 March 2017, https://www.iiss.org/en/events/ events/archive/2016-a3c2/march-1194/ deterrence-at-sea---indias-evolving-options-104a.

30 Government of India, 'India–Vietnam Joint Statement During State Visit of President of Vietnam to India', 3 March 2018, http://www.mea.gov.in/ bilateral-documents.htm?dtl/29535/ IndiaVietnam+Joint+Statement+during +State+visit+of+President+of+Vietnam +to+India+March+03+2018.

31 Government of India, 'Delhi Declaration of the ASEAN–India Commemorative Summit to Mark the 25th Anniversary of ASEAN–India Dialogue Relations', New Delhi, 25 January 2018, http://mea.gov.in/ bilateral-documents.htm?dtl/29386/ Delhi+Declaration+of+the+ASEANInd ia+Commemorative+Summit+to+mark +the+25th+Anniversary+of+ASEANIn dia+Dialogue+Relations.

32 Saha, 'The Quad in the Indo-Pacific'.

33 Rajat Pandit, 'Eye on China: India Steps Up Naval Deployments, Kicks Off Nuclear Submarine Project', Times of India, 2 December 2017, https:// timesofindia.indiatimes.com/india/ eye-on-china-india-steps-up-naval-deployments-kicks-off-nuclear-submarines-project/articleshow/61882815.cms.

34 Rahul Roy-Chaudhury, 'India Emerges as World's Big Defence Spender', India Global Business, March 2018, http://www.indiaglobalbusiness. indiaincorporated.com/india-emerges-worlds-big-defence-spender/.

35 Government of India, 'India–France Joint Statement During State Visit of President of France to India', 10 March 2018, http://www.mea.gov.in/bilateral-documents.htm?dtl/29596/IndiaFrance +Joint+Statement+during+State+visit+ of+President+of+France+to+India+Ma rch+10+2018.

Review Essay

Governing Fantasyland

John A. Gans, Jr

Fantasyland: How America Went Haywire – A 500-Year History
Kurt Andersen. New York: Random House, 2017. $30.00. 462 pp.

In late October 2016, a few days before the US presidential election, a poll of more than 1,000 Americans asked respondents not who they wanted to win but who they *believed* would win the contest between Republican businessman Donald Trump and Democrat Hillary Rodham Clinton, a former secretary of state and US senator.[1] Nearly 70% of those surveyed were sure Clinton would win, an assumption shared by much of official Washington, as well as by observers in capitals, boardrooms and military headquarters around the world. Even the Republican candidate himself was pessimistic about his chances, according to recent reports on the mood at Trump Tower in New York at the end of the campaign.[2]

With Trump's surprising triumph, he took the helm of a country that had 'passed through the looking glass and down the rabbit hole', says journalist Kurt Andersen in his ambitious new book, *Fantasyland* (p. 6). According to Andersen, the 2016 election is the epitome of half a millennium of American acceptance of, and addiction to, the 'supernatural and miraculous' (p. 5), the preposterous and absurd. The election is cited as just the latest example in a long litany of fantastic episodes, though the author nearly loses his balance

John A. Gans, Jr, runs the Global Order Program at the University of Pennsylvania's Perry World House and is a fellow at the German Marshall Fund. These views are his own.

Survival | vol. 60 no. 3 | June–July 2018 | pp. 195–202   DOI 10.1080/00396338.2018.1470774

trying to prove just how far 'overboard' the citizens of Fantasyland have gone (p. 5).

The author blames the American people themselves for Trump's unlikely and unexpected victory, and for the nation's descent into fantasyland. But this judgement lets too many institutions and individuals, including journalists like Andersen, off the hook. The 2016 election was not decided only by Trump's successes, Clinton's failures or Russia's interference, but by the collapsing credibility of American elites. It is that deficit, which only grew with the mis-forecasting of the election itself, that poses the biggest risk to the United States as it faces a complicated and potentially dangerous world.

NEW YORK TIMES BESTSELLER

FANTASYLAND

How America
Went Haywire

A 500-YEAR HISTORY

KURT ANDERSEN

'Experts be damned'

Having published his diagnosis in 2017, Andersen sees the symptoms of an addiction to fantasy among Americans dating back to the country's earliest days. He tracks the journeys of fanatical migrants from the pews of European churches to the ports of New World cities, noting that such immigrants tended not just to survive the journey to the United States, but to thrive once there. In the years that followed, according to Andersen, the descendants of these believers have, amid religious fads, gold and land frenzies, business revolutions and cultural upheavals, given themselves over 'to all kinds of magical thinking, anything-goes relativism, and belief in fanciful explanation, small and large fantasies that console or thrill or terrify' (p. 5).

Despite an onslaught of historical examples – Joseph McCarthy's anti-communist purge, Walt Disney's amusement parks, Hugh Hefner's centrefolds – there is little besides Andersen's personal perspective holding *Fantasyland* together. An American himself, Andersen believes he has experienced his country's descent first-hand, and he has prepared a history of it that conforms with his own reaction to, and worries about, the phenomenon. Writing as a Nebraskan 'born in the middle of the century in the middle of the country to middle-class parents' (p. 150), Andersen argues that Americans are susceptible to fantasies because of who they are. 'Being American', he argues, 'means we can believe any damn thing we want, that our beliefs are equal or superior to anyone else's, experts be damned' (p. 7). Because he so rarely directs his gaze beyond America's shores, his assessment that Americans are 'much more' inclined to believe in the supernatural 'than the other billion or two people in the rich world' (p. 5) feels like a stretch. There are surely more than a few fantasy-loving Germans, Italians, Chinese and Indians out there, but the author takes little notice of them.

Nor does Andersen care much for America's religious affinities. The book's unapologetic bias against religion, organised or not, is its author's most exhausting and counterproductive preoccupation. Andersen's easy and occasionally slapdash dispatch of the core beliefs of much of humanity hurts his argument in the end. Despite his willingness to concede that, in addition to the harmful variety, there are victimless and even helpful fantasies, no religion receives the benefit of the doubt.

Although Andersen admits there are some virtues of fantastical thinking, he worries more about the drawbacks. Believing anything, according to the author, eventually means 'the world turns inside out, and no cause-and-effect connection is fixed. The credible becomes incredible and the incredible credible' (p. 7). As a result, Americans have proven particularly zealous, if not downright crazy, about the religious, the nationalist, the fabulist and the occasional con. They have shown a tendency to panic over witches, communism, Satan and more, and to fall for salesmen, shamans, showmen and charlatans. And they have seen gunmen on grassy knolls and in black helicopters where none exist.

Andersen is worried about how much worse America's fantastic thinking has grown over the last half-century. He cites two major developments which he believes have accelerated the country's descent into delusion. The first is the arrival in the 1960s of what Andersen describes as a 'new rule set' for Americans' 'mental operating systems' (p. 9). During that turbulent decade, personal truth came to be seen as more important than objective facts, as summed up by the exhortation to 'do your own thing, find your own reality' (p. 9). The later and more consequential development was the arrival of a new era of information and communications driven by technological developments at the end of the twentieth century, which have allowed America's fantasies to look and feel far more real.

The author concedes that psychologists believe that stress can trigger delusions, and that fantasy can provide not just distraction but genuine relief from the pressures of day-to-day life. Yet the shocks that attended the dawn of the twenty-first century, including the 9/11 attacks and the global financial crisis, receive scant attention in his book. The past 20 years have, after all, seen more than enough change to make even rational individuals seek the comfort and comradeship offered by the conspiracy theories available on the World Wide Web and elsewhere.

Even innocent escapism, however, has become, in Andersen's opinion, the cause of a national unravelling. Although the author acknowledges that the United States is still relatively rich, powerful and free, he argues that 'our drift toward credulity, doing our own thing, and having an altogether uncertain grip on reality has overwhelmed our other exceptional national traits and turned us into a less-developed country as well' (p. 11). As Americans become less attuned to the real world, their country becomes less able to manage challenges and pursue opportunities, both at home and abroad.

'It will not end'

Andersen's '500-year history' of American freak-outs includes relatively little discussion of foreign policy, save a few mentions of the Cold War. Yet it is in the global arena where America's fantastical thinking – the wishful and whimsical judgements that have underpinned several of the country's wars and other foreign-policy larks – is exposed to the harshest light. Despite being mugged by reality time and again, fantasyland's foreign policy has proven remarkably persistent.

While the 1960s is accorded no fewer than five chapters in Andersen's book, the war that dominated that decade is only briefly discussed. This is surprising given that the Vietnam War is among the best – and bloodiest – examples of how wrong American fantasies can go. Driven by trumped-up fears about communist infiltration at home and the prospect of another domino falling to communism abroad, American policymakers drew a line in Southeast Asia and sent hundreds of thousands of Americans to fight –

and die – over it. More than a decade of combat would eventually reveal that these driving concerns were largely fantastical.

Yet the Vietnam model of American foreign policy has been used again and again, particularly when the Cold War ended and especially after the 9/11 attacks. With few external constraints, Washington, either encouraged by or encouraging popular fears, has time and again sent American forces abroad in search of monsters to destroy. The costs of these misadventures have been high, not just in terms of casualties (American and otherwise), but also in undermining the credibility of the foreign-policy elites and institutions who promoted each decision.

After 9/11, the United States embarked on a 'global war on terror'. Even as scholars and experts took pains to explain that it was fantasy to believe that a tactic as old as time could be defeated, policymakers in Washington proceeded to set an unrealistically high bar for success. In the days after the 2001 attacks, then-president George W. Bush declared, 'Our war on terror begins with al Qaeda, but it does not end there. It will not end until every terrorist group of global reach has been found, stopped and defeated.'[3] Seventeen years later, the fight drags on.

The Iraq War was perhaps the most fantastical episode of this endless ordeal. Not only did the country play no role in 9/11, it was militarily contained in the wake of the 1991 Gulf War. Yet Saddam Hussein, armed with what many assumed to be a massive WMD programme, was enough of a bogeyman to whip the nation into a frenzy for a war that resulted in the deaths of more than 4,000 Americans and many more Iraqis, and ultimately threw the Middle East's power dynamics badly off kilter.

Another casualty of the Iraq War, and the broader 'war on terrorism', has been Washington's credibility. As America's latest fantasy foundered in the deserts of the Middle East with few apologies or admission of failure, Bush's popularity, and that of his political party, took a beating. Barack Obama, who publicly challenged the core assumptions of the foreign-policy establishment, resoundingly won the White House from the Republicans. And soon after, when Washington's elites, Democrat and Republican alike, began to warn of a new threat, this time at home, few Americans heeded their expert advice.

'Breakdown of a shared public reality'

Unsurprisingly, Andersen draws a crooked line through all this woeful history to the campaign and election of Donald Trump. While some might interpret Trump's presidency, and the 'post-truth, alternative facts' moment he has both fostered and benefited from, as 'some inexplicable and crazy *new* American phenomenon' (p. 11, emphasis in original), Andersen sees Trump as 'empirical proof' of his book's argument. Indeed, he admits to finding Trump's rise and victory 'a little gratifying' (p. 417). The author has had a long, contentious relationship with the president, having covered, and satirically needled, Trump for decades as a journalist. He suggests that Trump was smart and strategic enough to run for president at a moment when the 'critical mass of Americans had decided politics were all a show and a sham' (p. 421). As such, Trumpism is the 'ultimate extrapolation and expression of attitudes and instincts that have made America exceptional for its entire history' (p. 11).

If anything, Andersen's account demonstrates that neither Americans' tendency to believe, nor the willingness of charlatans to take advantage of this tendency, are new phenomena. Indeed, Trump's pitch was built on the politics of numerous nationalist and populist predecessors, such as McCarthy. Even the campaign slogan he embroidered on red hats, 'Make America Great Again', was recycled from president Ronald Reagan.

What was new in 2016 was not that Americans refused to listen to reason, but how damaged the voices of reason had become. No one can say that there were no warnings about Trump. Throughout the campaign, experts from nearly every field – including, for example, the two 2012 contenders for president, Obama and Republican governor Mitt Romney – explained how abnormal Trump's message was and how dangerous his promised policies could prove to be. Their warnings fell on enough deaf ears in Pennsylvania and other swing states to allow Trump to eke out a narrow electoral-college victory.

That victory is but one example of how the expertise of American elites and institutions has proven insufficient to counteract the allure of fantasy and its most adept peddlers, including Trump. This is probably in part because of technological progress: information, and misinformation, is moving faster and faster. There is a cyclical element to this problem as well. Andersen's chapters track the ebbs and flows of incredulity, and after a hyper-rational presidency like Obama's, perhaps it was just time for a more fantastical one. Just as likely is that, after almost two decades of war and crisis during which political, military, corporate and cultural messengers have over-promised and under-delivered, America's rational voices no longer command the respect they might otherwise have done.

Many of these same voices have offered criticisms of Trump's decisions, on trade and climate change, Russia, North Korea and more, every day since his inauguration. But by suggesting (incorrectly so far) that each presidential tweet risks the end of American leadership in the world, or worse, a Third World War, these already compromised advocates for a more rational course are only further weakening themselves at a moment fraught with risk. There are real dangers ahead, as China continues to rise, Russia continues to provoke and terrorists continue to threaten. Credibility-starved elites should be focused on picking their fights and getting them right.

American 'bender'?

Andersen correctly points out that for much of American history, 'fantasist and realist impulses existed in rough balance, with a powerful animating tension between' them. The balance served as a kind of societal motor in which 'every idiosyncratic vision and dreamy ambition' was 'permitted to ignite – but with control mechanisms and gaskets and a sturdy engine block' that kept the 'contraption from blasting apart' (pp. 430–1).

This evocative imagery suggests a way forward. Andersen blames fantasy addicts for how badly imbalanced America has become and writes of his hope that the nation's 'bender', the consequence of 'guzzling too much fantasy cocktail for too long', is a relatively short detour (p. 11). To him and many others, the 2016 presidential election and its effects represent rock bottom, a national wake-up call to start seeing the world for what it is and to allow rational impulses to dominate for a while.

But a smarter course, for a country in which one person's fantasy is another's American dream, and where revolutionary thinkers have frequently improved how people live, think, create and fight, may be to shore up its engine block. Andersen's book should serve as a reminder not just of how fantastical American thinking can become, but also how vital its most realistic thinkers are. If the nation's more rational voices are strengthened, they can once again serve to balance those less worried about reality. Rebuilding credibility is never easy, especially in the midst of a bender, but the first step for American elites is admitting there is a problem.

Notes

1   Jennifer Agiesta, 'Poll: Most See a Hillary Clinton Victory and a Fair Count Ahead', CNN, 25 October 2016, https://www.cnn.com/2016/10/25/politics/hillary-clinton-2016-election-poll/index.html.

2   Michael Wolff, 'Donald Trump Didn't Want to Be President', *New York*, 3 January 2018, http://nymag.com/daily/intelligencer/2018/01/michael-wolff-fire-and-fury-book-donald-trump.html.

3   George W. Bush, 'Address Before a Joint Session of the Congress on the United States Response to the Terrorist Attacks of September 11', 20 September 2001, available from the American Presidency Project at http://www.presidency.ucsb.edu/ws/?pid=64731.

Book Reviews

Africa
'Funmi Olonisakin

Another Fine Mess: America, Uganda, and the War on Terror
Helen C. Epstein. New York: Columbia Global Reports, 2017.
£10.99/$14.99. 262 pp.

Two decades ago, Uganda's President Yoweri Museveni was considered one of 'a new breed of African leaders', a characterisation popularised by former US president Bill Clinton. The leaders of Uganda, Rwanda, Ethiopia and Eritrea seemed atypical – reforming and progressive – in a region that was grappling with the challenges of armed conflict and long-term authoritarian rule. Subsequent events have led many to question the accuracy of this perception.

Helen Epstein locates Museveni at the epicentre of a post-Cold War 'storm' in which US alliances with a select group of African dictators, intended to address terrorism (among other threats), fuelled six wars in eastern and central Africa (p. 20). Millions died, and a new terrorist group, al-Shabaab, emerged. Epstein argues that not only has Museveni's government done well out of this, but that the Ugandan president succeeded in manipulating his American and European benefactors in the service of his own agenda. Uganda in this period received more than $20 billion in aid and debt relief, in addition to heavy military assistance. The author's ultimate conclusion is that the interconnected wars and related insecurities in Rwanda, Congo, Sudan, South Sudan and Somalia were intensified or reignited by Museveni; and that the US, along with its European partners, enabled much of the violence by providing development aid. It is a compelling argument.

US support to Museveni's government began shortly after a militant Islamist government came to power in Sudan. Uganda received assistance to train the

Survival | vol. 60 no. 3 | June–July 2018 | pp. 203–210   DOI 10.1080/00396338.2018.1470777

Sudan People's Liberation Army, which would wage a long war in Sudan. In retaliation, Sudan armed the Lord's Resistance Army rebel group in northern Uganda (p. 83). Museveni would later play a role in the events that preceded the Rwandan genocide in 1994. Three years before the genocide, the Rwandan Patriotic Front, trained and armed by Uganda, invaded Rwanda (p. 103). Epstein finds the US complicit in this invasion: Uganda acquired ten times more American weapons in 1991 than at any time in the previous ten years, and US foreign aid to the country was almost doubled.

Following the Rwandan genocide, the new Rwandan army pursued *genocidaires* into the Democratic Republic of the Congo (DRC) and forced many Hutu refugees to return. Then the armies of Rwanda and Uganda, alongside the Alliance of Democratic Forces for the Liberation of Congo (which the two countries had trained), invaded the DRC, toppled Mobutu Sese Seko and installed Laurent Kabila as president. Both countries returned to war in 1998 after a falling out with Kabila, who was assassinated in 2001 and replaced by his son, Joseph. Epstein finds the Ugandan army to have been complicit in the looting of mineral resources in the DRC around this time. Museveni is also found to have made a significant contribution to the escalation and prolongation of conflict in Somalia and South Sudan.

Epstein explains how Museveni was able to pull this off. His rise to power in Uganda coincided with a post-Cold War climate in which militant Islam was on the rise. Several African states seen as being predisposed to supporting militant Islam were designated as 'state sponsors of terror', while others were deemed to be 'failed states' and therefore potential breeding grounds for terrorists. An equally urgent concern was that Africa's rich natural-resource endowment – unexploited gold, diamonds, uranium and oil, among others – could fall under the control of such states. Uganda's neighbours, including Sudan, Somalia and the DRC, were seen as critically important to US national security. Museveni became an indispensable ally. Epstein makes a convincing case that he also helped himself.

Congo's Violent Peace: Conflict and Struggle Since the Great African War
Kris Berwouts. London: Zed Books, 2017. £16.99/$24.95. 193 pp.

In this study of the unstable peace that has become a feature of life in the DRC, Kris Berwouts identifies three mutually reinforcing features of a conflict that has simmered for the last two decades: the perennial struggle for power in Kinshasa; export of the Rwandan civil war into the DRC; and the illegal exploitation of the country's mineral resources.

The so-called Great African War began in 1996, when Rwanda and Uganda supported the relatively weak Alliance of Democratic Forces for the Liberation of Congo in a rebellion that toppled Mobutu Sese Seko. Rwanda and Uganda returned to war in 1998, this time against Laurent Kabila. Angola, Zimbabwe and Namibia, meanwhile, joined the war on Kabila's side. All of these actors participated in the illegal exploitation of the DRC's natural resources.

Although an All-Inclusive Agreement was signed in Pretoria in 2002; a transitional government became operational in 2003; troops deployed by foreign governments left the country; and the 2006 elections legitimised Laurent's son Joseph as president following his father's assassination, a stable peace eluded the DRC. Several non-state armed groups, both foreign and Congolese, remained. Eastern Congo in particular was the site of considerable instability. Ineffective security-sector reform saw actors such as rebel leader Laurent Nkunda gain influence (p. 73). It took cooperation between the Rwandan and Congolese governments to flush out Nkunda's National Congress for the Defence of the People, and to dismantle the Democratic Forces for the Liberation of Rwanda in North Kivu. Although the contested 2011 election results consolidated Kabila's power, instability returned in 2012 with the Rwanda-supported M23 insurgency, which decimated Goma. A UN-led operation was required to halt the rebellion.

Berwouts rejects claims that the regional war and the plundering of the DRC's natural resources are the root causes of instability, pointing instead to the historical evolution of complex patterns of interaction between the environment and governance in the region. Even before colonialism, kingdoms and clans competed for access to land in eastern Congo due to increasing demographic pressure. Population movements were fluid as kingdoms expanded and contracted. Colonialism would introduce a permanency to the boundaries with Rwanda under German control and Congo under King Leopold II of Belgium. Land tenure and use became monetised. A policy in which migrant labourers (particularly Rwandans) came to work on colonial plantations created a dichotomy between foreigners and indigenous people, which would create tensions over land and the status of migrants.

Mobutu manipulated these policies to serve his political ends. The Law on Nationality, passed in 1972, accorded citizenship to anyone who had immigrated to the Congo before 1960. Hence, Rwandan populations in eastern Congo could enjoy citizenship rights. Mobutu revised this law in 1981 so that only those residents whose ancestors were in the Congo before 1885 were entitled to citizenship. This paralysed the country's political life. Scheduled elections could not be held, for example. The rapid militarisation of communities in the Kivu region warned of the instability that was to come. Given Kabila's failure to address the underlying causes of the regional war that ensued, and to hold elections in 2016, it seems reasonable to predict further instability.

The Horn of Africa: State Formation and Decay
Christopher Clapham. London: C. Hurst & Co., 2017.
£17.99/$27.95. 224 pp.

Christopher Clapham successfully depicts the Horn of Africa as much more than the disaster zone it is widely perceived to be. The Horn is an anomaly in Africa: it is the only region in which secessionist movements have secured independence for portions of existing states. This is significant for a continent whose post-colonial leaders agreed to preserve the borders inherited from colonial times to prevent rampant wars. The Horn is further distinguished by the fact that the Ethiopian empire was the only indigenous sub-Saharan African state to have survived the period of colonial domination. The region is also distinctive in geographical terms: Clapham describes it as one of the most 'seismologically active' areas in the world (p. 8).

Notwithstanding external influences, the dynamics of state formation and reconstruction in the Horn are 'home grown', according to Clapham. The densely populated 'highland core', covering areas from Asmara to Addis Ababa, is conducive to arable farming, adaptable to hierarchical governance and practises Orthodox Christianity in the main. In sharp contrast, the less densely populated, pastoralist 'lowland periphery', which includes much of the Somali territories, resists hierarchical governance while relying on social organisation based on lineage. The dominant religion here is Sunni Islam. Clapham notes that among pastoralist communities, borders are not rigidly defined, and the state constitutes an alien form of domination. However, people of the 'highland periphery' are mostly excluded from existing state structures.

A struggle for power in the Horn eventually led to intra- and inter-state wars and state failure. In 1991, the Tigrayan People's Liberation Front (TPLF) emerged victorious in Ethiopia, while the Eritrean People's Liberation Front (EPLF) took power in Eritrea after engaging in guerrilla warfare for a quarter of a century. Meanwhile, contestation among warring clans and warlords in Somalia led to the disintegration of the state.

Reconstruction efforts were confronted with the contradictions inherent in the Horn's geophysical character and political history. In Ethiopia, the TPLF essentially inherited a state, albeit one it sought to change (ethnic federalism replaced an over-centralised state, for example). The EPLF, meanwhile, did not inherit state institutions in Eritrea. It sought to create its own type of state, rejecting all other models, whether African or Western.

The war between Ethiopia and Eritrea from 1998 to 2000 was a major blow to the reconstruction of Eritrea, which was decisively beaten (p. 120). Illiberal as Eritrea's state-building process might have been, it benefited from a highland-core population accepting of centralised, disciplined, hierarchical governance (p. 135). In Somalia, things have been much more complex. Characteristic of the lowland periphery, the country's weakly organised insurgencies have been unable to transform into effective governments. Rather, they seem to have gravitated toward indigenous forms of social organisation, particularly along clan lines.

Of the Somali territories, only Djibouti has managed to effectively adopt a regular pattern of statehood. The interventions in central Somalia focusing on the capital city of Mogadishu have produced tragic consequences. Somaliland has a stable governance arrangement; and Puntland has built a relatively effective system of administration. The social base provided by pastoralism has persisted (p. 142).

Clapham seems convinced that the Horn will remain in flux as the interactions between highland and lowland, Islam and Christianity, and various forms of settled governance and statelessness produce constant change (p. 193).

Understanding Zimbabwe: From Liberation to Authoritarianism
Sara Rich Dorman. London: C. Hurst & Co., 2016.
£17.99/$27.95. 347 pp.

Sara Rich Dorman provides a robust explanation for the longevity of the Mugabe-led regime in Zimbabwe, analysing the interests, coercive power and underlying public discourse that sustained the Mugabe regime over a 37-year period.

Zimbabwe's trajectory typifies nationalist movements that fought and won wars of liberation, particularly in the way its government has sought to project a coherent national narrative. Dorman argues that, beyond serving to legitimise the regime, post-independence rhetoric of a hard-fought liberation and expectations of unity and solidarity often masks internal contradictions and struggles within nationalist movements. She suggests that the liberation struggle that culminated in Mugabe's rise to power in Zimbabwe was non-monolithic, and indeed 'profoundly ambiguous' (p. 30).

Dorman identifies several contributing factors to the survival and longevity of the Mugabe regime. For most of the ten years that followed independence, the regime focused on a politics of inclusion. Successes in the liberation war and a sizeable victory in the independence elections enabled the new government to bring the disparate elements of the nationalist movement together. By shifting public discourse to 'unity, development and nationalism', the nationalist movement was successfully demobilised. At the same time, the regime's legislative and security powers borrowed much from the oppressive laws of the Rhodesian state. The signing of the Unity Accord, in which the former opposition party was merged with the ruling party to create the Zimbabwe African National Union–Patriotic Front (ZANU–PF), ushered Zimbabwe toward a one-party state (p. 42).

Mugabe's regime would experience increasing contestation in the following decade because of damaging allegations of corruption and economic downturn. New forces of political opposition were also emerging amid a growing and vibrant civil society. Still, the regime succeeded in stymying the debate among academics, lawyers and the student community about the logic of a socialist, one-party state. Dorman argues compellingly that the regime's durability during this period can be attributed to a combination of 'strategic policy responses, rhetoric and the distribution of benefits' (p. 113).

The relationship between the state and society began to show signs of increasing polarisation from around 1998 as civil society became more confident and articulate. The establishment of a National Constituent Assembly triggered a debate in which the regime's development agenda and liberation credentials were challenged. The regime established a Constitutional Commission and called for a referendum on a new constitution in 2000, which it lost. By then, the nationalist rhetoric that had served its purpose in previous decades had lost some of its effectiveness.

Continuing economic challenges, corruption and declining social services were soon to create real problems for the regime. Following its defeat in the referendum, it began to dabble in the politics of exclusion by distributing 'incentives' to select groups (p. 141). The subjects of land reform and the needs of war veterans became more prominent. Dorman shows how the regime's 'discursive and material strategies' came under threat as the economy continued to decline and the country's infrastructure collapsed (p. 186). The opposition struggled to assert itself in the face of the government's exclusionary politics, and was subject to intimidation, including violent attacks.

ZANU–PF's defeat in the parliamentary elections of 2008 gave prominence to the opposition Movement for Democratic Change for the first time. The violence that surrounded the presidential elections, which went into a second round of voting, was also unprecedented. The signing of a Global Political Agreement, which allowed for power-sharing between Mugabe and prime minister Morgan Tsvangirai, only served to strengthen Mugabe and ZANU–PF, whose control of the country's security institutions remained intact. Winner-take-all politics became the order of the day. In the absence of a convincing alternative narrative of citizenship and nationhood, the ground was ceded to 'nationalist public intellectuals' (p. 212).

One year after the publication of this book, Robert Mugabe resigned as president of Zimbabwe. ZANU–PF immediately took steps to consolidate itself in power.

Continental Shift: An Investigative Journey into Africa's 21st Century
Kevin Bloom and Richard Poplak. London: Portobello Books, 2016. £14.99. 419 pp.

Continental Shift is the product of Kevin Bloom and Richard Poplak's ten-year quest to discover what defines Africa, a mission that took them to at least one-third of the continent's 54 states. Here, the authors present findings from research undertaken in ten of the countries visited between 2011 and 2015, each of which illustrates some aspect of the significant change being seen on the continent. Along the way, they offer a gripping narrative about twenty-first-century Africa.

Despite the prevalence of the 'Africa rising' narrative, which suggests that Africa is experiencing unprecedented economic growth and the emergence of a middle class, the evidence suggests that the rise in earning power is neither consistent nor sustainable. In Namibia, for example, the authors illustrate the double-edged nature of China's economic presence. On the one hand, an abundance of low-cost, Chinese-made products offers opportunities to Namibian youth to engage in informal economic activities, thus enhancing their social mobility (p. 17). On the other hand, the influx of thousands of Chinese workers into a construction industry largely controlled by Chinese firms poses a challenge for the local labour force and the country's labour laws.

Botswana, by all accounts, has been a success story for decades, consistently registering the highest per capita growth of any country in Africa over an extended period. It is also rated highly in terms of economic freedom and the independence of the judiciary (p. 53). Bloom and Poplak describe how these values were severely tested when China's largest firms took over the construction of prestigious projects, including hydropower. Botswana's institutions did not buckle under the pressure of public controversy, but rather subjected Chinese firms and their performance to close scrutiny (p. 85).

In the DRC, the authors consider the controversial but significant issue of Africa's mines. Noting that the country has a mineral reserve estimated to be worth three-quarters of the combined GDP of Europe and the US (p. 191), they discuss the effects of competing interests among neighbouring states, multinationals and some state-owned corporations, with an emphasis on the competition between China and the West. The signing of what was to become one of the largest deals in Sino-African history in 2007, promising the DRC's resources in exchange for infrastructure, signalled the consolidation of China's position as a significant actor in Africa (pp. 197–8).

Nigeria stands out in the authors' analysis not least for its size, and for the rich cultural output of 'Nollywood', the country's film industry. This home-grown project has survived in spite of the failures of the state – indeed, it could be seen as a response to these failings – and receives neither Chinese nor Western assistance (p. 135). The authors highlight Nollywood's disruptive power as an industry with a massive local consumer base, describing it as a necessary African resource (p. 170).

Bloom and Poplak also present impressive findings from Ethiopia, where they interrogate the 'supremely controversial and yet supremely important matter of Africa's farms' (p. 256). They also visit South Sudan, where the lessons of history are ostensibly being used to create a state from scratch; and Central African Republic, where the struggle against a historical narrative imposed from the outside continues.

The authors conclude that Africa's greatest strengths – 'her ethnic diversity, growing population, vast landmass and boundless commodities' (p. 356) – are also the continent's greatest weaknesses.

Latin America
Russell Crandall

China, the United States, and the Future of Latin America
David B.H. Denoon, ed. New York: New York University Press, 2017. $38.00. 419 pp.

Back in spring 2005, the George W. Bush administration held a National Security Council deputies committee meeting on a novel topic: China's interests in Latin America. Before the turn of the century, US policymakers had given little thought to any serious Chinese gambit in Washington's historic geopolitical backyard. Overnight, or so it seemed at the time, China was vastly expanding its economic, political and military footprint in the region, leaving US policymakers flummoxed. Adding to the policy anxiety, nativist politicians – almost exclusively Republicans – were 'seeing Red' in China's actions and thus clamouring for an aggressive American defence of its hemispheric privileges and dominion.

In the past 20 years, China has made itself into a vital actor in the Middle East, Africa and Latin America. In each of these areas, it appears that economic, political, military and technological agency are of primary importance to Beijing. Between 2007 and 2012, Sino-Latin American trade surged from $100 billion to $250bn, eclipsing Chinese trade with the European Union. Indeed, China is now the biggest trading associate of more than half of the economies in the hemisphere.

Edited by New York University scholar David H. Denoon, *China, the United States, and the Future of Latin America* shows us that one of the principle challenges in evaluating the state of Chinese involvement in Latin America is deciphering what this opaque regime actually covets in the region. Does it merely desire a stable supply of trade, especially primary-resource imports? Or, as hawkish Republicans continue to insist, are there ulterior, more deleterious (at least from Washington's perspective) motives in play?

Professor Denoon explains that, unlike in the South China Sea, where Beijing's construction of airfields and military outposts is a threatening and ongoing development, there is no equivalent threat in the western hemisphere – for now. It is not out of the question, though, that China would at some point develop a significant military or strategic relationship with leftist regimes in Nicaragua, Cuba or Venezuela. In an excellent, sober chapter, Professor R. Evan Ellis writes that Beijing's security strategy in the region is 'principally long-term and indirect', and 'widely misunderstood' (p. 341). He contends that US policymakers will invariably play a role, for good or ill, in shaping China's

 DOI 10.1080/00396338.2018.1470778

engagement. The last thing Washington should do is try to summarily check Beijing's presence in the region. Much better, he thinks, would be to shape China's permanent involvement through bilateral and multilateral consultation and exercises. He rightly adds that excluding China from Latin America – assuming this could even be accomplished – would not necessarily be good either for US goals or for those of other governments in the hemisphere. With the Trump administration pushing its white-nationalist, America First agenda at home and abroad, we should not look for nuance, and thus success, on this key topic for the foreseeable future.

Close but No Cigar: A True Story of Prison Life in Castro's Cuba
Stephen Purvis. London: Weidenfeld & Nicolson, 2017. £18.99.
256 pp.

When British-born developer and architect Stephen Purvis – the author of this riveting but analytically incomplete memoir – first visited Cuba in 1997, he found there a desperate, almost starving population and a central government badly short of cash. He writes, for example, of walking into a massive grocery store that contained only a single aisle of 5 kilogram cans of Polish pickled cabbage and bags and bags of local sugar. 'The whole country felt and smelt like a pair of tramp's trousers', he recalls, 'held up by nothing more than old string and forlorn duty' (p. 17).

Despite this arresting first impression, three years later Purvis moved to Havana with his spouse and four young children to pursue attractive investment opportunities – high-end hotels, factories and even a shipping port – in the economically reforming but politically static system that might be called Castro Inc. One would normally have expected this to be a lucrative but otherwise unexceptional instance of an expat living in a hybrid capitalist–communist regime, except that, as part of Raúl Castro's draconian 'anti-corruption' campaign of 2012, the Cuban intelligence service summarily arrested Purvis for graft associated with his firm, the Coral Capital Group. Overnight, the British national found himself behind bars at the infamous La Condesa prison, with its KGB-designed cells and interrogation/torture rooms. He writes of being informed by a security agent, using the Orwellian language so common of totalitarian regimes, that he had been 'provisionally charged with revelations of state security and illegal activities'. 'These are serious crimes', the agent went on. 'We need to know many things and it is easier for you to concentrate here' (p. 26). On some days, Purvis might endure three interrogation sessions; on others, nary a one. Naturally, he became despondent, recalling that the 'walls [began] to sing to me' as he spent day after day in the 'dungeon' (p. 65). And then, in a move that was nearly as arbitrary as his initial imprisonment, Purvis was released following a 'trial' in a kangaroo court and returned to Britain. He had been in custody for 12 months.

Purvis's harrowing account is a grim but necessary reminder that there are two Cubas: one evoked by the Buena Vista Social Club and classic American cars, and the other by 'Castro's Zoo', as the author calls it, referring to the prison in which businessmen like Purvis, along with other 'non-desirables' such as homosexuals and dissidents, are imprisoned. Given how much the Cuban regime relies on the rapacious, hypocritical Tío Sam (Uncle Sam to English speakers) as a convenient foil to justify its own repression and political monopoly, there is a case to be made that the United States should be more attentive to the dungeon-like practices in its own domestic prisons.

Cuban Revolution in America: Havana and the Making of a United States Left, 1968–1992
Teishan A. Latner. Chapel Hill, NC: University of North Carolina Press, 2018. $39.95. 351 pp.

On a torrid day in Havana in August 1967, the Trinidad-born, US civil-rights and black-power activist Stokely Carmichael spoke at an international solidarity conference of leftist intellectuals, politicians and revolutionaries. The fiery orator made no bones about what was at stake in Cuba and across the world, declaring,

> We share with you a common struggle; we have a common enemy. Our enemy is white Western imperialist society … Our struggle is to overthrow this system, which feeds itself and expands itself through the economic and cultural exploitations of nonwhite, non-Western peoples. (p. 1)

Writing in *Cuban Revolution in America*, historian Teishan A. Latner describes how the 1959 Cuban Revolution's self-declared ideology of social equality and justice deeply resonated with dissident Americans in the late 1960s and 1970s, especially those who, like Carmichael, actually visited or lived on the island. Sickened by incessant reports of wrongdoing by the American military in far-off Vietnam, these activists were drawn to what they saw as a socialist utopia just off the Florida coast. One of the author's most fascinating chapters discusses the notorious US-based Venceremos Brigade, a motley assortment of New Left, anti-war, feminist, Black Panther and nationalist Puerto Rican activists, in addition to many others who shared a deep distaste for US hegemony and racism.

Extolling Havana's gains in health, literacy and education, the Brigade was the largest pro-Cuba solidarity organisation in the world for many years. Latner reminds us, however, that this love affair had its limits, especially after Fidel Castro endorsed Moscow's invasion of Czechoslovakia in August 1968.

Latner believes that the Castro regime's embrace of American dissidents was driven by a mixture of ideological compatibility and realpolitik vis-à-vis its chief Western imperialist foe, the United States. This being the Cold War, however, the other shoe was bound to drop. According to Latner, Carmichael's 1967 trip might have triggered the US government's more aggressive stance toward pro-Cuba organisations, which were seen as being complicit in Cuban-backed acts of domestic terrorism. One US senator, for example, denounced the Venceremos Brigade as 'missiles in human forms' (p. 9). US intelligence agencies became convinced that it was in Havana, and not Moscow, where American radicals would find the most support.

The FBI in Latin America: The Ecuador Files
Marc Becker. Durham, NC: Duke University Press, 2017. $26.95.
322 pp.

Back in the 1980s, Marc Becker volunteered with an international non-governmental organisation working in Nicaragua's mountain highlands to document attacks on civilians by the Reagan administration-backed Contra guerrillas. Roughly three decades later, Becker, now a historian, returns to the topic of US imperial machinations in its geopolitical backyard in this highly readable and lively tome. FBI surveillance in Latin America started under Franklin Roosevelt as a wartime effort initially intended to keep tabs on a swelling Nazi presence in the region. Yet Becker makes the case that FBI chief J. Edgar Hoover used the 700-agent Special Intelligence Service (SIS) throughout the decade to spy on Latin American leftists and communists as well, especially after the Nazi regional threat had dissipated after 1943. The author reminds us that this particular instance of overseas snooping corresponded with a short period in the 1940s during which US officials – especially in the State Department – were inclined to support, or at least not to subvert, leftist political organisations and ideologies. If there were concerns about such groups in Latin America, Becker reasons, it was because they posed a potential threat to American corporate profits in the region, and not simply because they espoused communist ideas. Becker observes that in these pre-CIA years (the agency was founded in 1947), the FBI's intelligence reporting reveals a disconnect between American hysteria about communism and the 'lack of danger' that these parties actually posed to US security interests in the region

(p. 3). In the case of Ecuador, examined in detail in the book, the communist threat turned out to be infinitesimal: by the end of the SIS programme in 1947, the FBI had concluded that the country's communist party was 'one of the weakest and most ineffective' in Latin America (p. 238).

Readers of *The FBI in Latin America* should keep in mind that the author appears to have a Marxist ideological bias that almost certainly influences his depiction of events. He seems to take the arguments and statements of Latin American communists or anti-imperialists at face value, and even to tacitly endorse them, noting, for example, that the history of FBI surveillance 'excited' him 'not because of what it might tell us about U.S. imperial adventures in Latin America … but because of the insights spying might provide on popular movements' struggles to create a more just and equal society' (p. viii). Contrast this with his characterisation of Hoover's obsession with 'an alleged communist threat' (p. 9), or the FBI's 'fixation on a communist menace that allegedly emanated out of Moscow' (p. 5). Still, there is much to be learned from Becker's account of a little-known episode in the history of America's foremost *domestic* law-enforcement agency in a part of the globe where American influence has an admittedly chequered track record.

Acting Globally: Memoirs of Brazil's Assertive Foreign Policy
Celso Amorim. Michael Marsden, trans. Lanham, MD: Hamilton Books, 2017. £31.95/$46.99. 458 pp.

It might as well be ancient history: the tenure of Luiz Inácio Lula da Silva as president of Brazil, during which he became one of the most beloved leaders in the country's history and effortlessly ushered in steady economic growth, a rising middle class and political continuity – and with that, an assertive and confident foreign policy. Fast forward about a decade to 2018, and Brazilian politics couldn't look more different. Lula finds himself in prison, beginning a 12-year sentence for corruption and money laundering, his political legacy in tatters, and the heady days of Brazil's international assertiveness little more than a distant dream.

Celso Amorim, Lula's foreign minister for eight years and the man behind Brazil's expanded diplomatic reach, attempts to protect his own legacy in this memoir. He explains the behind-the-scenes dynamics of three major foreign-policy initiatives for Brazil: the Iran nuclear agreement, its recognition of Palestine and other diplomatic initiatives in the Middle East, and the Doha round of international trade agreements. Bolstered by diligent note-taking during his time in office, Amorim is able to recreate these episodes with remarkable detail. In so doing, he provides Brazil's side of the story.

It is fair to say that none of these initiatives had any staying power. The Doha round had fizzled by 2015, Brazilian efforts in relation to the Middle East did not contribute to the peace process, and the nuclear deal brokered by Turkey and Brazil fell apart at the end of 2009 after being rejected by the United Nations. While the terms of Brazil's deal were similar to a previous plan supported by the United States, Iran had accumulated enough enriched uranium since this prior attempt to cause the deal to be seen as a pretext for avoiding UN demands. Brazil's significant effort to 'give diplomacy a chance' failed to stop the sanctions that Brasília so desperately wanted to avoid.

Amorim doesn't hide his frustration toward the Obama administration for this perceived snub. He writes that Obama viewed Lula with a 'mixture of admiration and condescension' (p. 12), and refers to then-secretary of state Hillary Clinton's 'typical imperial arrogance' (p. 42). Blaming the failure of the brokered agreement on an elite club of traditional powers actively shutting out new entries to international diplomacy, Amorim concludes that the 'global political system is still incapable of absorbing the changes that have taken place in the geometry of power' (p. 66).

Yet there is a reason why *Foreign Policy* once named Amorim the world's best foreign minister. In 2003, Brazil secured a larger seat at the table for developing countries at the WTO's Cancún conference; and Brazil's effective leadership within the G20 gave it and other developed countries a more respected voice in international governance. Because of diplomats like Amorim, the term 'BRIC' is today more than just an investment banker's acronym. As one of Brazil's great elder statesmen, he was instrumental in pushing Brazil into the global arena.

In *Acting Globally*, Amorim is ultimately optimistic that developing powers like Brazil will one day play a decisive role in international diplomacy, arguing that 'inevitably that will happen, even if the wait lasts twenty or thirty years. And when it happens it will help bring peace to the world' (p. 66). Thanks to Amorim, the world is one step closer to achieving that goal.

By Britta Crandall

Europe
Erik Jones

A Diary of the Euro Crisis in Cyprus: Lessons for Bank Recovery and Resolution
Panicos Demetriades. London: Palgrave Macmillan, 2017.
£31.99/$49.99. 215 pp.

Central banks are politically vulnerable because they are institutions, and thus need to have both structure and purpose to function effectively. Central bankers are vulnerable because they do not like to be embarrassed, maligned or threatened – particularly when such actions extend to their families. Both are vulnerable because they extend loans, but also withhold credit, actions that create both friends and enemies. All this suggests that central banks are more political than is commonly believed.

These are the insights that emerge from the diary kept by Panicos Demetriades during the 2013 Cypriot banking crisis, when he was governor of the Central Bank of Cyprus (CBC). His book is essential reading for anyone who wants to understand the politics that surrounds so-called 'politically independent' central banks. It is also a cautionary tale about the unintended consequences of participating in Europe's single market. Demetriades is sceptical of both Europe and the euro. Nevertheless, he is quick to recognise that only the smooth functioning of the eurozone prevented an already bad situation from getting worse.

Demetriades explains that the 'business model' of Cyprus was always flawed. Politicians and bankers colluded to specialise in a particular form of offshore banking that relied on excessive risk-taking and regulatory forbearance. It was a confidence game that grew out of the personal relationships tying together the centre-right of the political spectrum and the largest Cypriot banks. The president of Cyprus, Nicos Anastasiades, felt personal responsibility for the Bank of Cyprus; the finance minister, Michael Sarris, was the former head of the Cypriot bank Laiki; and one of Demetriades's predecessors as central-bank governor, Afxentis Afxentiou, who governed the CBC for two decades, had millions of euros – as did members of his family – at risk.

It is no surprise, therefore, that many top politicians and business leaders in Cyprus took it personally when the CBC had to wind up Laiki and restructure the Bank of Cyprus, then the country's two largest banks. In response, Anastasiades publicly blamed Demetriades. The government dismissed the deputy governor of the CBC and rewrote the rules regarding board membership and responsibilities. Meanwhile, Demetriades and his family received credible death threats. Ultimately, Demetriades recognised that he could no longer run

Survival | vol. 60 no. 3 | June–July 2018 | pp. 217–223   DOI 10.1080/00396338.2018.1470779

the bank effectively. When he resigned, it was clear that Anastasiades had 'got what he wanted' (p. 177).

As Demetriades tells it, the European Union played only a supporting role in this drama. EU membership enhanced the ability of Cypriot banks to attract deposits. Participation in the single currency ensured those banks remained liquid even as they grew far beyond the underlying Cypriot economy. Once the crisis struck, the EU played a more ambivalent role. The European Central Bank was supportive, but only within limits. The Eurogroup was determined to test a new formula for banking resolution despite the fact — and probably because — this would help to break the Cypriot business model. The damage to the CBC as a central bank, and to Demetriades as the central banker, was collateral to this objective. Demetriades makes it clear that European institutions could have done more to protect his and his institution's political independence, but chose not to. That neglect is another political vulnerability to add to the list.

Banking on Markets: The Transformation of Bank–State Ties in Europe and Beyond
Rachel A. Epstein. Oxford: Oxford University Press, 2017.
£55.00/$70.00. 214 pp.

The close relationship between governments and banks is as old as it is strong. In that sense, there is little about Panicos Demetriades's story (see previous review) that surprises. Governments rely on banks to create money, finance debt and service the national economy. That reliance is particularly strong when the country faces economic crisis. In such moments, governments may have to call upon banks for vital support, offering their willingness to protect them from foreign competitors and domestic regulators in exchange. Policymakers may opt to liberalise capital markets to take advantage of access to savings abroad, while promising not to endanger the control and influence that banks wield.

This state–bank symbiosis is what Rachel Epstein explores in her fascinating study of how the recent economic and financial crisis unfolded in the countries of Central and Eastern Europe. Epstein notes that governments like to protect their banks, because having control over (or access to) cooperative national financial institutions makes policymakers feel less vulnerable. Somewhat paradoxically, however, such economic nationalism actually puts policymakers at more risk, particularly when the domestic economy depends heavily on access to capital from abroad. Those governments that allowed large foreign banks to take controlling positions in their domestic markets, by contrast, turned out to be less vulnerable to capital flight than conventional wisdom would suggest. Rather than fleeing, these large foreign banks chose to hunker down and absorb their losses. Moreover, they did so out of strategic self-interest: having fought hard to gain access to new and potentially lucrative markets, the large multinational banks were more concerned to maintain a presence than to repatriate their assets.

Epstein's story about the experience of Central and Eastern European countries does not dismiss the conventional wisdom about states and banks altogether. Governments that allow foreign financial conglomerates to dominate their domestic markets get neither the developmental outcomes in periods of stability, nor the cooperation in times of crisis, that domestic banks could offer. In essence, governments have to trade policy discretion for a more stable financial funding model. Not all governments are willing to accept that bargain. Indeed, the transition from communism to capitalism may have offered a unique environment for policymakers to reconsider state–bank relations in ways that more vested interests would find abhorrent. The story of Cyprus looms large in the background of Epstein's analysis even if it is not a case she chose to analyse; the parallel case of Slovenia gets more attention (and leads to a similar disastrous outcome as the government tries to hold on to its domestic banks).

Nevertheless, there are signs elsewhere in Europe that bank–state ties are undergoing a process of transformation. The creation of a European Banking Union with a single supervisory mechanism, regulatory rulebook and resolution board goes a long way toward constraining the instruments of national control. A pooled mechanism for deposit insurance, resolution funding and direct bank recapitalisation could liberate European banks even further from the tutelage of national politicians. It is still too early to tell whether Western European governments will find themselves as estranged from their home-grown financial institutions as are the governments of Central and Eastern Europe. What is clear is that the old relationship between states and banks deserves careful reconsideration. Epstein's book is a critical first step in that direction.

The End of Europe: Dictators, Demagogues, and the Coming Dark Age
James Kirchick. New Haven, CT: Yale University Press, 2017.
£12.99/$17.00. 273 pp.

The End of Europe starts off by announcing that 'Europe today is breaking apart … and slowly heading down the once unfathomable path to war' (pp. 1–2), and ends by insisting that 'such a collapse would usher in nothing less than a new dark age' (p. 230). In between, it focuses on four key points: Russia is meddlesome; democracy is fragile; Muslim immigration is subversive; and the left is anti-Semitic. And yet the book is not a rant. Indeed, it is subtle, informative, well written and even persuasive. True, there are occasional errors of fact, and even more attempts at manipulation: the author's decision to highlight a 14-year-old Palestinian refugee's musings about a world without Israel is but one illustration (p. 134). Nevertheless, this is journalism, not scholarship. The book is meant to be read, not studied. James Kirchick is skilled at his craft, which involves stirring readers' emotions to hold their attention.

There is no prize for guessing where Kirchick falls on the political spectrum, or what the broad contours of his world view are. Robert Kagan's appearance in the acknowledgements foretells the author's claim that 'so allergic are Europeans to the use of military force, and so anemic are their resources, that the thought of picking a side [in Syria] and seeing it through to victory was unimaginable' (p. 131). Then again, the predictable bits of this book are the least interesting. They are also unprovocative, except perhaps for the uninitiated. The relevant arguments have already been made in the debates surrounding previous books by authors like Kagan and Christopher Caldwell.

What Kirchick adds to his themes — and what makes this book worth reading — is his reflection on the role and creation of collective memory. This represents a genuinely new field of scholarly interest, one that is attracting a great deal of attention because of its real-world implications. Readers do not have to agree with Kirchick on the set pieces of his argument to share his horror at the prospect of Hungary repainting its role in the Holocaust in vibrant new hues. This rewriting of history is not just an offence to the memory of those who suffered, it is also an open door to those who would repeat the same atrocities. Moreover, the process involves much more than the building of monuments or museums. Kirchick finds a similar revisionism in the failure to protect the remaining Jewish population in France, in the institutionalised anti-Semitism of the British Labour Party – which he calls 'the most influential anti-Semitic institution in the Western World' (p. 141) – and the use of the term 'Nazi' to vilify the political opposition in Ukraine.

Kirchick's repeated references to the Holocaust should not mislead readers into thinking that his message is confined to the fate of the world's Jewish community. His point is that, if people can rewrite the history of such a high-profile, unambiguously horrific episode, then there is no telling what they could do to histories that are nuanced and subtle. Russian President Vladimir Putin, for instance, might press his case that Russians can only survive under authoritarian rule because that has always been their fate; and that democracy is a failed experiment and always has been. If we do not push back against the rewriting of clear-cut, painful histories, then we should not be surprised if we lose sight of the bolder and more beautiful accomplishments of Western civilisation at the same time.

Memory Laws, Memory Wars: The Politics of the Past in Europe and Russia
Nikolay Koposov. Cambridge: Cambridge University Press,
2017. £22.99/$29.99. 321 pp.

Memory and history are not the same thing. Memory exists in the present, history in the past. Memory evolves (active voice); history is revised (passive voice). Sometimes memory can and should be manipulated to ensure that the lessons of the past are never forgotten. History, on the other hand, should not be manipulated. Instead, historians should be left in peace to practise their craft. These are just a small handful of the insights that emerge in Nikolay Koposov's fascinating study of the rationale for writing 'memory laws' and the unintended conflicts these laws can create.

Following Koposov's argument in this book is no easy task. This is partly due to the multiple agendas that underlie it. The author is a historian, and hence is at least as interested in recounting how legislators came up with the idea of writing laws concerning the ways in which people remember (celebrate, revere and reconcile themselves with) the past, as he is in presenting an argument about how this kind of legislation leads to conflict. Anyone looking merely to dip into this book is advised that the conclusion is much tighter than the introduction. More conventional readers should know that its principal argument only emerges on page nine; the definition of 'memory' shows up on page 48; and the prose that surrounds these analytical building blocks consists of tightly interwoven digressions containing distractingly interesting observations.

The core of the argument is worth untangling because of what it implies about the vulnerability of the popular imagination. Koposov suggests that the end of ideology robbed Western society of its purpose. If there is no utopia to be created, then there is no future. (The echoes of Francis Fukuyama's 'end of history' are manifest.) Nevertheless, progressives can strive to make the world a better place by remembering humanity's tragic failures and promising never to repeat them. Given that, in many ways, memory laws rose to prominence as Western governments prohibited efforts to deny, minimise or relativise the Holocaust, this particular genocide features prominently.

The Western project to protect the memory of the Holocaust was progressive, both in tackling persistent anti-Semitism and in underpinning a wider appreciation of universal human rights. The use of legal instruments to do so, however, opened up the possibility for abuse. Koposov shows how Central and Eastern European countries used similar legislative acts to privilege specific national histories. For many of these countries, the goal was to put fascism and communism on an equal footing as external sources of victimisation. In this way, governments sought to whitewash their national experiences in order to escape, rather than reconcile themselves with, the lessons of the past. Often these countries — notably Hungary and Poland — were the most vigorous in rebelling against communism, and are the most prosperous in the region. At stake is whether these governments have embraced Western liberal democracy or distorted it.

For some countries, the manipulation of popular memory has a more openly anti-democratic agenda. The goal is not simply to escape responsibility for past failings, but also to relocate political agency (and the legitimacy that goes with it) from the individual or the cultural collective to the state. Koposov shows how Vladimir Putin, for example, is using the politics of memory to recast Russia as a 'state sovereignty' rather than a 'nation state'. In so doing, Putin is not only elevating himself above the Russian people, but also asserting the primacy of memory over history. In other words, what matters most is not what happened, but how the people feel about it today. This is a terrifying prospect, and not just for professional historians. Koposov has written a challenging book on a new and unfamiliar topic. It deserves to be widely read.

Communism's Shadow: Historical Legacies and Contemporary Political Attitudes
Grigore Pop-Eleches and Joshua A. Tucker. Princeton, NJ: Princeton University Press, 2017. £24.95/$29.95. 336 pp.

Popular attitudes may be another form of memory. If so, they are surely closer to muscle memory than to narrative memory. This is the conclusion Grigore Pop-Eleches and Joshua Tucker draw as they look for the legacies of communism in the survey responses of people who lived under communist rule and try to explain why large, multinational surveys about attitudes toward a range of social and political institutions reveal that respondents who lived under communism or in post-communist countries are more sceptical about democracy, more critical of the market and more supportive of the welfare state than respondents who did not share in that experience. The difference cannot be explained by the conditions that prevail in post-communist countries: people living in such countries may be unhappy with their lot, but their unhappiness is not the source of their attitudinal uniqueness. Rather, the length of time they spent under communism and the intensity with which they were socialised to accept communist values appear to be of far greater importance.

Any socialisation that did take place was more likely to be a result of what communists did than what they said. Communists had much to say about gender equality, for example, and yet Pop-Eleches and Tucker found little evidence that survey respondents in post-communist countries expressed more support for gender equality than respondents elsewhere. Indeed, once the authors control for variables related to living under communism or living in a post-communist environment, they find evidence to suggest that sexism may be even more prominent among Central and Eastern Europeans than elsewhere (although, to be fair, these findings are often not statistically significant). The point is simply that ideology matters less than experience in shaping attitudes, and communist regimes were no more respectful of gender equality in practice than their non-communist counterparts elsewhere. Incentives matter as well. People who experienced adulthood under communism were more likely to have been socialised than were people whose experience ended after childhood despite having been educated in communist schools.

What is less clear from this research is the extent to which these differences in attitude translate into differences in political behaviour. Pop-Eleches and Tucker place their work clearly in the 'behaviouralist' camp so as to distinguish the legacies they identify from the more widely studied persistence of institutions and political or social groups after the fall of communism. The scholastic nomenclature should not create confusion, however. We can speculate about how such attitudes will feed into policy, politics or protest, and yet the causal mechanisms are not self-evident. The dynamics of mobilisation are unclear, and cannot be understood without some consideration of both institutions and narratives.

Pop-Eleches and Tucker are well aware of the limitations of their contribution. This is refreshing at a time when scholars often seem only too eager to overstate their findings. What Pop-Eleches and Tucker offer is a new toolkit for taking advantage of the wealth of survey data that is being harvested both across and within countries. They also point to socialisation dynamics that are likely to emerge over time whenever the mixture of political, economic and social institutions that define society have a kind of underlying ideological coherence. This is a chilling prospect when the ideology boils down to 'the state is always right' (p. 299). Here both Nikolay Koposov and James Kirchick could easily join the conversation (see the reviews of their books above). Communism has cast a long shadow, and yet the shadow of post-communism may prove even darker.

Environment and Resources
Jeffrey Mazo

The Extinction Market: Wildlife Trafficking and How to Counter It
Vanda Felbab-Brown. London: C. Hurst & Co., 2017. £20.00.
406 pp.

More than 35,000 species of plant and animal – about 2% of the total known to science – are protected to various degrees under the 1975 Convention on International Trade in Endangered Species of Wild Flora and Fauna (CITES). For about 1,000 species considered to be threatened with extinction, trade other than for strictly regulated scientific purposes is prohibited. International trade in the other 34,000 vulnerable species requires export permits or re-export certificates, which are issued subject to conditions set out in CITES. Yet demand for many of the listed species as a source of food (subsistence or luxury), traditional medicines and prestige items has led to poaching, smuggling and a black-market economy worth an estimated $20 billion per year.

In *The Extinction Market*, Brookings Senior Fellow Vanda Felbab-Brown explores the complex causes and nature of this illegal economy. She draws on her expertise in transnational organised crime and the global drugs trade to weigh policy responses such as bans and strict law enforcement, regulated legal trade, engaging and incentivising local communities, targeting money laundering and focusing on demand reduction. Felbab-Brown devotes only a couple of pages (pp. 66–8) to why the loss of biodiversity and ecosystems services matters. She spends much more time on the secondary consequences of the illegal trade, such as how criminalisation can increase such losses and damage local and national economies, create threats to public health, undermine the rule of law and exacerbate the threat of violent conflict.

The book's unifying theme is the comparison between trade in illegal drugs and illegal wildlife. The scale of the global drugs economy is an order of magnitude greater than the illegal wildlife trade (p. 57), while the resources devoted to combating drugs are yet another order of magnitude larger (p. 4). Felbab-Brown identifies the structural similarities between the drugs and wildlife trades (barriers to entry, dispersion of supply, labour-intensiveness, detectability of flows, nature and dispersion of consumption and demand) and differences that affect the usefulness of different policies in each case – and in different circumstances within each illicit economy. The author's key finding is that policy outcomes are highly context sensitive and contingent; there is no one-size-fits-all approach and therefore flexibility and frequent reassessment are critical. 'This, the central finding of the book, may be the one that very few readers want to hear' (p. 29).

Given this contingency, and the complex trade-offs between successes and side effects, a secondary theme of *The Extinction Market* is the debate about values: local versus global; the rights of individuals versus the imperative of states; human welfare versus animal. Most of the demand, and much of the supply, in the illegal wildlife trade comes from East and Southeast Asia, and Africa (although the US is the second-largest market, after China). Some suppliers and consumers of wildlife products argue that restrictive policies are a form of cultural (or actual, vestigial) imperialism. Felbab-Brown navigates these fraught waters with sensitivity, while making her own values and cultural biases explicit. The result is a nuanced, detailed and thoughtful analysis that not only offers lessons for conservation policy, but uses conservation as a mirror to further inform global drugs policy.

Burn Out: The Endgame for Fossil Fuels
Dieter Helm. New Haven, CT: Yale University Press, 2017.
£20.00/$35.00. 281 pp.

Changing Energy: The Transition to a Sustainable Future
John H. Perkins. Oakland, CA: University of California Press,
2017. £24.00/$29.95. 343 pp.

'It is remarkable', writes Oxford energy-policy professor Dieter Helm in *Burn Out*, 'how little has changed on the energy front in the last thirty-five years. Indeed, many of today's energy fault lines go back at least to the beginning of the twentieth century' (p. 3). The energy mixture, the main producers and consumers, the geopolitics, and the market shares of private and state-owned companies are broadly the same now as they were in 1980, with the main exception being the advent of fracking and the shift towards natural gas. The conventional wisdom reflected in the energy outlooks published by the major international oil companies and by the International Energy Agency (IEA) likewise expects the next 35 years or so, to 2050, to show more continuity than change.

This wisdom, Helm points out, is wholly inconsistent with the ambitions of limiting climate change embodied in the 2015 Paris agreement. Yet the 'carbon crunch', as the externalities of climate-change impacts make fossil fuels increasingly costly even as their production costs remain stable or decline, is only one of three 'predictable surprises' or 'known unknowns' that Helm argues will transform the world both economically and geopolitically. The second is the end of the commodity supercycle; Helm sees the recent fall in oil and gas prices as the new normal, a return to the stability experienced during most of the twentieth century, rather than a temporary blip. In fact, as he points out, repeated IEA projections of oil prices since the 1970s have been so bad that it would have been more accurate simply to extrapolate the then-current price (p. 17). The final surprise is the nascent yet profound revolution in materials and technology, including 3D printing, robotics and artificial intelligence.

Although the precise shape of the world in 2050 is impossible to predict, it will be one of radical change and discontinuity, relying mainly on electrical power using new technologies for generation, storage and use. Unlike the fossil-fuel economy, the electric economy will be structured around fixed-cost contracts for access to supply, just as access to broadband is based on monthly access charges rather than usage charges, independent of the amount of energy used. In such an economy, growth in demand doesn't much matter, so long as generation rests on zero-carbon technologies.

This vision may recall Lewis Strauss's often-mocked 1954 prediction that the next generation would enjoy electricity 'too cheap to measure'. But as I argued in a Politics and Strategy blog post ('Fusion and Forecasting') five years ago, Strauss wasn't wrong, only premature. In fact, Helm's main departure from the conventional wisdom is in the matter of timing. The latter does not deny the transformational impact of Helm's three predictable surprises, just that they will have any significant impact until after mid-century. Helm relies on an optimistic view of future progress, but one which stands on firm ground. The extraordinary speed of the shale-gas revolution is a harbinger of future change: 'the key features of our energy transformation now are speed and the multitude of *simultaneous* advances' (p. 242, emphasis in original).

The geopolitical consequences of this new economy will be profound. Helm sees the United States, with its technological depth and maturity, as the biggest potential winner, both in absolute terms and compared to Europe and to China, which will find its economic model strongly challenged by the new reality. The Middle Eastern oil powers and Russia will all likely be significant losers. Here too, the shale-gas revolution is a portent of things to come.

Helm speaks with confidence and authority, but *Burn Out* sometimes lacks the depth of data and analysis that a self-described challenge to an embedded conventional wisdom should provide. It reads, in fact, like an executive summary of a more complex report. For the reader looking for more context, more data and more confidence, John H. Perkins's *Changing Energy* would make an excellent companion. Perkins, an emeritus professor of environmental and energy studies and a senior fellow with the US National Council for Science and the Environment, has produced a work on energy's past, present and future that would make both an excellent textbook and a reference work that should be on the shelves of anyone whose occupation even peripherally involves the future of global energy. Seven chapters provide a comprehensive and clear grounding in the history and science of energy production, sources, use and risks (including climate change, geopolitical tensions, and environmental and health impacts). A further four chapters cover the practicality of a 'fourth energy transition' from the 'big four' fuels (coal, oil, gas and uranium) to an economy based on renewables. Analysing in turn the criteria for the acceptability of renewable energy sources (five traditional criteria and four new criteria for sustainability) and the degree to which different sources meet these criteria, Perkins concludes that such an economy is at least theoretically possible. Of the renewable sources, solar and wind score well across most criteria other than time of use. Energy efficiency is, however, far and away the best overall energy 'source'.

Yet Perkins to a large degree embodies the conventional wisdom that Helm is challenging. In his chapter on barriers and challenges to the fourth energy transition, Perkins pays lip service to the idea of new technologies, but his analysis is grounded in the current investment and political environment, as well as the extrapolation of existing technologies. Helm assumes that most of these barriers will be swept away by his three predictable surprises. So while Perkins concludes that energy efficiency, for example, will be one of the most important components of the sustainable-energy economy, Helm sees it as merely part of a temporary transition to a world in which energy will be too cheap to meter. The difference is Helm's belief in the speed of technological discovery, so that solar cells, for example, could harvest more of the light spectrum than the current meagre 7%. As Helm puts it, 'the future of electricity is probably solar, but not as we know it' (p. 6).

Unstable Ground: Climate Change, Conflict, and Genocide
Alex Alvarez. Lanham, MD: Rowman & Littlefield, 2017. $34.00.
212 pp.

Storming the Wall: Climate Change, Migration, and Homeland Security
Todd Miller. San Francisco, CA: City Lights, 2017. $16.95. 270 pp.

It might seem an odd choice for an author such as Alex Alvarez to use the Balkan and Central African conflicts of the 1990s as his main case studies in a chapter on 'Linking Climate Change and Conflict' (ch. 3). There is an active debate over whether modern wars and genocides such as those in Darfur and Syria are climate related, but Kosovo and Rwanda are more often invoked as counter-examples by those who tend to downplay the climate link. In *Unstable Ground*, however, Alvarez, author of one of the standard textbooks on the causes of violence and genocide, uses these cases precisely to 'illustrate the processes and mechanisms through which an apparently stable society can descend into war and genocide as a result of bad leadership, social, political and economic instability, and a resurgence of ethnic nationalism, prejudice and xenophobia' (p. 6).

In effect, he is using these wars – and the Balkan conflicts in particular – as control cases in his attempt to isolate the specific pathways linking climate change and violence. As Alvarez sums it up, climate change will create conditions and mindsets conducive to intergroup hostility and tension, in turn enabling ethnic and communal violence, wars and genocide (p. 89). This is not inevitable, but structural, psychological and ideological factors will combine with environmental change to heighten the risks. In subsequent chapters, Alvarez focuses tightly on two specific aspects of the complex nexus between climate and conflict. Chapter four looks at the role of water scarcity in the Arab Spring (the Syrian civil war in particular) and the Darfur conflict, and discusses the risks of both rising sea levels and drought more widely. Chapter five covers the ways in which climate change may lead to widespread population displacement and cross-border migration, and how such displacements (regardless of cause) become sources of tension and conflict. He examines, for example, the political and sociocultural backlash against immigrants in many parts of the world, and the changing nature of borders.

The themes, conclusions and most of the case studies in *Unstable Ground* are familiar; several older books cover much the same territory, my own 2010 *Climate Conflict* among them. One weakness Alvarez shares with many of these is a failure to assess the consequences of likely climate futures in favour of a reliance on worst-case climate scenarios. His strength is his undeniable expertise in the causes of violence and genocide. This informs in particular his concluding chapter on resilience and conflict prevention, and his chapter (ch. 2) on the origins of war and the genocidal impulse, which contains a particularly useful unpacking and taxonomy of different forms of conflict, including riots, pogroms, war and genocide. *Unstable Ground* is up to date, well informed and closely argued, and is a valuable contribution to the debate on climate change as a threat multiplier for national and human security.

Todd Miller, in contrast, is a journalist with 15 years' experience in issues involving the US–Mexico border. Unlike Alvarez, who casts his particular perspective widely, in *Storming the Wall* Miller falls into the trap of thinking his narrow focus is necessarily central. 'The theater for future climate battles', he asserts, 'will be the world's ever thickening border zones and not, as national security forecasts constantly project, in communities where individuals fight each other for scarce resources' (pp. 29–30). Besides being a fallacy of the familiar, this mischaracterises the consensus of the climate-security community. It is notable, moreover, that Miller says that it was as late as 2015 that he first heard the issue of climate refugees addressed from the security perspective, and that he describes the security response to climate change as a threat multiplier as 'an adaptation program for the rich and powerful' (p. 42). He wears his ideology on his sleeve, and it is sometimes difficult to recognise the key players in the climate-security debate – and their arguments – in his portrayals.

This is not to say that Miller's expertise, focus and ideological perspective are without value. Contrarian views are always helpful, if not as correctives then at least as reality checks. Treated as an adjunct to the chapter in *Unstable Ground* on migration and border issues, *Storming the Wall* is a useful amplification and complement to Alvarez's analysis. Miller, however, does not – like Alvarez – just assume worst-case climate scenarios, but also cherry-picks the most extreme threat forecasts based on those scenarios, offering a worst-case picture of the sociopolitical consequences of population displacement and migration. *Storming the Wall* itself embodies a worst-case and unpersuasive scenario for the sociopolitical consequences of climate migration, and of the national-security response to climate refugees.

In 2015, the Intergovernmental Panel on Climate Change, having assessed more than a decade of research and analysis, concluded that an effect of climate change on population displacement, migration and civil conflict – let alone its magnitude – could not be detected with any degree of confidence. The social, economic and environmental drivers of migration and conflict are so varied, and interact in such complex ways, that it is difficult – if not impossible – to isolate the effect or magnitude of *any* individual factor empirically. It is not to be expected that climate change would be any different. Alvarez's and Miller's reliance on worst-case climate scenarios means they shed little light on the question of magnitude. But bringing a wider range of disciplines, methodologies and expertise to bear on the question is one way of increasing confidence in the climate–conflict link.

A Completed Life

Chiara Kessler

I

I made my grandmother a smoothie. I made it carefully and consciously, watching how the colours and flavours blended as we sat in her bright, airy living room, surrounded by her paintings, carpets, books, porcelain and photographs. The silver cookie jar was where it had been for as long as I could remember, on the little round table where we would place our drinks as we looked over the narrow but carefully tended garden. My parents, uncles, aunts and cousins, nervous but composed, chattered among themselves. My grandmother was a proud, elegant woman despite her fragile figure, her words as commanding as her character. As she drank my smoothie I felt grateful for this gesture, remembering the moment a few weeks earlier when my mother had called to tell me that grandma had chosen a date. When the doorbell rang at last, the tension was broken by my grandmother's soft and oddly cheerful murmur, 'Well, *finally*!'

The physician told us that we would have to wait in the living room, but before long we found ourselves crowding around the bed on which she lay, feeling a mixture of sadness and awe at the fragility of life deepened by the melancholic French song she had asked to be played, and which my father had gone to great lengths to find.

My grandmother went peacefully, and my feelings of sadness competed with ones of gratitude. I was 18 years old, and it was the first time I perceived that the inevitability of death does not exclude a degree of

Chiara Kessler is a Master's student at the Johns Hopkins School of Advanced International Studies.

Survival | vol. 60 no. 3 | June–July 2018 | pp. 231–236   DOI 10.1080/00396338.2018.1470782

choice, and that this small measure of freedom, enabled by the legal right to a planned and assisted departure from this life, can be a way of honouring our human dignity.

II

In most of the world, euthanasia is considered to be criminal homicide. In the Netherlands, however, where my grandmother was euthanised, euthanasia and assisted suicide are regulated by the Termination of Life on Request and Assisted Suicide Act, which applies exclusively to patients who are considered to be suffering unbearable pain with little, if any, prospect of improvement. The law entered into force in April 2002, making the Netherlands the first country in the world to legalise euthanasia and assisted suicide.

Last year, 6,760 people were relieved from 'intractable suffering' in the Netherlands through this method, and it is estimated that 85,600 requests for such assistance are submitted yearly. This does not mean that euthanasia and assisted suicide is not a highly sensitive issue, however. In fact, it played a central role in the prolonged negotiations to form the Dutch cabinet in 2017. The current cabinet, Prime Minister Mark Rutte's third (or 'Rutte–III'), represents a coalition of four parties: the centre-right People's Party for Freedom and Democracy (VVD) and Christian Democratic Appeal (CDA); the centre-left Democrats 66 (D66); and the Christian Union (ChristenUnie), which sides with both right- and left-wing parties depending on the issue. The first time these four parties attempted to form a coalition, the negotiations broke down in a matter of hours due to disagreement between the D66 and the Christian Union. The main point of disagreement was the former's plans to draft new legislation – the so-called 'completed life act' – which would allow, under very strict conditions, people over the age of 75 who felt that their life was 'complete' to resort to euthanasia. Unsurprisingly, the two parties espousing Christian principles – the CDA and the Christian Union – strongly opposed this plan. Although the four parties finally formed a government 225 days after the elections took place, the issue of completed-life euthanasia remains highly controversial, and is likely to remain a serious point of contention in the current government.

The discussion concerning completed life was sparked in 2010, when a citizen's initiative ('Uit Vrije Wil') submitted a petition to the government. In response, the government commissioned an exploratory study of the social dilemmas raised by the completed-life issue and the options available within the current legal framework.

In February 2016, the Advisory Committee on Completed Life presented its final report, concluding that it would not be desirable to extend the legal possibilities for euthanasia and assisted suicide. However, rather than ending the debate, the report only added fuel to the fire. It was in the wake of this report that D66 announced its plan to draft a new law. The government, then consisting of the liberal VVD and social-democratic PvdA (the Rutte–II cabinet), sided with D66, thus overruling the advice of the committee.

III

The position of the VVD and D66 centres on concepts of self-determination and autonomy. Holders of this position believe that individuals should be able to make autonomous decisions on matters concerning their own life, including on euthanasia, abortion and marriage. The Christian position as represented by the CDA and the Christian Union, on the other hand, holds that human life deserves full legal protection, from conception to the end of life.

Opponents of the completed-life bill frequently make the 'slippery slope' argument, according to which tolerating voluntary euthanasia (especially in the context of completed life) could eventually lead to unacceptable practices such as *non*-voluntary euthanasia. Another serious concern is that it can be extremely difficult to establish whether an individual truly wishes to die. What if someone is in fact experiencing extreme but reversible loneliness, or a transitory bout of depression? What if candidates have decided that their life has become redundant and feel pressure to die in order to reduce the burden on their families and society? In such cases, is there not a societal duty to offer them psychological assistance and to help them find meaning in their lives instead of 'simply' granting their wish to die? Of course, it is possible to question whether *any* decision can be truly autonomous, given that decisions always take place in a social context.

These concerns are legitimate and need to be taken seriously. As the populations of industrialised societies age and medical advances contribute to lengthening life expectancies, we must think about sustainable, long-term solutions to the loneliness and economic hardship often experienced by the elderly. The completed-life discussion, however, is above all a question of principle. If a person truly feels that his or her life is complete, and makes a voluntary and autonomous decision to die according to strictly defined criteria and with professional guidance, there seems no reason to criminalise this choice. We do not have a duty to live. The proposed completed-life bill is about upholding the right of all people to make their own decisions.

The Netherlands is a largely secular country with a strong liberal-democratic tradition and a deeply engrained culture of tolerance and pragmatism. Its liberal policies on drugs, gay marriage, prostitution, abortion and euthanasia are well known around the world. It is also well known, however, that the Netherlands is under pressure from the same difficult dynamics that are threatening other wealthy liberal democracies in Europe and beyond. These include, famously, pressures from immigration and a large Muslim minority that are straining the country's established reputation for tolerance. And they include the demographic and budgetary pressures from an ageing population that render the moral-philosophical debates around end-of-life issues even more tangled and fraught.

The central question of whether completed-life euthanasia is justifiable hinges on whether unbearable and hopeless suffering should be limited to physical suffering, or whether it could be extended to include psychological suffering as well. Neither form of suffering is easily measured, but it is clear that psychological pain involves a degree of subjectivity and complexity which makes the completed-life discussion even more difficult than the question of euthanasia in the more limited context of physical suffering. It should be acknowledged, however, that it is often impossible to make a clear distinction between physical and mental suffering – indeed, they are strongly interrelated. Therefore, in my eyes there would have been no moral grounds on which to deny my grandmother the choice to step out of life, to refuse her wish to be remembered as the woman she was, to relieve her from her physical and psychological suffering, and to grant us the gift of an intimate, loving farewell.

THE SECURITY OF
PARTNERSHIP.

AT LOCKHEED MARTIN,
WE'RE ENGINEERING A BETTER TOMORROW.®

Global security encompasses a broad spectrum of challenges. Today's leaders look to companies with wide-ranging capabilities, technological expertise and broad perspectives to solve complex challenges. Our global team partners with customers and approaches each challenge as our own. When it comes to success in complex environments, we know partnerships make a world of difference.

Learn more at lockheedmartin.com

LOCKHEED MARTIN

ONE JOURNEY.
ALL WALKS
OF LIFE.

Every person's story is unique. But when we come together, we can do amazing things. Boeing is proud to support the work of the International Institute for Strategic Studies, and to lend its expertise and voice on matters of global and critical Asia-Pacific security issues.